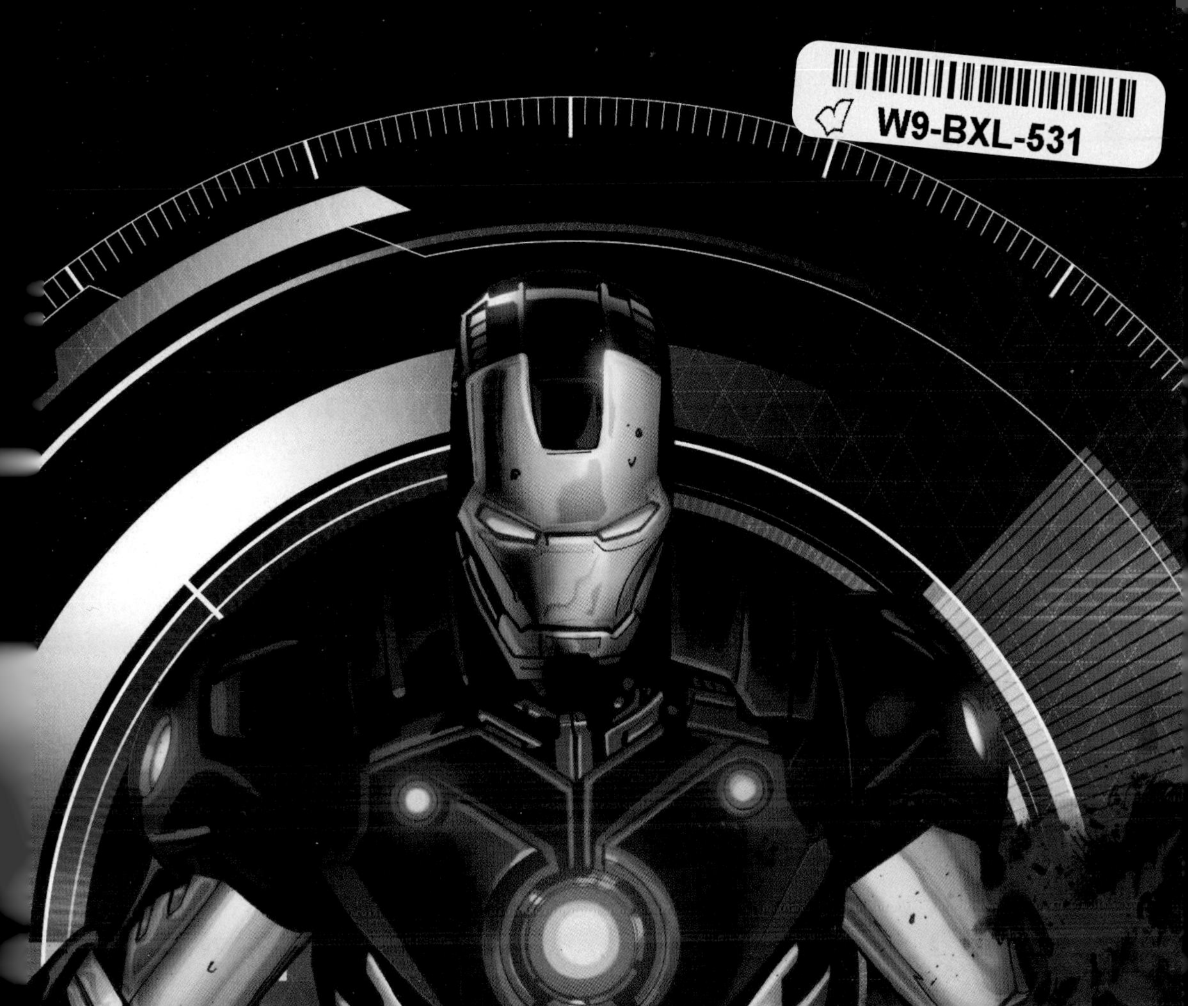

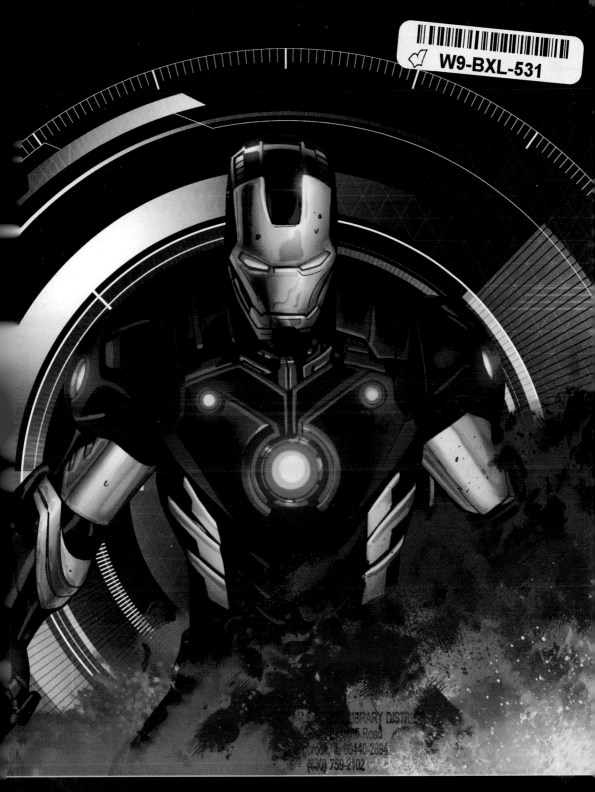

IRON MAN

BELIEVE

IRON MAN VOL. 1: BELIEVE. Contains material originally published in magazine form as IRON MAN #1-5. First printing 2014. ISBN# 978-0-7851-6665-8. Published by MARVEL WORLDWIDE, INC., a subsidiary of MARVEL ENTERTAINMENT, LLC. OFFICE OF PUBLICATION: 135 West 50th Street, New York, NY 10020. Copyright © 2012 and 2014 Marvel Characters, Inc. All rights reserved. All characters featured in this issue and the distinctive names and likenesses thereof, and all related indicia are trademarks of Marvel Characters, Inc. No similarity between any of the names, characters, persons, and/or institutions in this magazine with those of any living or dead person or institution is intended, and any such similarity which may exist is purely coincidental. **Printed in the U.S.A.** ALAN FINE, EVP - Office of the President, Marvel Worldwide, Inc. and EVP & CMO Marvel Characters B.V.; DAN BUCKLEY, Publisher & President - Print, Animation & Digital Divisions; JOE QUESADA, Chief Creative Officer; TOM BREVOORT, SVP of Publishing; DAVID BOGART, SVP of Operations & Procurement, Publishing; C.B. CEBULSKI, SVP of Creator & Content Development; DAVID GABRIEL, SVP of Print & Digital Publishing Sales; JIM O'KEEFE, VP of Operations & Logistics; DAN CARR, Executive Director of Publishing Technology; SUSAN CRESPI, Editorial Operations Manager; ALEX MORALES, Publishing Operations Manager; STAN LEE, Chairman Emeritus. For information regarding advertising in Marvel Comics or on Marvel.com, please contact Niza Disla, Director of Marvel Partnerships, at ndisla@marvel.com. For Marvel subscription inquiries, please call 800-217-9158. **Manufactured between 12/20/2013 and 1/27/2014 by R.R. DONNELLEY, INC., SALEM, VA, USA.**

10 9 8 7 6 5 4 3 2 1

Tony Stark is a technological visionary...a famous, wealthy and unparalleled inventor. With the world's most advanced and powerful suit of armor, Stark valiantly protects the innocent as an invincible bright knight known as...

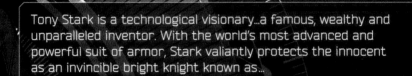

IRONMAN

KIERON GILLEN
WRITER

GREG LAND
PENCILER

JAY LEISTEN
INKER

GURU-eFX
COLORIST

VC'S JOE CARAMAGNA
LETTERER

GREG LAND & **GURU-eFX**
COVER ART

JON MOISAN
ASSISTANT EDITOR

MARK PANICCIA
EDITOR

COLLECTION EDITOR: **JENNIFER GRÜNWALD**
ASSISTANT EDITORS: **ALEX STARBUCK** & **NELSON RIBEIRO**
EDITOR, SPECIAL PROJECTS: **MARK D. BEAZLEY**
SENIOR EDITOR, SPECIAL PROJECTS: **JEFF YOUNGQUIST**
SVP PRINT, SALES & MARKETING: **DAVID GABRIEL**
BOOK DESIGNER: **RODOLFO MURAGUCHI**

EDITOR IN CHIEF: **AXEL ALONSO**
CHIEF CREATIVE OFFICER: **JOE QUESADA**
PUBLISHER: **DAN BUCKLEY**
EXECUTIVE PRODUCER: **ALAN FINE**

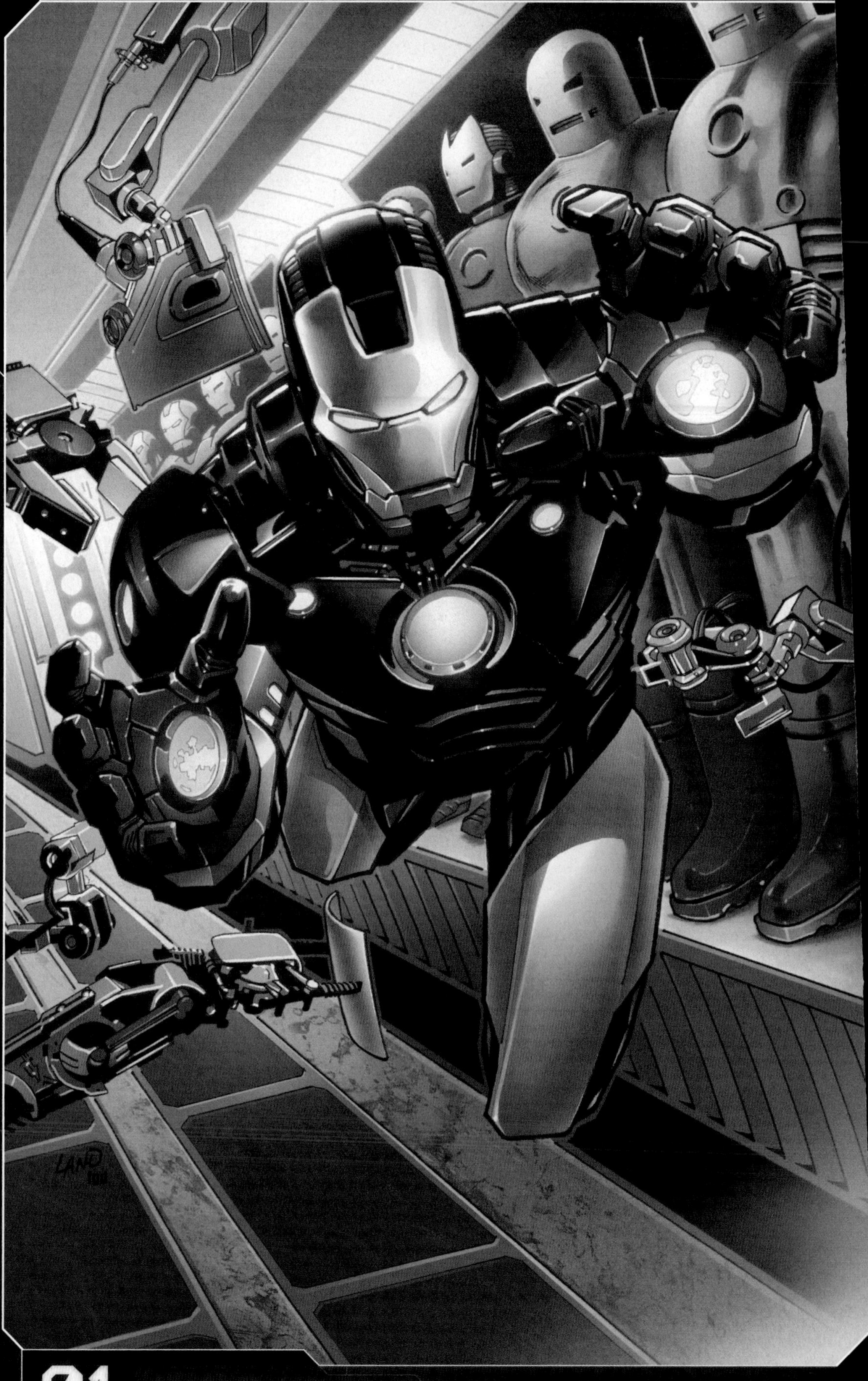

01 DEMONS AND GENIES

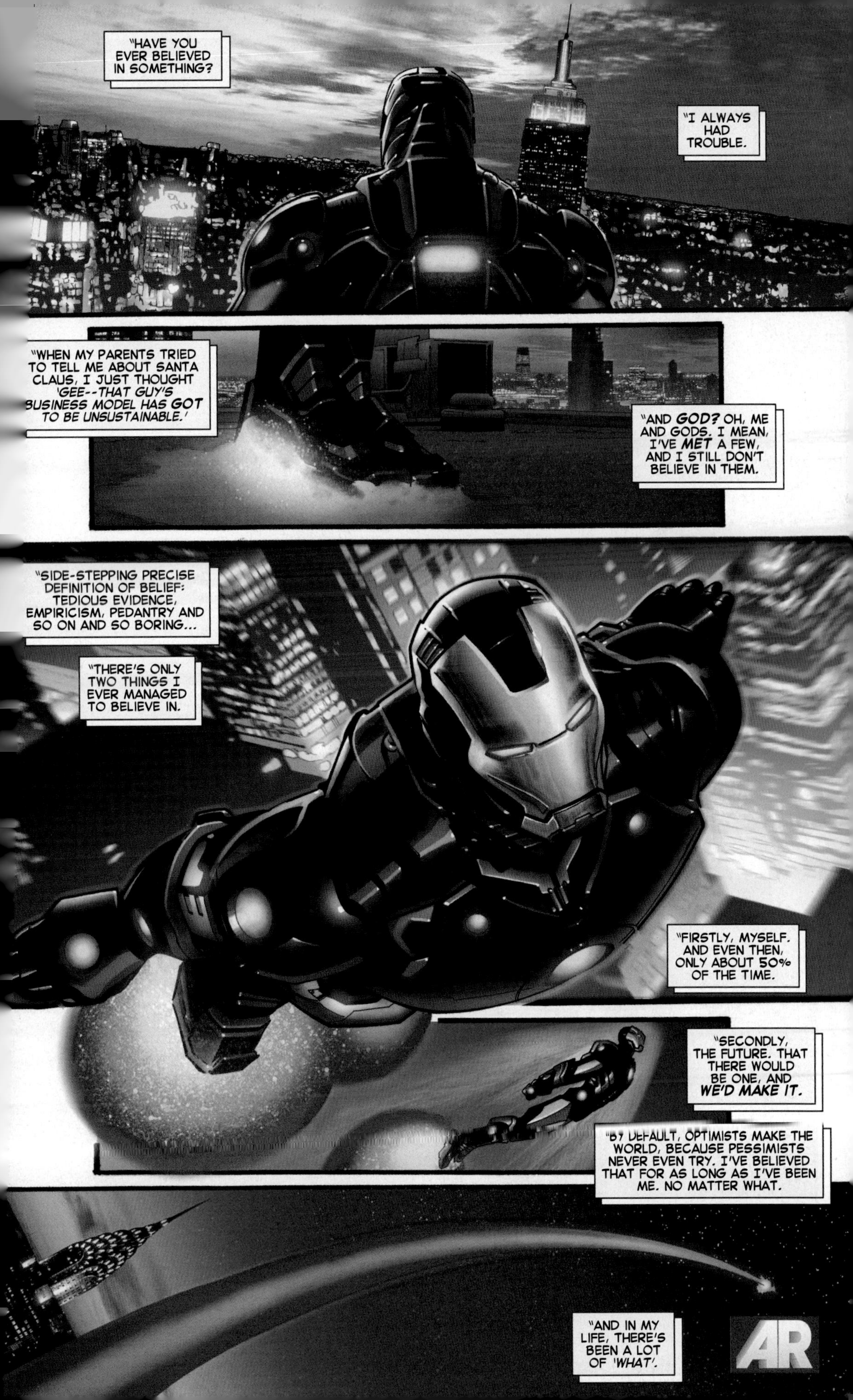
"HAVE YOU EVER BELIEVED IN SOMETHING?
"I ALWAYS HAD TROUBLE.
"WHEN MY PARENTS TRIED TO TELL ME ABOUT SANTA CLAUS, I JUST THOUGHT 'GEE--THAT GUY'S BUSINESS MODEL HAS GOT TO BE UNSUSTAINABLE.'
"AND GOD? OH, ME AND GODS. I MEAN, I'VE MET A FEW, AND I STILL DON'T BELIEVE IN THEM.
"SIDE-STEPPING PRECISE DEFINITION OF BELIEF: TEDIOUS EVIDENCE, EMPIRICISM, PEDANTRY AND SO ON AND SO BORING...
"THERE'S ONLY TWO THINGS I EVER MANAGED TO BELIEVE IN.
"FIRSTLY, MYSELF. AND EVEN THEN, ONLY ABOUT 50% OF THE TIME.
"SECONDLY, THE FUTURE. THAT THERE WOULD BE ONE, AND WE'D MAKE IT.
"BY DEFAULT, OPTIMISTS MAKE THE WORLD, BECAUSE PESSIMISTS NEVER EVEN TRY. I'VE BELIEVED THAT FOR AS LONG AS I'VE BEEN ME. NO MATTER WHAT.
"AND IN MY LIFE, THERE'S BEEN A LOT OF 'WHAT'.

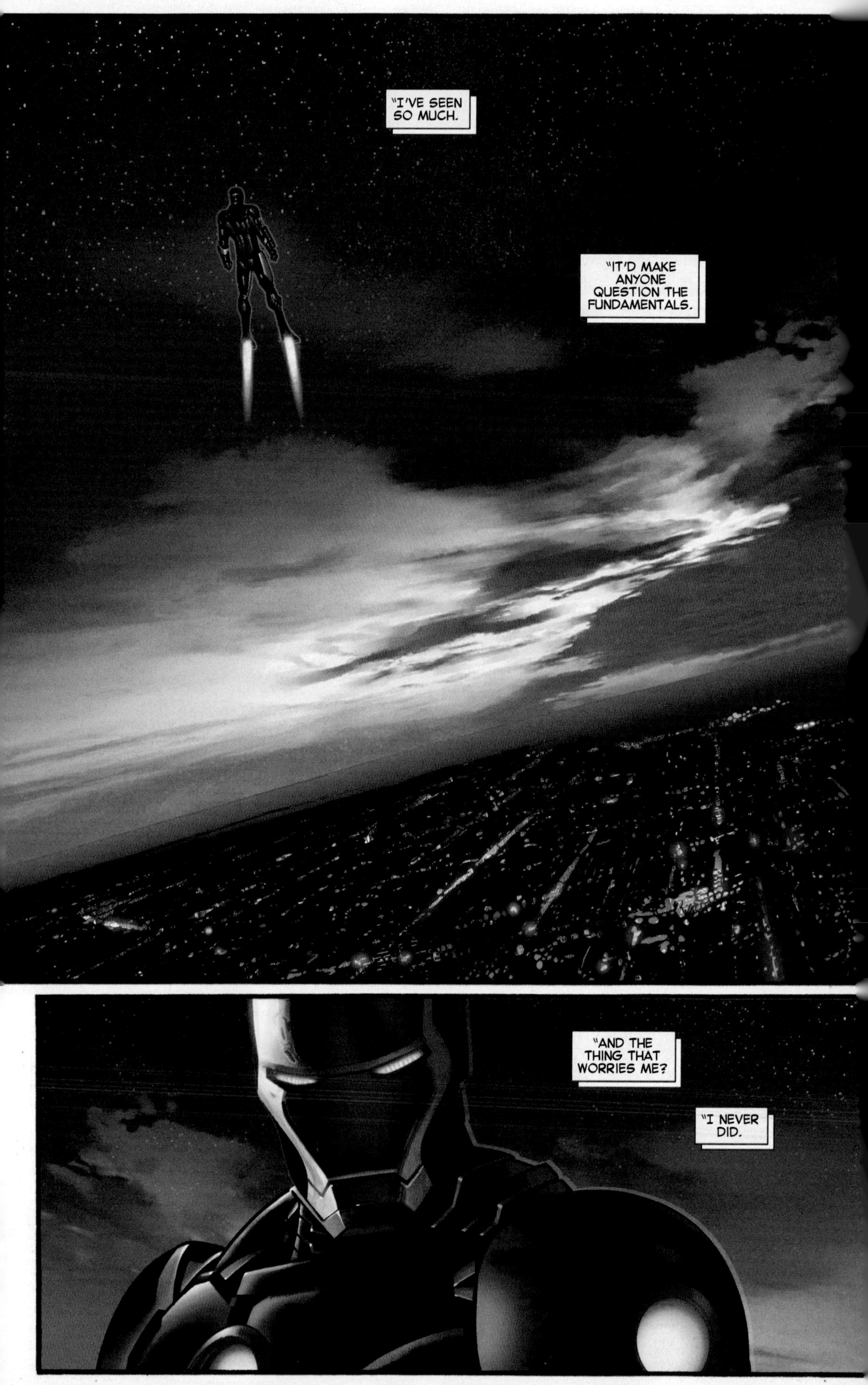
"I'VE SEEN SO MUCH.
"IT'D MAKE ANYONE QUESTION THE FUNDAMENTALS.
"AND THE THING THAT WORRIES ME?
"I NEVER DID.

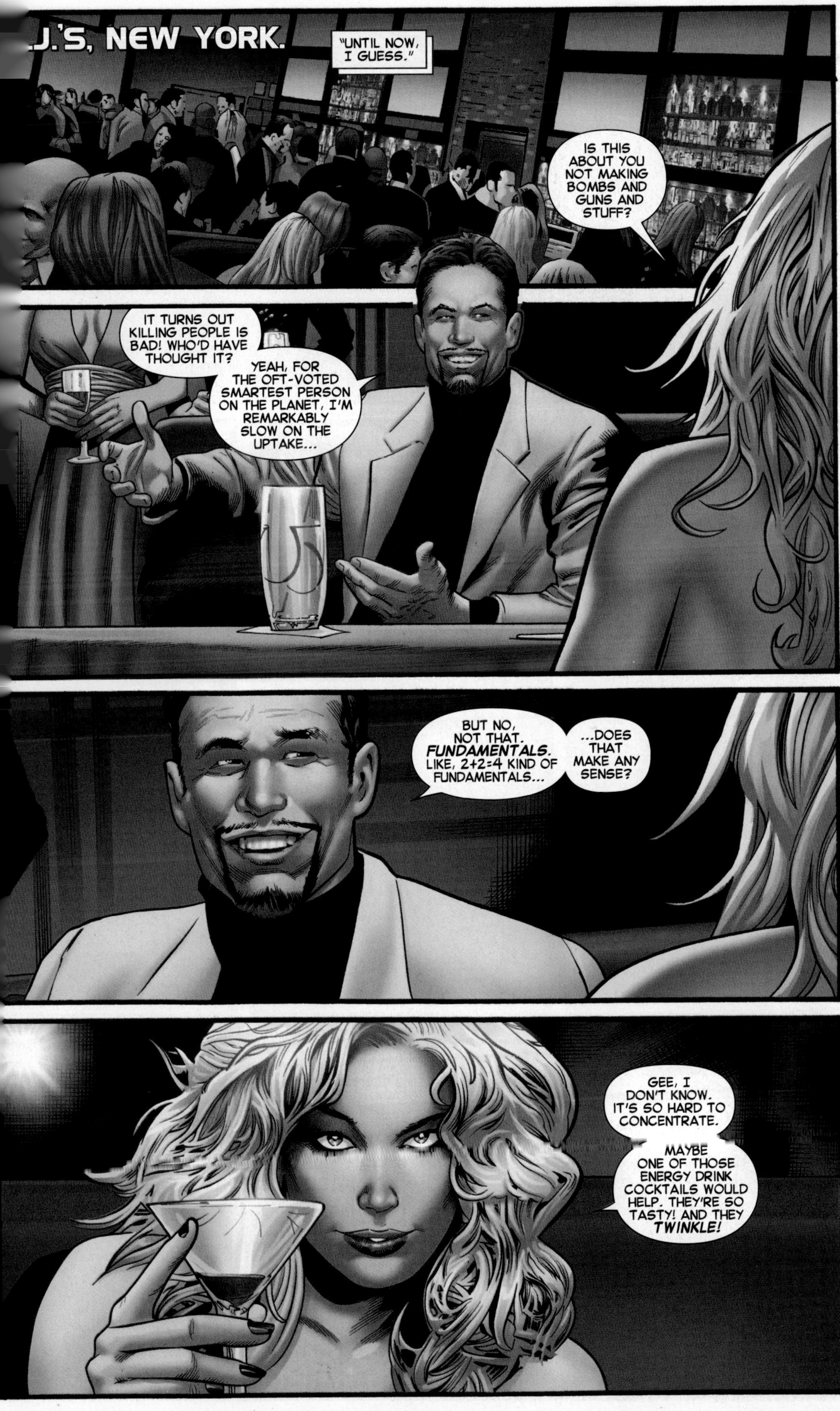
.J.'S, NEW YORK.
"UNTIL NOW, I GUESS."
IS THIS ABOUT YOU NOT MAKING BOMBS AND GUNS AND STUFF?
IT TURNS OUT KILLING PEOPLE IS BAD! WHO'D HAVE THOUGHT IT?
YEAH, FOR THE OFT-VOTED SMARTEST PERSON ON THE PLANET, I'M REMARKABLY SLOW ON THE UPTAKE...
BUT NO, NOT THAT. *FUNDAMENTALS.* LIKE, 2+2=4 KIND OF FUNDAMENTALS...
...DOES THAT MAKE ANY SENSE?
GEE, I DON'T KNOW. IT'S SO HARD TO CONCENTRATE.
MAYBE ONE OF THOSE ENERGY DRINK COCKTAILS WOULD HELP. THEY'RE SO TASTY! AND THEY *TWINKLE!*

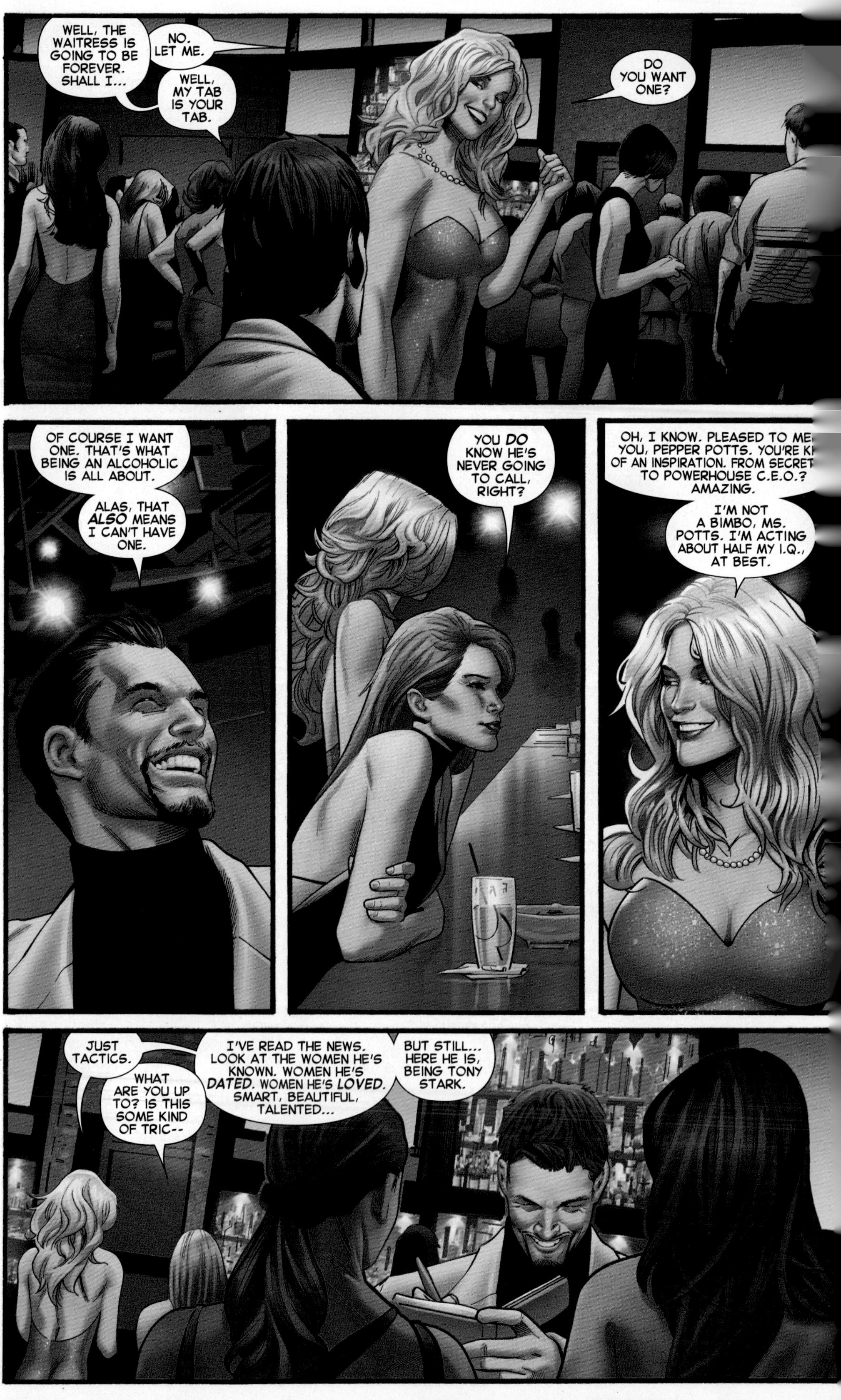
WELL, THE WAITRESS IS GOING TO BE FOREVER. SHALL I...
NO. LET ME.
WELL, MY TAB IS YOUR TAB.
DO YOU WANT ONE?
OF COURSE I WANT ONE. THAT'S WHAT BEING AN ALCOHOLIC IS ALL ABOUT.
ALAS, THAT *ALSO* MEANS I CAN'T HAVE ONE.
YOU *DO* KNOW HE'S NEVER GOING TO CALL, RIGHT?
OH, I KNOW. PLEASED TO ME YOU, PEPPER POTTS. YOU'RE K OF AN INSPIRATION. FROM SECRET TO POWERHOUSE C.E.O.? AMAZING.
I'M NOT A BIMBO, MS. POTTS. I'M ACTING ABOUT HALF MY I.Q., AT BEST.
JUST TACTICS.
WHAT ARE YOU UP TO? IS THIS SOME KIND OF TRIC--
I'VE READ THE NEWS. LOOK AT THE WOMEN HE'S KNOWN. WOMEN HE'S *DATED*. WOMEN HE'S *LOVED*. SMART, BEAUTIFUL, TALENTED...
BUT STILL... HERE HE IS, BEING TONY STARK.

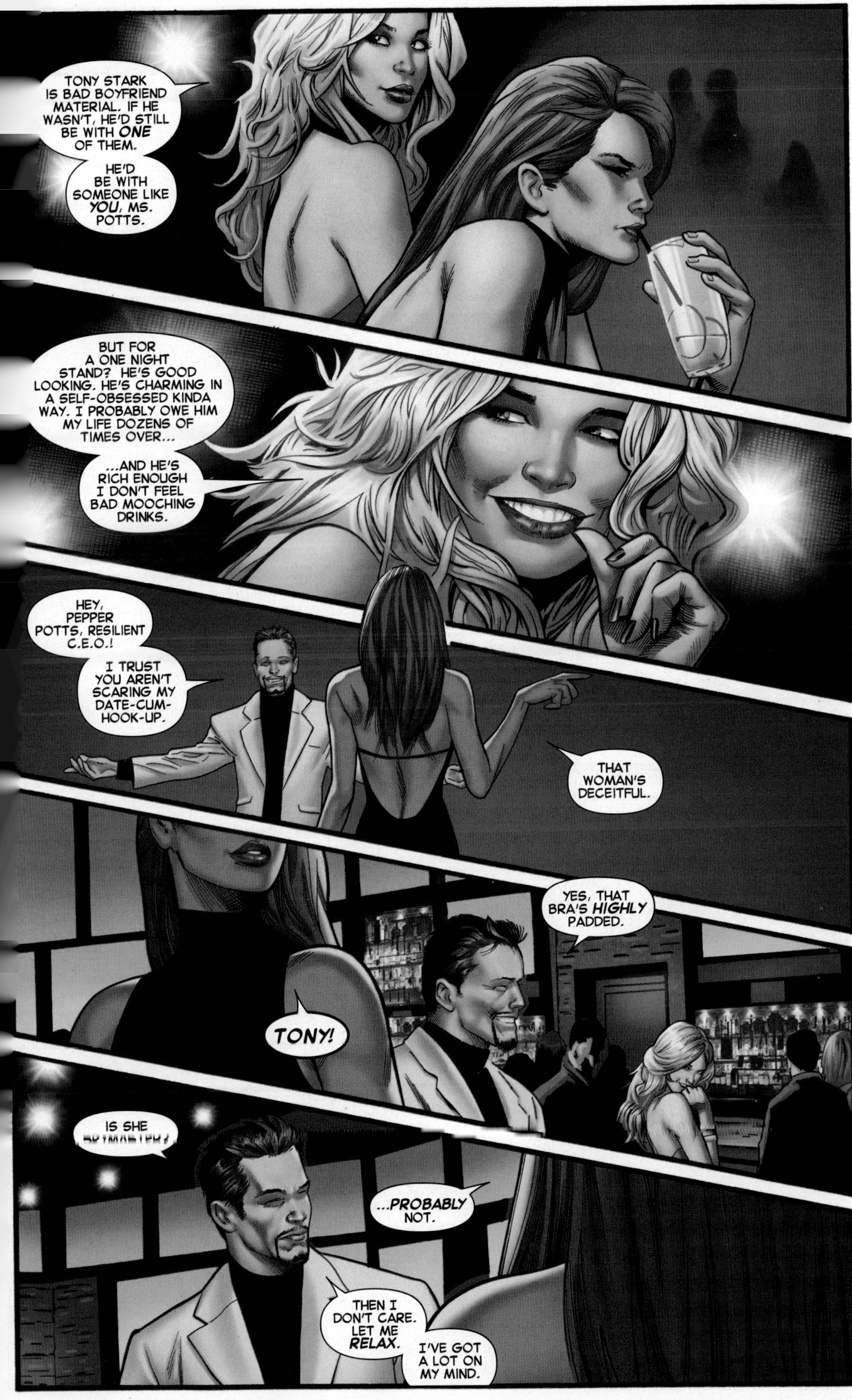
TONY STARK IS BAD BOYFRIEND MATERIAL. IF HE WASN'T, HE'D STILL BE WITH ONE OF THEM.
HE'D BE WITH SOMEONE LIKE YOU, MS. POTTS.
BUT FOR A ONE NIGHT STAND? HE'S GOOD LOOKING. HE'S CHARMING IN A SELF-OBSESSED KINDA WAY. I PROBABLY OWE HIM MY LIFE DOZENS OF TIMES OVER...
...AND HE'S RICH ENOUGH I DON'T FEEL BAD MOOCHING DRINKS.
HEY, PEPPER POTTS, RESILIENT C.E.O.!
I TRUST YOU AREN'T SCARING MY DATE-CUM-HOOK-UP.
THAT WOMAN'S DECEITFUL.
YES, THAT BRA'S HIGHLY PADDED.
TONY!
IS SHE
...PROBABLY NOT.
THEN I DON'T CARE. LET ME RELAX.
I'VE GOT A LOT ON MY MIND.

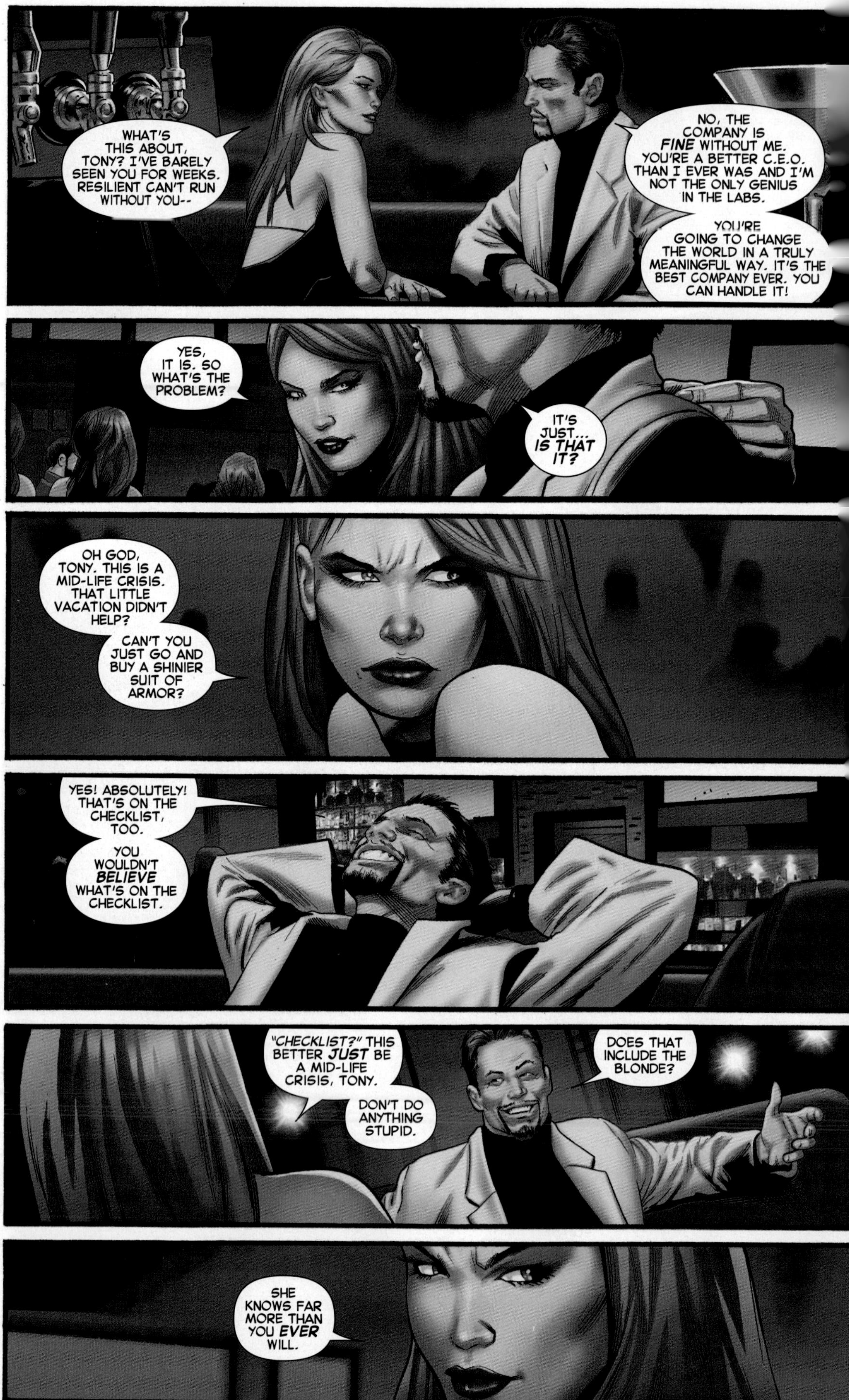
WHAT'S THIS ABOUT, TONY? I'VE BARELY SEEN YOU FOR WEEKS. RESILIENT CAN'T RUN WITHOUT YOU--
NO, THE COMPANY IS *FINE* WITHOUT ME. YOU'RE A BETTER C.E.O. THAN I EVER WAS AND I'M NOT THE ONLY GENIUS IN THE LABS.
YOU'RE GOING TO CHANGE THE WORLD IN A TRULY MEANINGFUL WAY. IT'S THE BEST COMPANY EVER. YOU CAN HANDLE IT!
YES, IT IS. SO WHAT'S THE PROBLEM?
IT'S JUST... *IS THAT IT?*
OH GOD, TONY. THIS IS A MID-LIFE CRISIS. THAT LITTLE VACATION DIDN'T HELP?
CAN'T YOU JUST GO AND BUY A SHINIER SUIT OF ARMOR?
YES! ABSOLUTELY! THAT'S ON THE CHECKLIST, TOO.
YOU WOULDN'T *BELIEVE* WHAT'S ON THE CHECKLIST.
"CHECKLIST?" THIS BETTER *JUST* BE A MID-LIFE CRISIS, TONY.
DON'T DO ANYTHING STUPID.
DOES THAT INCLUDE THE BLONDE?
SHE KNOWS FAR MORE THAN YOU *EVER* WILL.

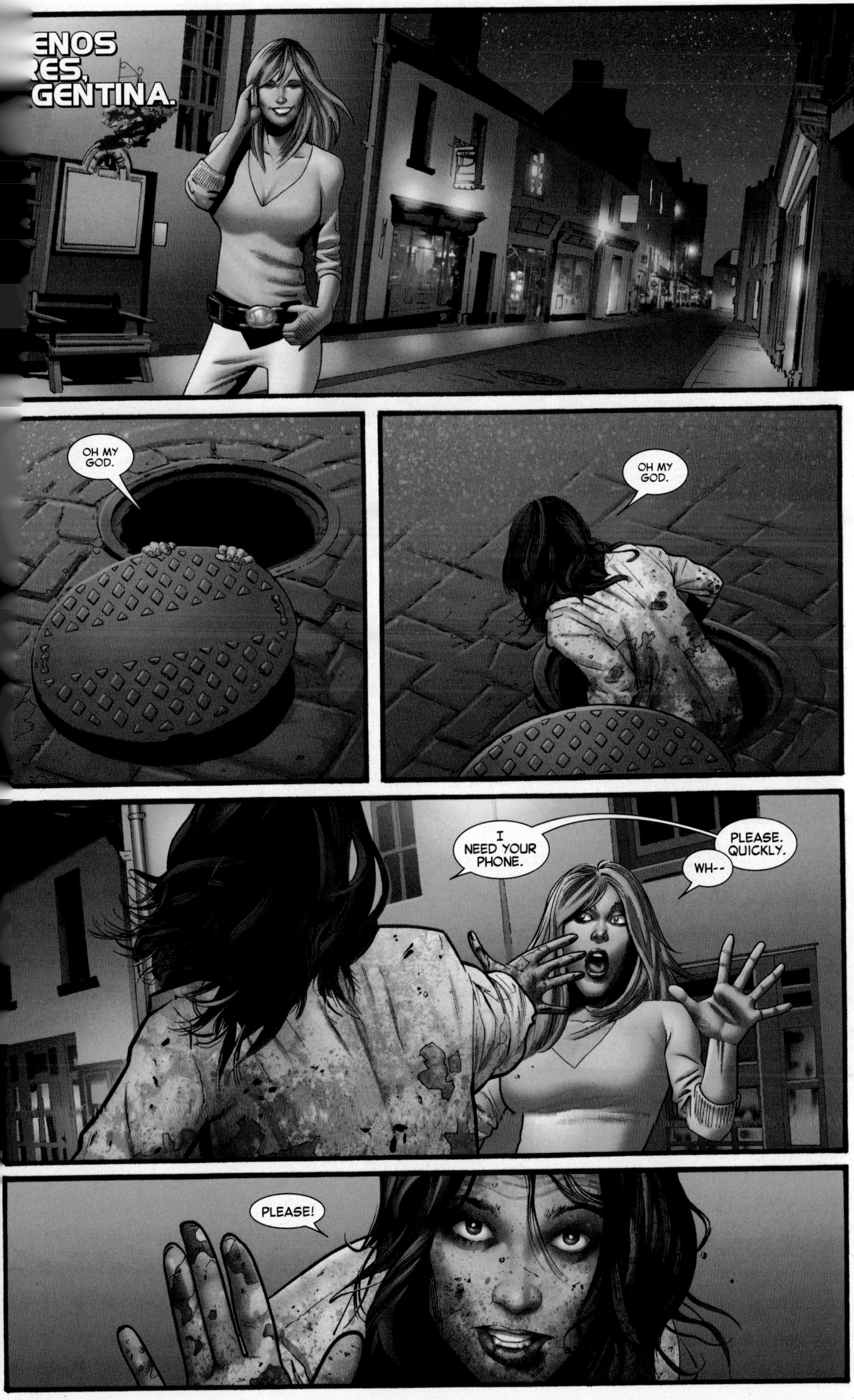
ENOS
RES,
GENTINA.
OH MY GOD.
OH MY GOD.
I NEED YOUR PHONE.
WH--
PLEASE. QUICKLY.
PLEASE!

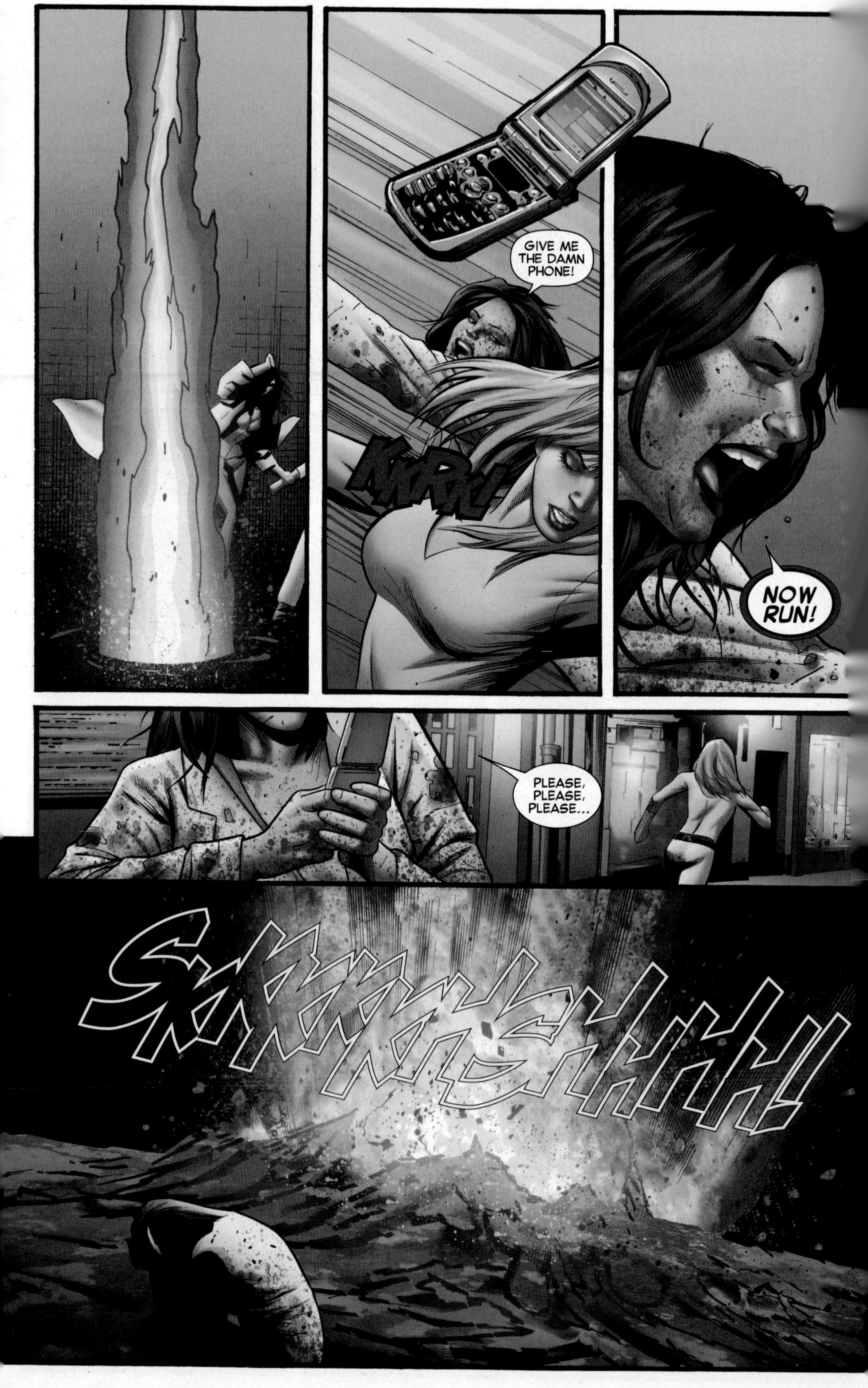
GIVE ME THE DAMN PHONE!
KKRRK!
NOW RUN!
PLEASE, PLEASE, PLEASE...
SKRRRRAAASHHHH!

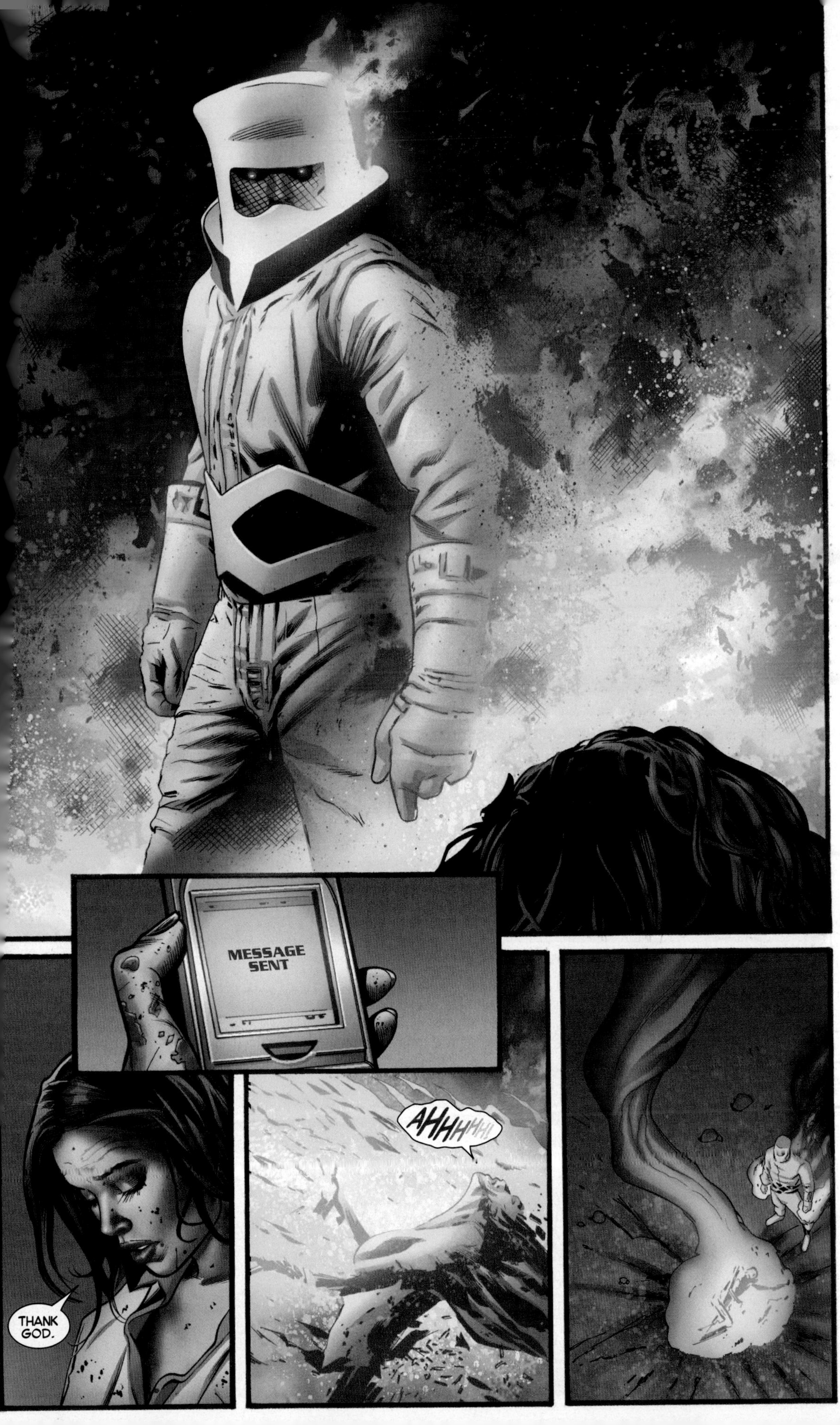
MESSAGE SENT
THANK GOD.
AHHHHH!

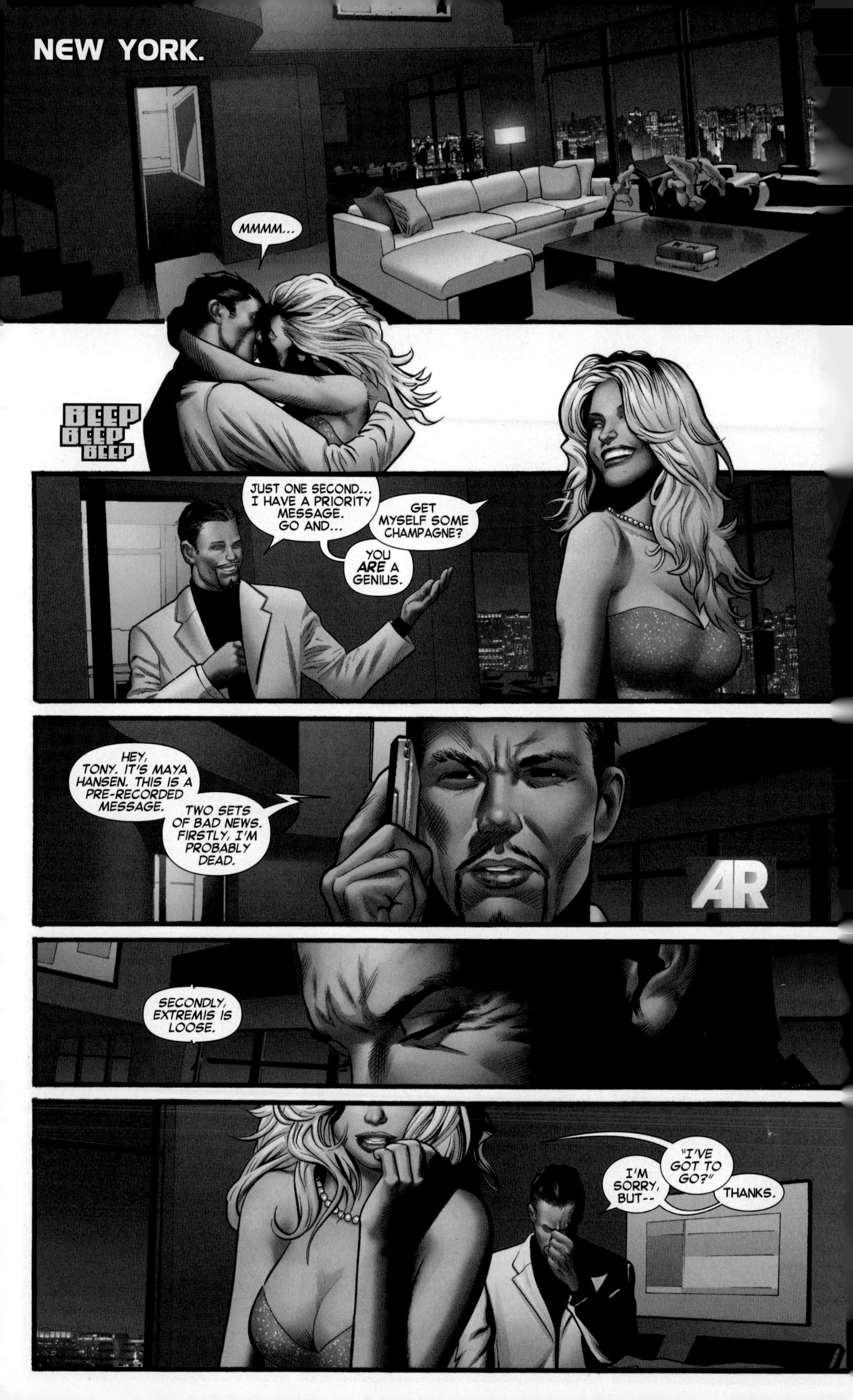
NEW YORK.
MMMM...
BEEP BEEP BEEP
JUST ONE SECOND... I HAVE A PRIORITY MESSAGE. GO AND...
GET MYSELF SOME CHAMPAGNE?
YOU ARE A GENIUS.
HEY, TONY. IT'S MAYA HANSEN. THIS IS A PRE-RECORDED MESSAGE.
TWO SETS OF BAD NEWS. FIRSTLY, I'M PROBABLY DEAD.
AR
SECONDLY, EXTREMIS IS LOOSE.
I'M SORRY, BUT--
"I'VE GOT TO GO?"
THANKS.

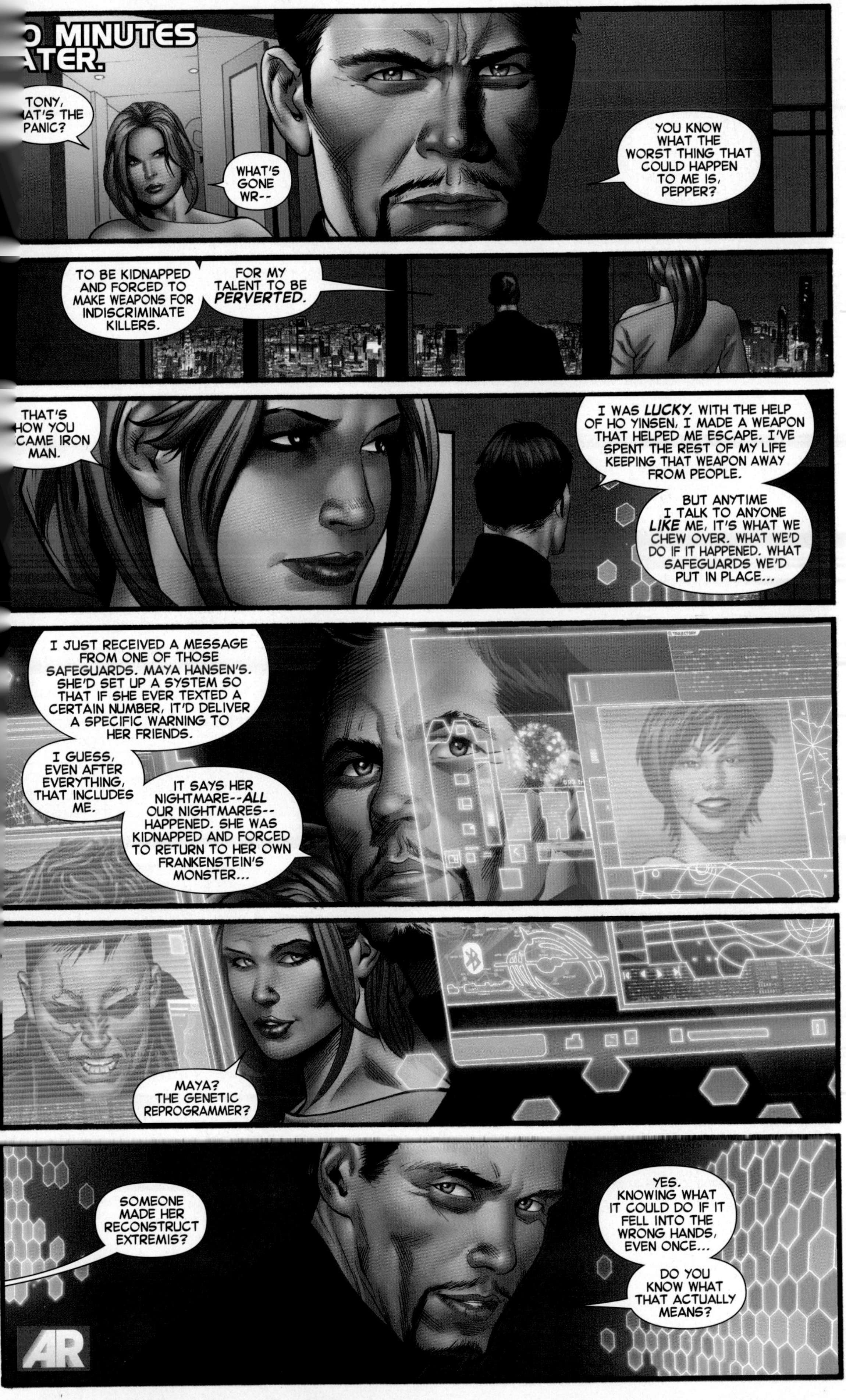

O MINUTES ATER.
TONY, AT'S THE PANIC?
WHAT'S GONE WR--
YOU KNOW WHAT THE WORST THING THAT COULD HAPPEN TO ME IS, PEPPER?
TO BE KIDNAPPED AND FORCED TO MAKE WEAPONS FOR INDISCRIMINATE KILLERS.
FOR MY TALENT TO BE PERVERTED.
THAT'S HOW YOU CAME IRON MAN.
I WAS LUCKY. WITH THE HELP OF HO YINSEN, I MADE A WEAPON THAT HELPED ME ESCAPE. I'VE SPENT THE REST OF MY LIFE KEEPING THAT WEAPON AWAY FROM PEOPLE.
BUT ANYTIME I TALK TO ANYONE LIKE ME, IT'S WHAT WE CHEW OVER. WHAT WE'D DO IF IT HAPPENED. WHAT SAFEGUARDS WE'D PUT IN PLACE...
I JUST RECEIVED A MESSAGE FROM ONE OF THOSE SAFEGUARDS. MAYA HANSEN'S. SHE'D SET UP A SYSTEM SO THAT IF SHE EVER TEXTED A CERTAIN NUMBER, IT'D DELIVER A SPECIFIC WARNING TO HER FRIENDS.
I GUESS, EVEN AFTER EVERYTHING, THAT INCLUDES ME.
IT SAYS HER NIGHTMARE--ALL OUR NIGHTMARES--HAPPENED. SHE WAS KIDNAPPED AND FORCED TO RETURN TO HER OWN FRANKENSTEIN'S MONSTER...
MAYA? THE GENETIC REPROGRAMMER?
SOMEONE MADE HER RECONSTRUCT EXTREMIS?
YES. KNOWING WHAT IT COULD DO IF IT FELL INTO THE WRONG HANDS, EVEN ONCE...
DO YOU KNOW WHAT THAT ACTUALLY MEANS?

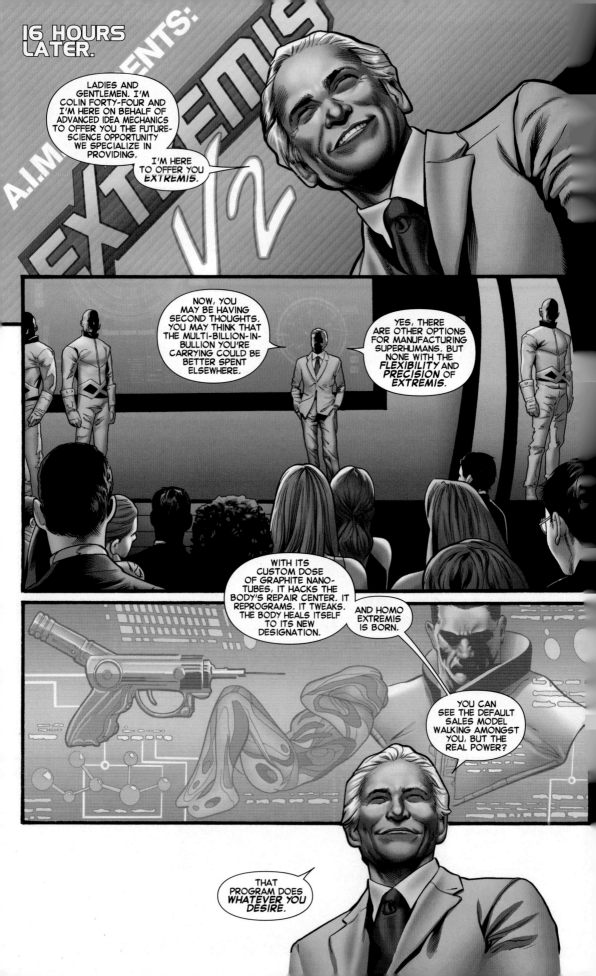

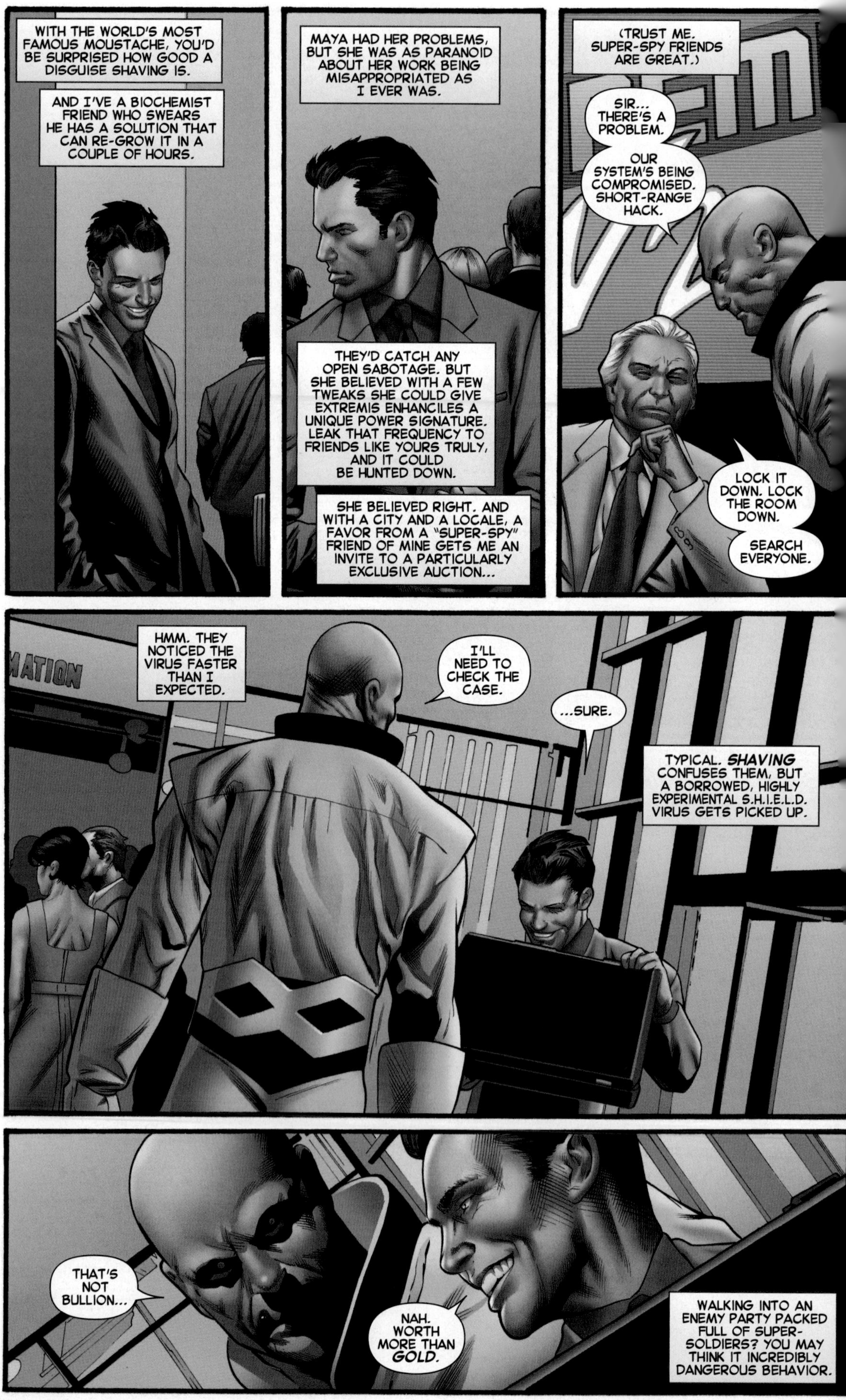
WITH THE WORLD'S MOST FAMOUS MOUSTACHE, YOU'D BE SURPRISED HOW GOOD A DISGUISE SHAVING IS.
AND I'VE A BIOCHEMIST FRIEND WHO SWEARS HE HAS A SOLUTION THAT CAN RE-GROW IT IN A COUPLE OF HOURS.
MAYA HAD HER PROBLEMS, BUT SHE WAS AS PARANOID ABOUT HER WORK BEING MISAPPROPRIATED AS I EVER WAS.
THEY'D CATCH ANY OPEN SABOTAGE. BUT SHE BELIEVED WITH A FEW TWEAKS SHE COULD GIVE EXTREMIS ENHANCILES A UNIQUE POWER SIGNATURE. LEAK THAT FREQUENCY TO FRIENDS LIKE YOURS TRULY, AND IT COULD BE HUNTED DOWN.
SHE BELIEVED RIGHT. AND WITH A CITY AND A LOCALE, A FAVOR FROM A "SUPER-SPY" FRIEND OF MINE GETS ME AN INVITE TO A PARTICULARLY EXCLUSIVE AUCTION...
(TRUST ME. SUPER-SPY FRIENDS ARE GREAT.)
SIR... THERE'S A PROBLEM.
OUR SYSTEM'S BEING COMPROMISED. SHORT-RANGE HACK.
LOCK IT DOWN. LOCK THE ROOM DOWN.
SEARCH EVERYONE.
HMM. THEY NOTICED THE VIRUS FASTER THAN I EXPECTED.
I'LL NEED TO CHECK THE CASE.
...SURE.
TYPICAL. SHAVING CONFUSES THEM, BUT A BORROWED, HIGHLY EXPERIMENTAL S.H.I.E.L.D. VIRUS GETS PICKED UP.
THAT'S NOT BULLION...
NAH. WORTH MORE THAN GOLD.
WALKING INTO AN ENEMY PARTY PACKED FULL OF SUPER-SOLDIERS? YOU MAY THINK IT INCREDIBLY DANGEROUS BEHAVIOR.

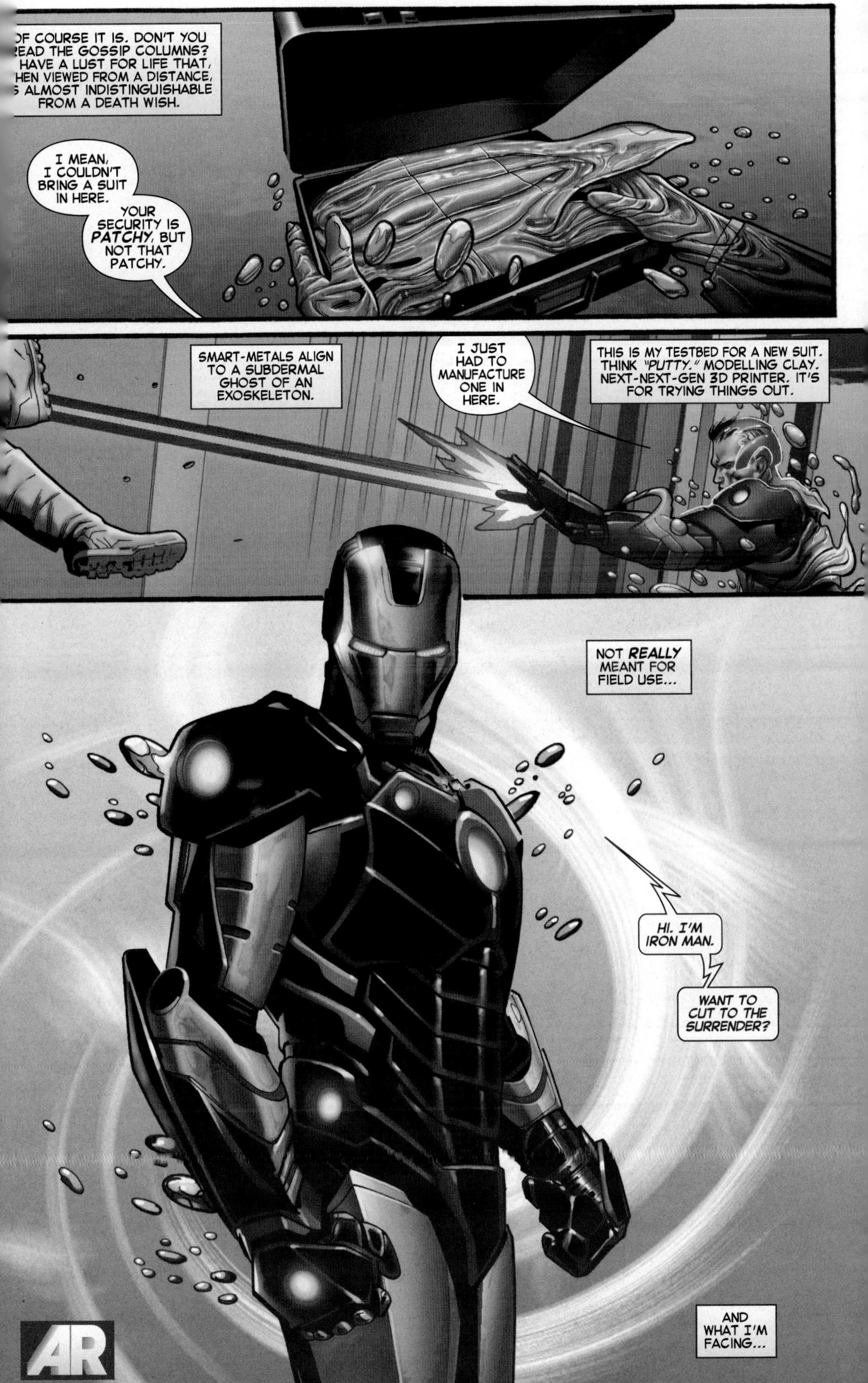
OF COURSE IT IS. DON'T YOU
READ THE GOSSIP COLUMNS?
HAVE A LUST FOR LIFE THAT,
HEN VIEWED FROM A DISTANCE,
S ALMOST INDISTINGUISHABLE
FROM A DEATH WISH.
I MEAN, I COULDN'T BRING A SUIT IN HERE.
YOUR SECURITY IS *PATCHY*, BUT NOT THAT PATCHY.
SMART-METALS ALIGN TO A SUBDERMAL GHOST OF AN EXOSKELETON.
I JUST HAD TO MANUFACTURE ONE IN HERE.
THIS IS MY TESTBED FOR A NEW SUIT. THINK *"PUTTY."* MODELLING CLAY. NEXT-NEXT-GEN 3D PRINTER. IT'S FOR TRYING THINGS OUT.
NOT *REALLY* MEANT FOR FIELD USE...
HI. I'M IRON MAN.
WANT TO CUT TO THE SURRENDER?
AND WHAT I'M FACING...

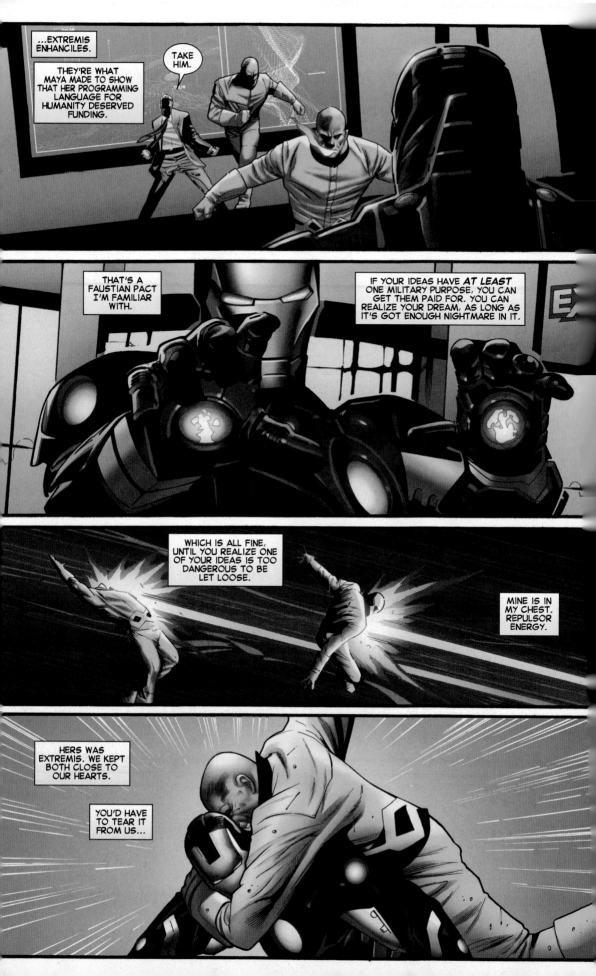

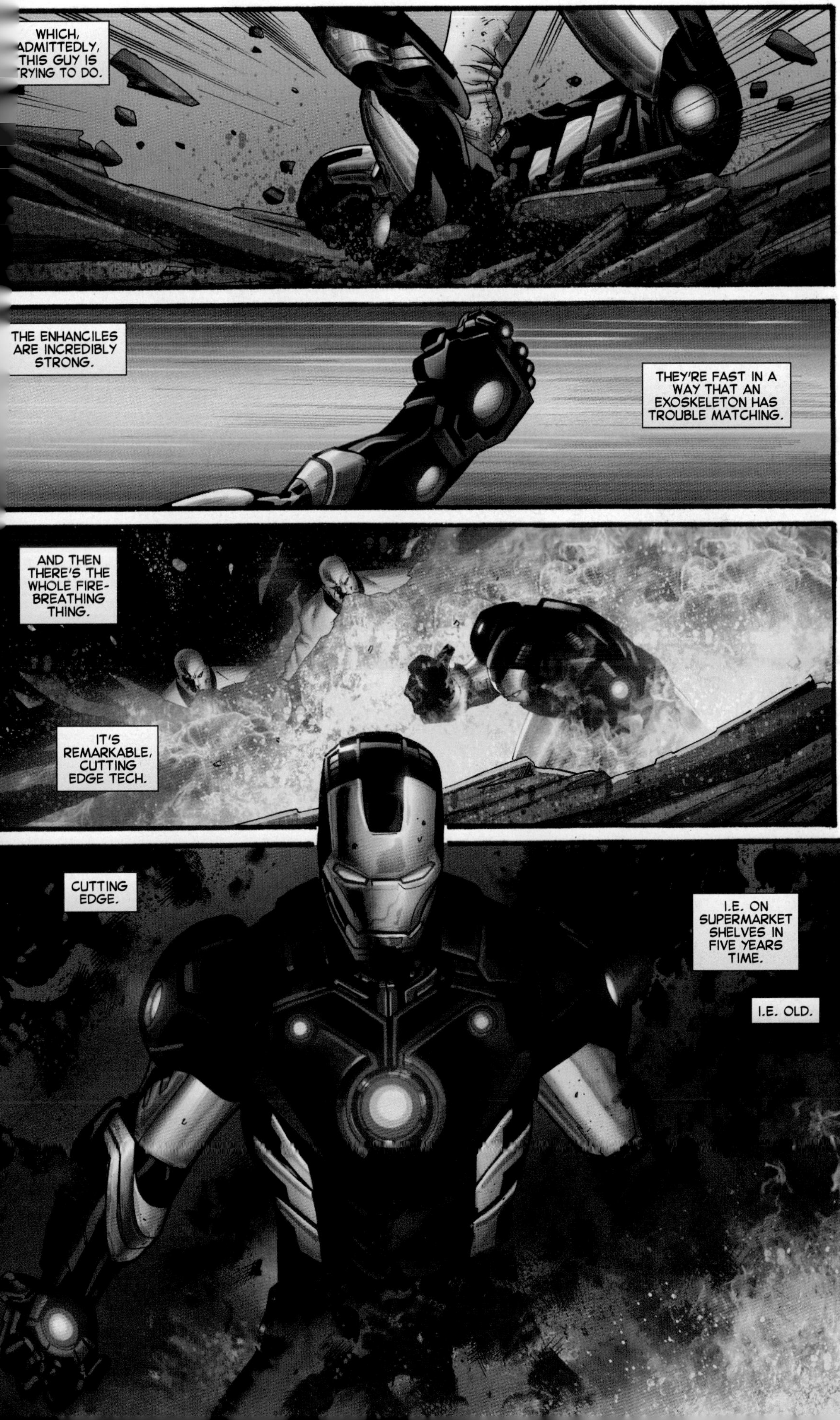
WHICH, ADMITTEDLY, THIS GUY IS TRYING TO DO.
THE ENHANCILES ARE INCREDIBLY STRONG.
THEY'RE FAST IN A WAY THAT AN EXOSKELETON HAS TROUBLE MATCHING.
AND THEN THERE'S THE WHOLE FIRE-BREATHING THING.
IT'S REMARKABLE, CUTTING EDGE TECH.
CUTTING EDGE.
I.E. ON SUPERMARKET SHELVES IN FIVE YEARS TIME.
I.E. OLD.

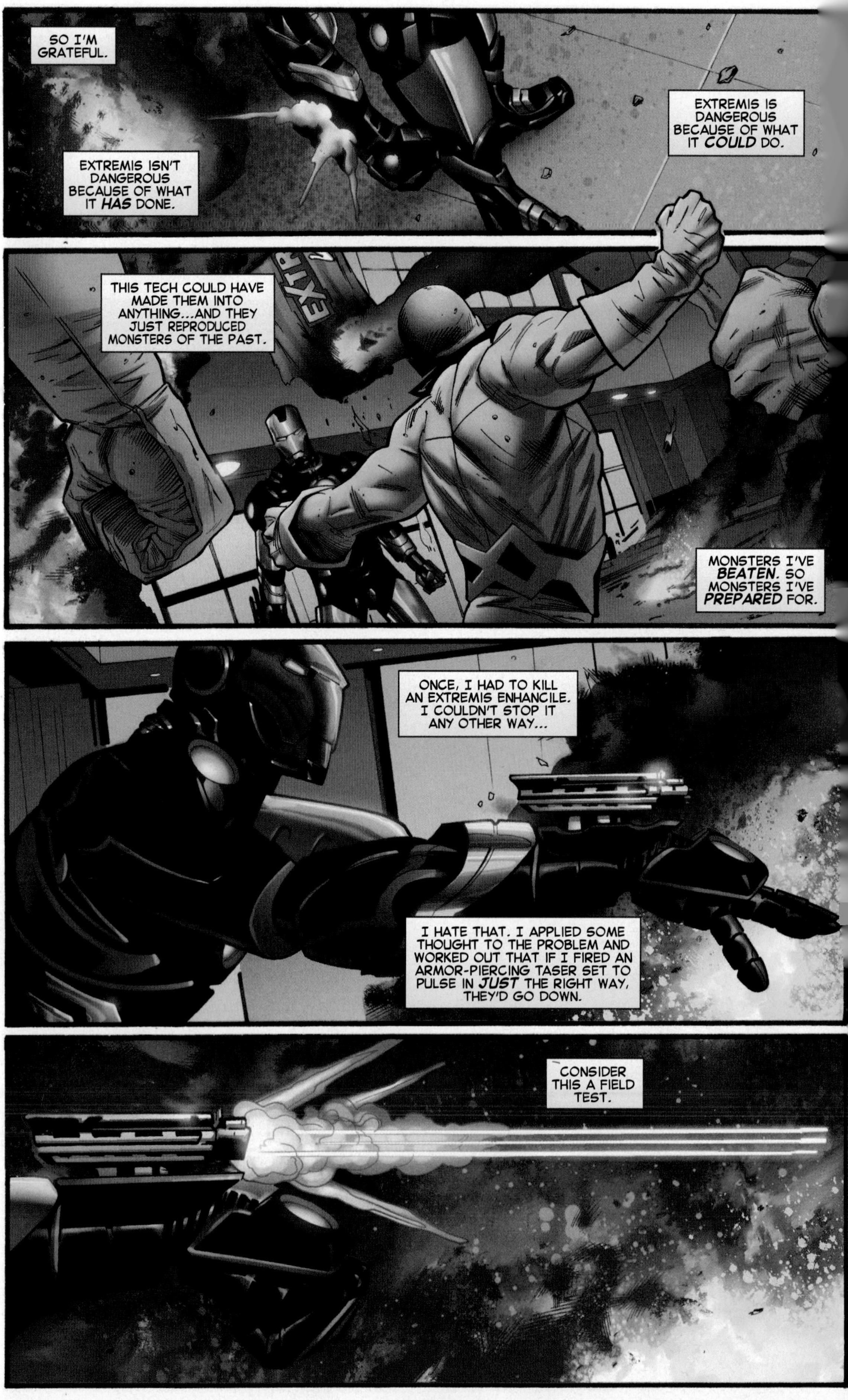
SO I'M GRATEFUL.
EXTREMIS ISN'T DANGEROUS BECAUSE OF WHAT IT *HAS* DONE.
EXTREMIS IS DANGEROUS BECAUSE OF WHAT IT *COULD* DO.
THIS TECH COULD HAVE MADE THEM INTO ANYTHING...AND THEY JUST REPRODUCED MONSTERS OF THE PAST.
MONSTERS I'VE *BEATEN.* SO MONSTERS I'VE *PREPARED* FOR.
ONCE, I HAD TO KILL AN EXTREMIS ENHANCILE. I COULDN'T STOP IT ANY OTHER WAY...
I HATE THAT. I APPLIED SOME THOUGHT TO THE PROBLEM AND WORKED OUT THAT IF I FIRED AN ARMOR-PIERCING TASER SET TO PULSE IN *JUST* THE RIGHT WAY, THEY'D GO DOWN.
CONSIDER THIS A FIELD TEST.

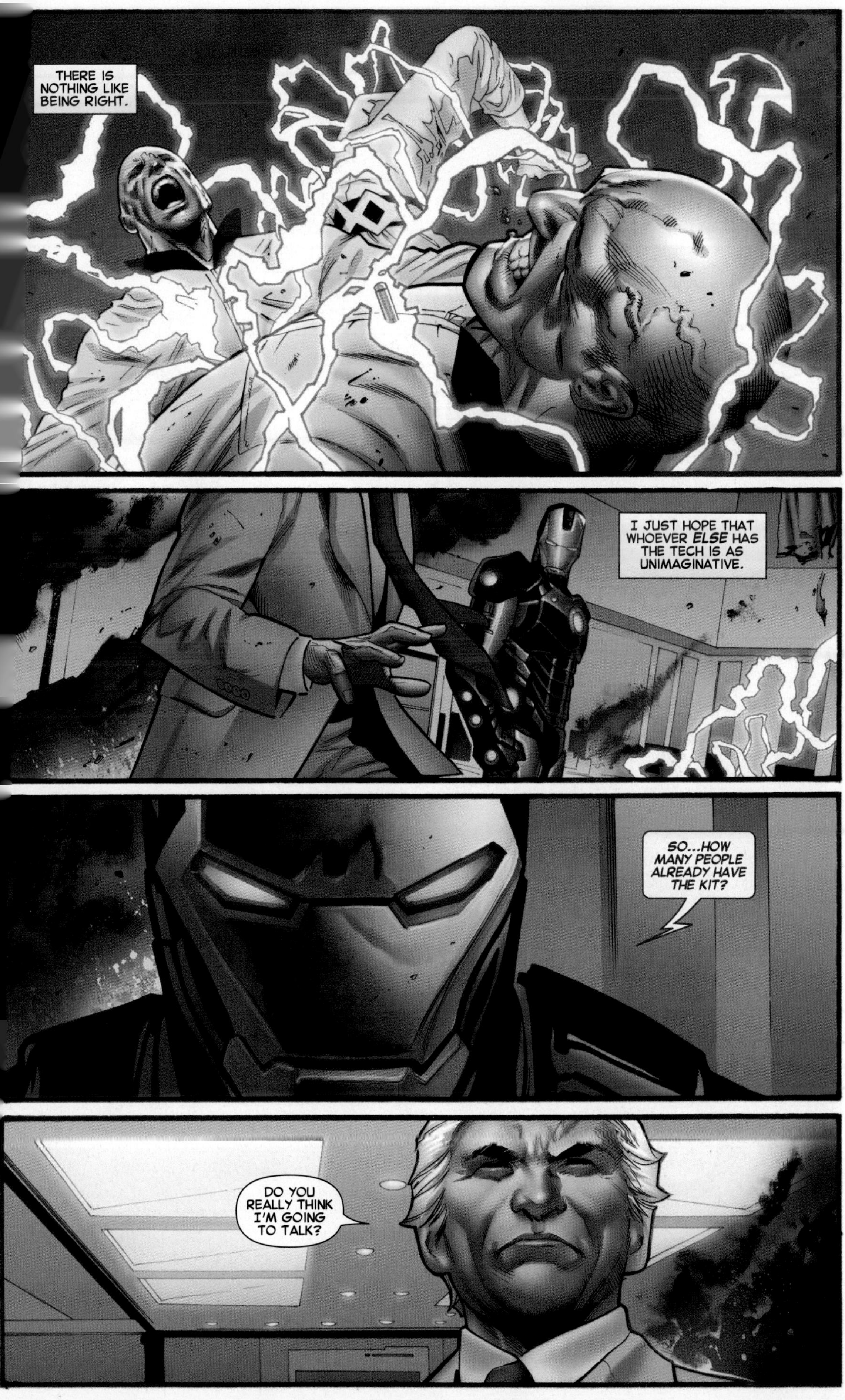
THERE IS NOTHING LIKE BEING RIGHT.
I JUST HOPE THAT WHOEVER ELSE HAS THE TECH IS AS UNIMAGINATIVE.
SO...HOW MANY PEOPLE ALREADY HAVE THE KIT?
DO YOU REALLY THINK I'M GOING TO TALK?

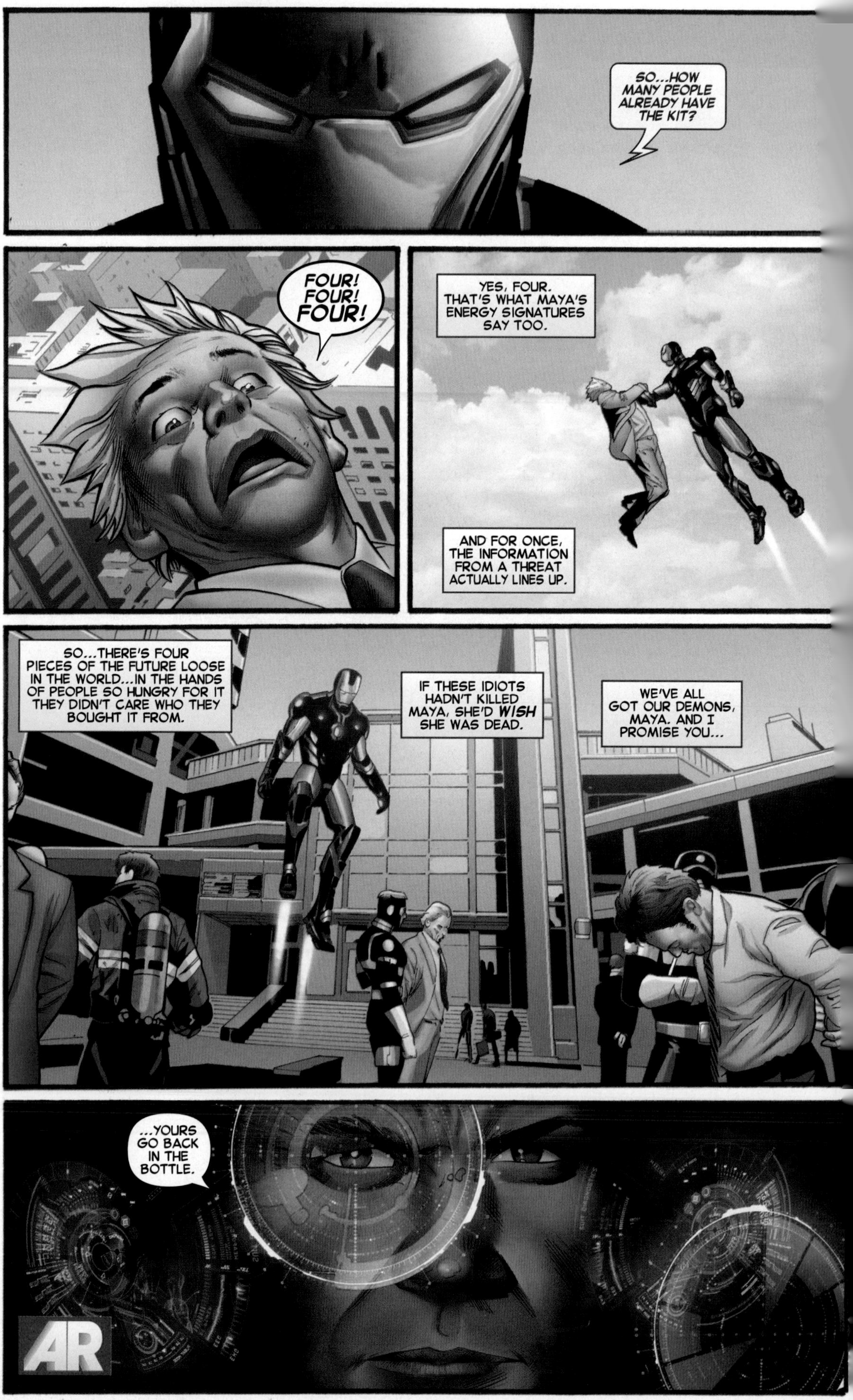
SO...HOW MANY PEOPLE ALREADY HAVE THE KIT?
FOUR! FOUR! FOUR!
YES, FOUR. THAT'S WHAT MAYA'S ENERGY SIGNATURES SAY TOO.
AND FOR ONCE, THE INFORMATION FROM A THREAT ACTUALLY LINES UP.
SO...THERE'S FOUR PIECES OF THE FUTURE LOOSE IN THE WORLD...IN THE HANDS OF PEOPLE SO HUNGRY FOR IT THEY DIDN'T CARE WHO THEY BOUGHT IT FROM.
IF THESE IDIOTS HADN'T KILLED MAYA, SHE'D WISH SHE WAS DEAD.
WE'VE ALL GOT OUR DEMONS, MAYA. AND I PROMISE YOU...
...YOURS GO BACK IN THE BOTTLE.
AR

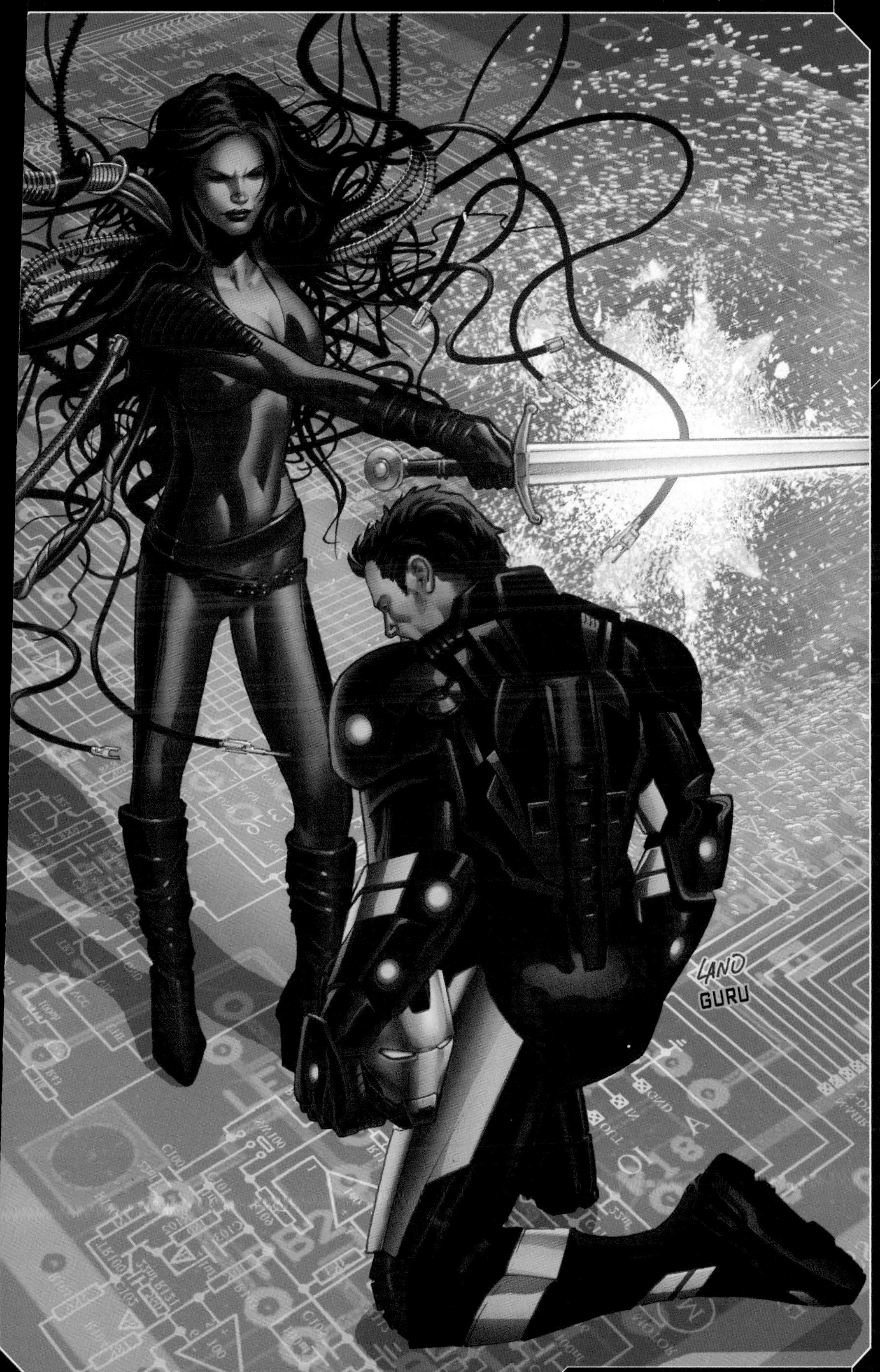
LAND
GURU

A GENTLEMAN'S WAGER 02

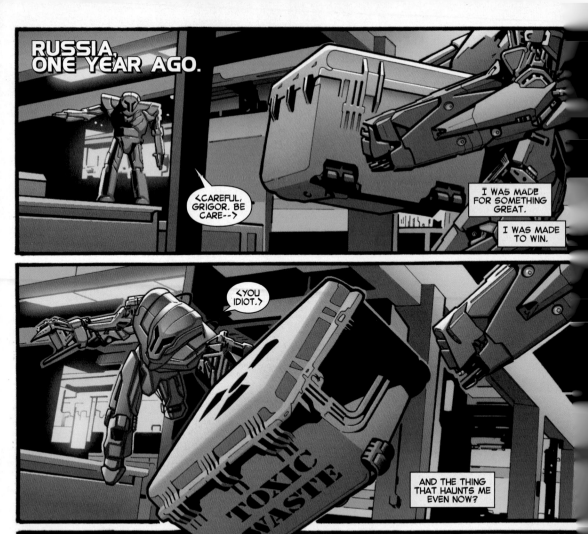

RUSSIA, ONE YEAR AGO.

<CAREFUL, GRIGOR. BE CARE--->

I WAS MADE FOR SOMETHING GREAT.

I WAS MADE TO WIN.

<YOU IDIOT.>

TOXIC WASTE

AND THE THING THAT HAUNTS ME EVEN NOW?

I NEVER EVEN HAD A CHANCE TO LOSE.

<TAKE YOUR TIME!>

<THE SUITS AREN'T MADE FOR SPEED.>

<THEY'RE BARELY MADE TO DO ANYTHING.>

ALEX DRAGUNO--

I'M WORKING.

IF YOU CALL IT THAT. CERTAINLY NOT THE WORK YOU WERE BORN TO DO.

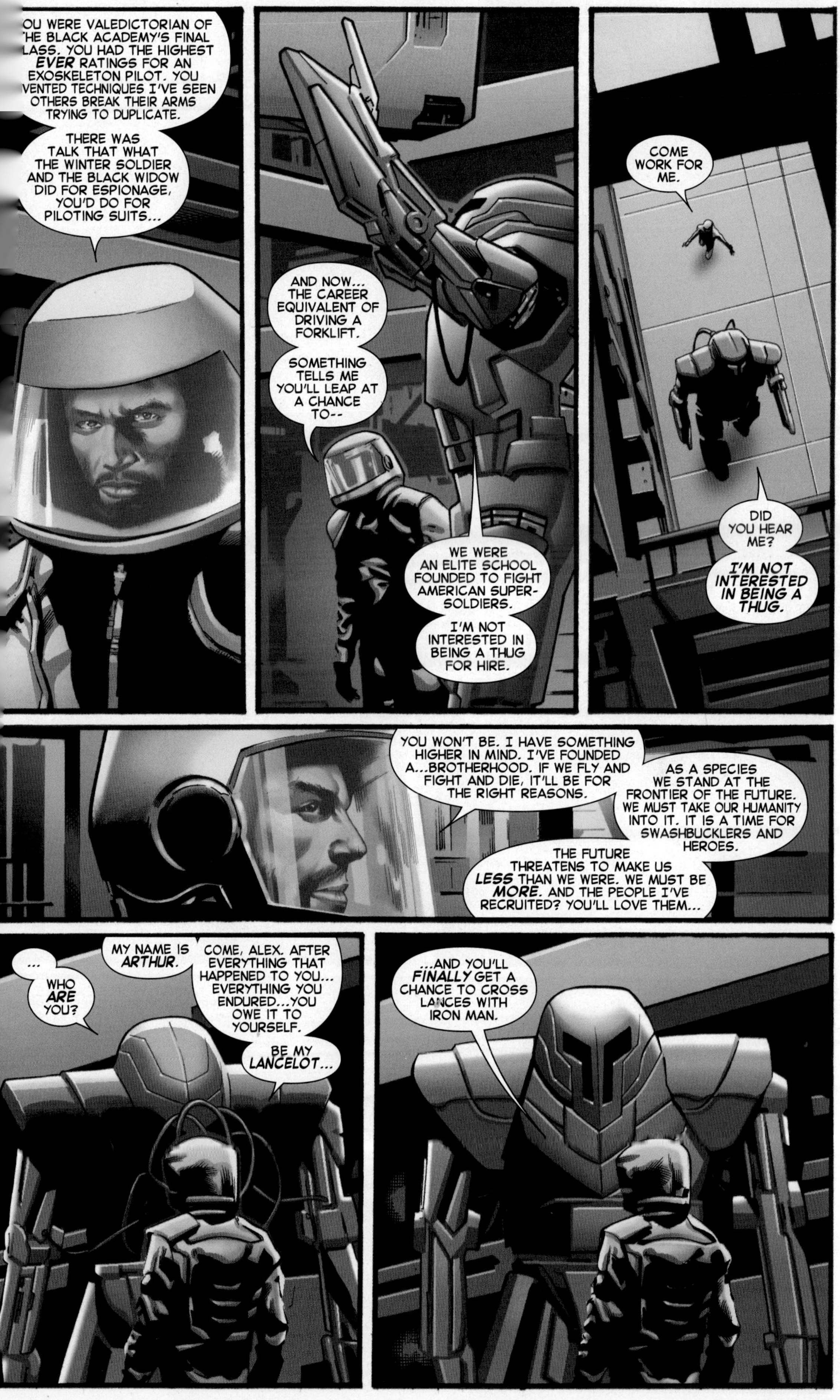

OU WERE VALEDICTORIAN OF HE BLACK ACADEMY'S FINAL LASS. YOU HAD THE HIGHEST EVER RATINGS FOR AN EXOSKELETON PILOT. YOU VENTED TECHNIQUES I'VE SEEN OTHERS BREAK THEIR ARMS TRYING TO DUPLICATE.
THERE WAS TALK THAT WHAT THE WINTER SOLDIER AND THE BLACK WIDOW DID FOR ESPIONAGE, YOU'D DO FOR PILOTING SUITS...
AND NOW... THE CAREER EQUIVALENT OF DRIVING A FORKLIFT.
SOMETHING TELLS ME YOU'LL LEAP AT A CHANCE TO--
WE WERE AN ELITE SCHOOL FOUNDED TO FIGHT AMERICAN SUPER-SOLDIERS.
I'M NOT INTERESTED IN BEING A THUG FOR HIRE.
COME WORK FOR ME.
DID YOU HEAR ME?
I'M NOT INTERESTED IN BEING A THUG.
YOU WON'T BE. I HAVE SOMETHING HIGHER IN MIND. I'VE FOUNDED A...BROTHERHOOD. IF WE FLY AND FIGHT AND DIE, IT'LL BE FOR THE RIGHT REASONS.
AS A SPECIES WE STAND AT THE FRONTIER OF THE FUTURE. WE MUST TAKE OUR HUMANITY INTO IT. IT IS A TIME FOR SWASHBUCKLERS AND HEROES.
THE FUTURE THREATENS TO MAKE US LESS THAN WE WERE. WE MUST BE MORE. AND THE PEOPLE I'VE RECRUITED? YOU'LL LOVE THEM...
... WHO ARE YOU?
MY NAME IS ARTHUR.
COME, ALEX. AFTER EVERYTHING THAT HAPPENED TO YOU... EVERYTHING YOU ENDURED...YOU OWE IT TO YOURSELF.
BE MY LANCELOT...
...AND YOU'LL FINALLY GET A CHANCE TO CROSS LANCES WITH IRON MAN.

SO WHAT'S THE STORY? BRIBES?

NO. THIS CIRCLE HAS *IMPRESSED* THEM. SYMKARIANS DON'T IMPRESS EASY, IN MY EXPERIENCE. SO, SOMEONE WHO REGISTERS ON THEIR COMPETENCE SCALE IS ALWAYS WELCOME TO STAY.

AFTER ALL, THEY BORDER *LATVERIA*. WHEN YOU HAVE *DOCTOR DOOM* AS A NEIGHBOR, I CAN SEE THE ATTRACTION OF HAVING A LITTLE INDEPENDENT DETERRENT IN YOUR GARDEN.

THOUGH LATVERIA ISN'T *THAT* BAD. THEIR LABOR LAWS ARE CHARMINGLY LENIENT. MAYBE YOU SHOULD THINK OF SETTING UP A FACTORY THERE...

TONY! DON'T EVEN JOKE.

SO WHAT ARE YOU GOING TO DO?

WHAT I HAVE TO.

WE CANNOT ALLOW EXTREMIS TECH TO BE IN ANYONE'S HANDS. MAYA WOULD COME BACK TO LIFE JUST TO KILL ME. I'LL SNEAK IN AND...

...WHAT'S THAT?

TONY STARK! THE CIRCLE INVITES YOU TO NEW AVALON, SYMKARIA, FOR A WAGER FOR CERTAIN TECHNOLOGIES. DETAILS TO FOLLOW VIA MORE TRADITIONAL MEANS.

I'D FROWN AT THE GRANDIOSITY IF I DIDN'T THINK IT WAS KINDA NEAT.

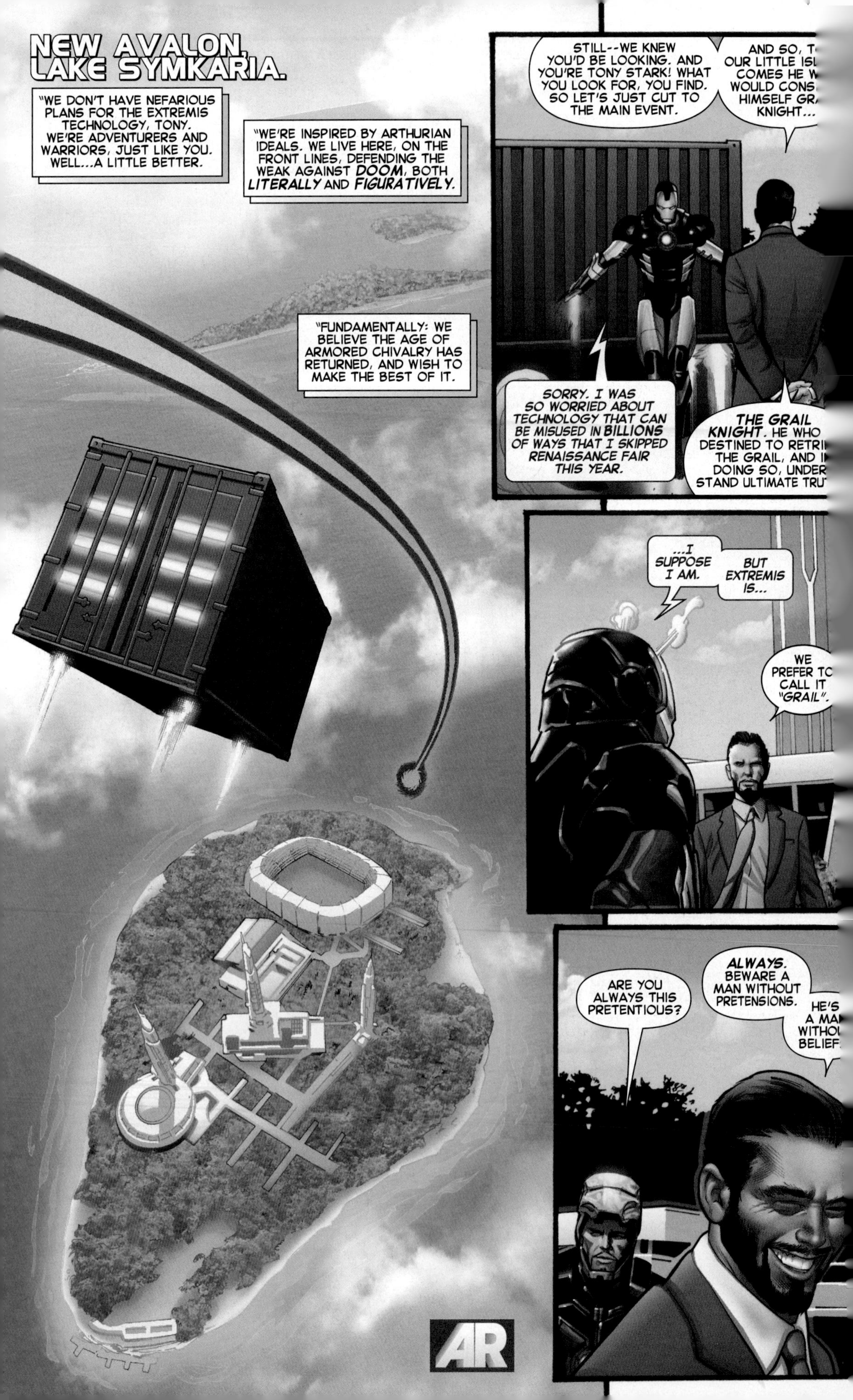

NEW AVALON, LAKE SYMKARIA.
"WE DON'T HAVE NEFARIOUS PLANS FOR THE EXTREMIS TECHNOLOGY, TONY. WE'RE ADVENTURERS AND WARRIORS, JUST LIKE YOU. WELL...A LITTLE BETTER.
"WE'RE INSPIRED BY ARTHURIAN IDEALS. WE LIVE HERE, ON THE FRONT LINES, DEFENDING THE WEAK AGAINST **DOOM**, BOTH ***LITERALLY*** AND ***FIGURATIVELY***.
"FUNDAMENTALLY: WE BELIEVE THE AGE OF ARMORED CHIVALRY HAS RETURNED, AND WISH TO MAKE THE BEST OF IT.
STILL--WE KNEW YOU'D BE LOOKING. AND YOU'RE TONY STARK! WHAT YOU LOOK FOR, YOU FIND. SO LET'S JUST CUT TO THE MAIN EVENT.
AND SO, T OUR LITTLE ISL COMES HE W WOULD CONS HIMSELF GRA KNIGHT...
*SORRY. I WAS SO WORRIED ABOUT TECHNOLOGY THAT CAN BE MISUSED IN **BILLIONS** OF WAYS THAT I SKIPPED RENAISSANCE FAIR THIS YEAR.*
THE GRAIL KNIGHT. HE WHO DESTINED TO RETRI THE GRAIL, AND I DOING SO, UNDER STAND ULTIMATE TRU
...I SUPPOSE I AM.
BUT EXTREMIS IS...
WE PREFER TO CALL IT *"GRAIL"*.
ARE YOU ALWAYS THIS PRETENTIOUS?
ALWAYS. BEWARE A MAN WITHOUT PRETENSIONS.
HE'S A MA WITHOU BELIEF.

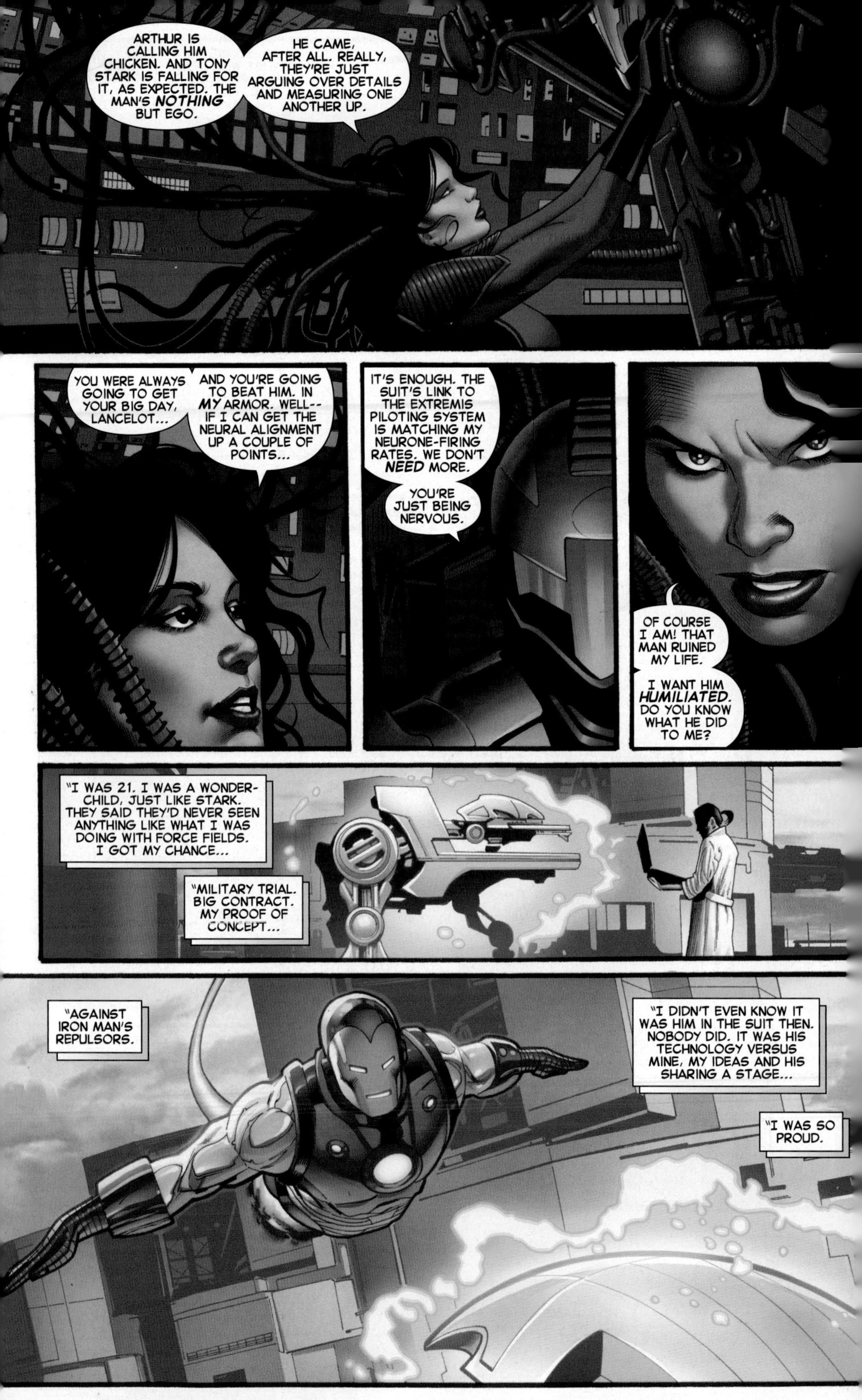
ARTHUR IS CALLING HIM CHICKEN. AND TONY STARK IS FALLING FOR IT, AS EXPECTED. THE MAN'S NOTHING BUT EGO.
HE CAME, AFTER ALL. REALLY, THEY'RE JUST ARGUING OVER DETAILS AND MEASURING ONE ANOTHER UP.
YOU WERE ALWAYS GOING TO GET YOUR BIG DAY, LANCELOT...
AND YOU'RE GOING TO BEAT HIM. IN MY ARMOR. WELL-- IF I CAN GET THE NEURAL ALIGNMENT UP A COUPLE OF POINTS...
IT'S ENOUGH. THE SUIT'S LINK TO THE EXTREMIS PILOTING SYSTEM IS MATCHING MY NEURONE-FIRING RATES. WE DON'T NEED MORE.
YOU'RE JUST BEING NERVOUS.
OF COURSE I AM! THAT MAN RUINED MY LIFE.
I WANT HIM HUMILIATED. DO YOU KNOW WHAT HE DID TO ME?
"I WAS 21. I WAS A WONDER-CHILD, JUST LIKE STARK. THEY SAID THEY'D NEVER SEEN ANYTHING LIKE WHAT I WAS DOING WITH FORCE FIELDS. I GOT MY CHANCE...
"MILITARY TRIAL. BIG CONTRACT. MY PROOF OF CONCEPT...
"AGAINST IRON MAN'S REPULSORS.
"I DIDN'T EVEN KNOW IT WAS HIM IN THE SUIT THEN. NOBODY DID. IT WAS HIS TECHNOLOGY VERSUS MINE, MY IDEAS AND HIS SHARING A STAGE...
"I WAS SO PROUD.

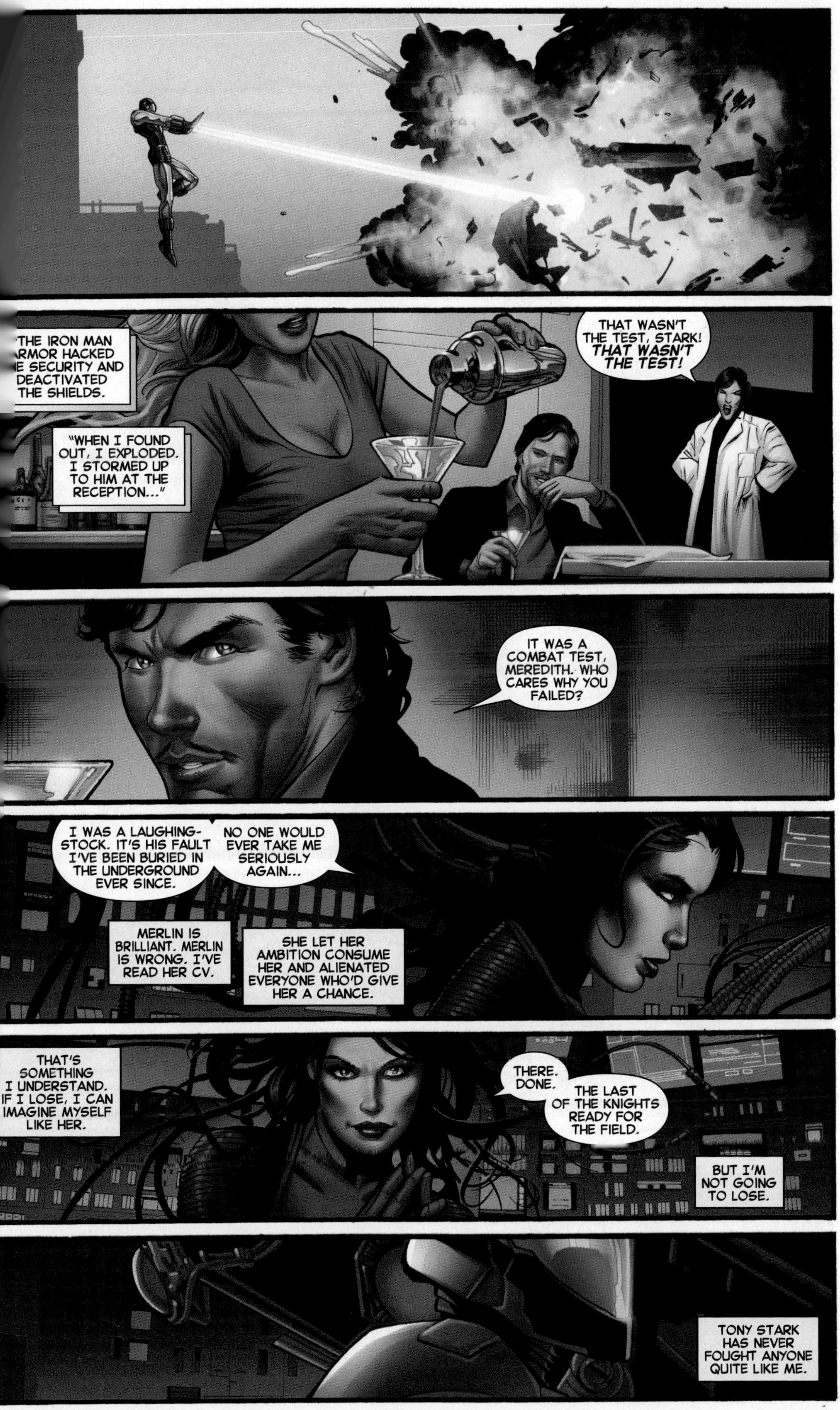
THE IRON MAN ARMOR HACKED E SECURITY AND DEACTIVATED THE SHIELDS.
"WHEN I FOUND OUT, I EXPLODED. I STORMED UP TO HIM AT THE RECEPTION..."
THAT WASN'T THE TEST, STARK! THAT WASN'T THE TEST!
IT WAS A COMBAT TEST, MEREDITH. WHO CARES WHY YOU FAILED?
I WAS A LAUGHING-STOCK. IT'S HIS FAULT I'VE BEEN BURIED IN THE UNDERGROUND EVER SINCE.
NO ONE WOULD EVER TAKE ME SERIOUSLY AGAIN...
MERLIN IS BRILLIANT. MERLIN IS WRONG. I'VE READ HER CV.
SHE LET HER AMBITION CONSUME HER AND ALIENATED EVERYONE WHO'D GIVE HER A CHANCE.
THAT'S SOMETHING I UNDERSTAND. IF I LOSE, I CAN IMAGINE MYSELF LIKE HER.
THERE. DONE.
THE LAST OF THE KNIGHTS READY FOR THE FIELD.
BUT I'M NOT GOING TO LOSE.
TONY STARK HAS NEVER FOUGHT ANYONE QUITE LIKE ME.

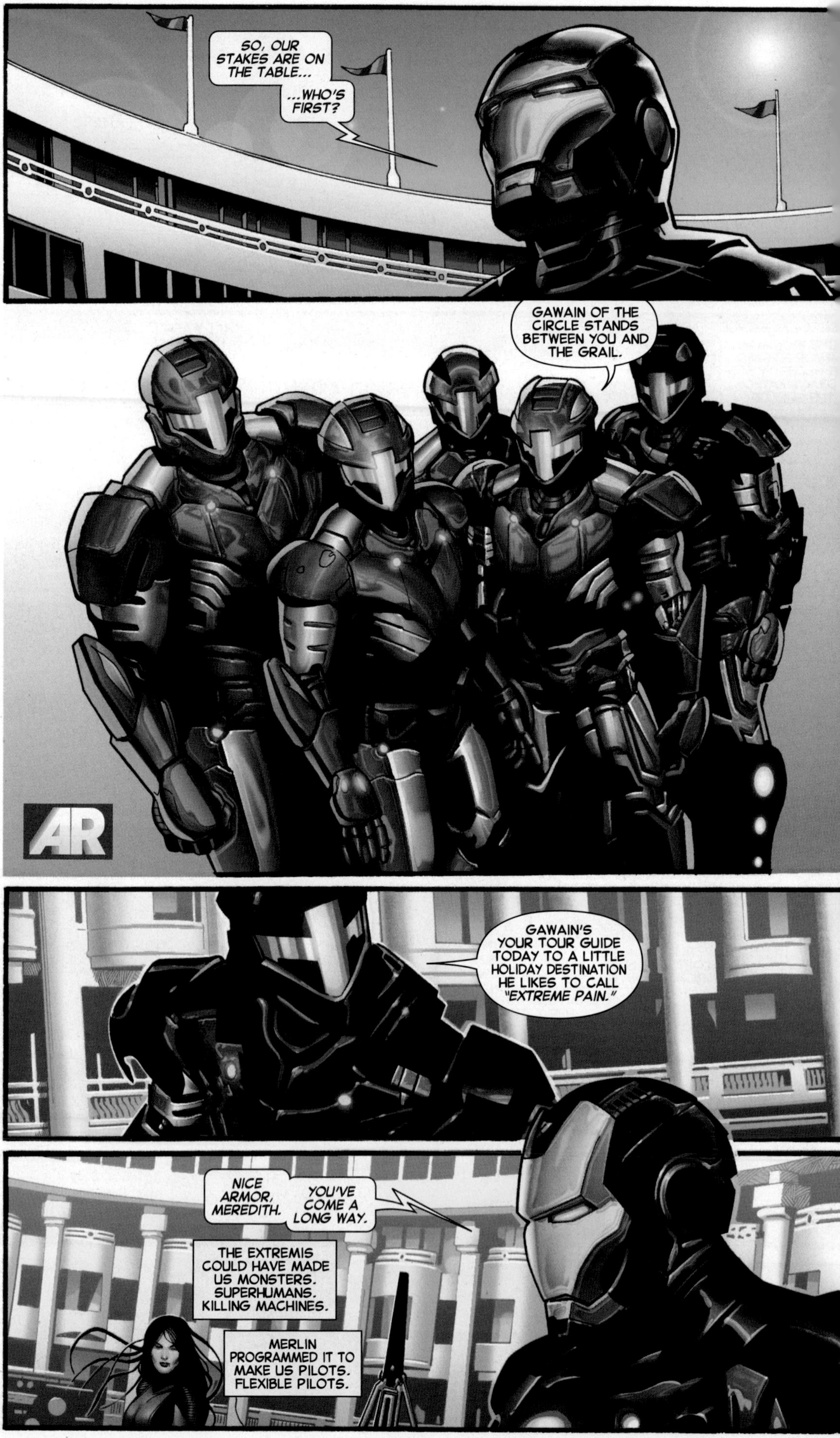
SO, OUR STAKES ARE ON THE TABLE...
...WHO'S FIRST?
GAWAIN OF THE CIRCLE STANDS BETWEEN YOU AND THE GRAIL.
GAWAIN'S YOUR TOUR GUIDE TODAY TO A LITTLE HOLIDAY DESTINATION HE LIKES TO CALL "EXTREME PAIN."
NICE ARMOR, MEREDITH.
YOU'VE COME A LONG WAY.
THE EXTREMIS COULD HAVE MADE US MONSTERS. SUPERHUMANS. KILLING MACHINES.
MERLIN PROGRAMMED IT TO MAKE US PILOTS. FLEXIBLE PILOTS.

...ARE NOW LIVING CONTROL ...EMS, DIRECTLY CONNECTED TO ...VER SUITS MERLIN BUILDS. IT'S ...RE-PROOFED. THE SUITS CAN ...OVE WHILE THE PILOTS ARE AS ...OD AS THEY CAN GET WHILE ...STILL REMAINING HUMANS.

...L, MOSTLY HUMAN. SOME MINOR ...OSTS, G-TOLERANCE AND SO ON, ...THEY'RE NOT THE SORT OF THINGS ...T GET YOU INTO THE AVENGERS.

COMPUTER?

YZZ?

DEPLOY THE ARMORY.

YZZ!

GIVE ME A SINGLE-OPPONENT LOAD-OUT.

THROW THE LATEST REPULSOR IN THERE. THE MARK IVa.

IT'S ABOUT FLEXIBILITY.

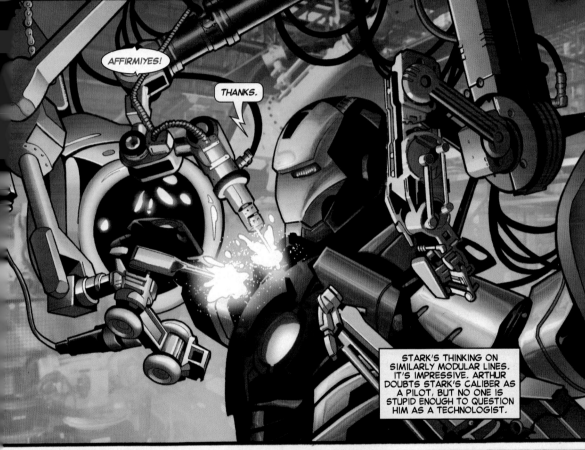

AFFIRMIYES!

THANKS.

STARK'S THINKING ON SIMILARLY MODULAR LINES. IT'S IMPRESSIVE. ARTHUR DOUBTS STARK'S CALIBER AS A PILOT, BUT NO ONE IS STUPID ENOUGH TO QUESTION HIM AS A TECHNOLOGIST.

READY WHEN YOU ARE, WAYNE.

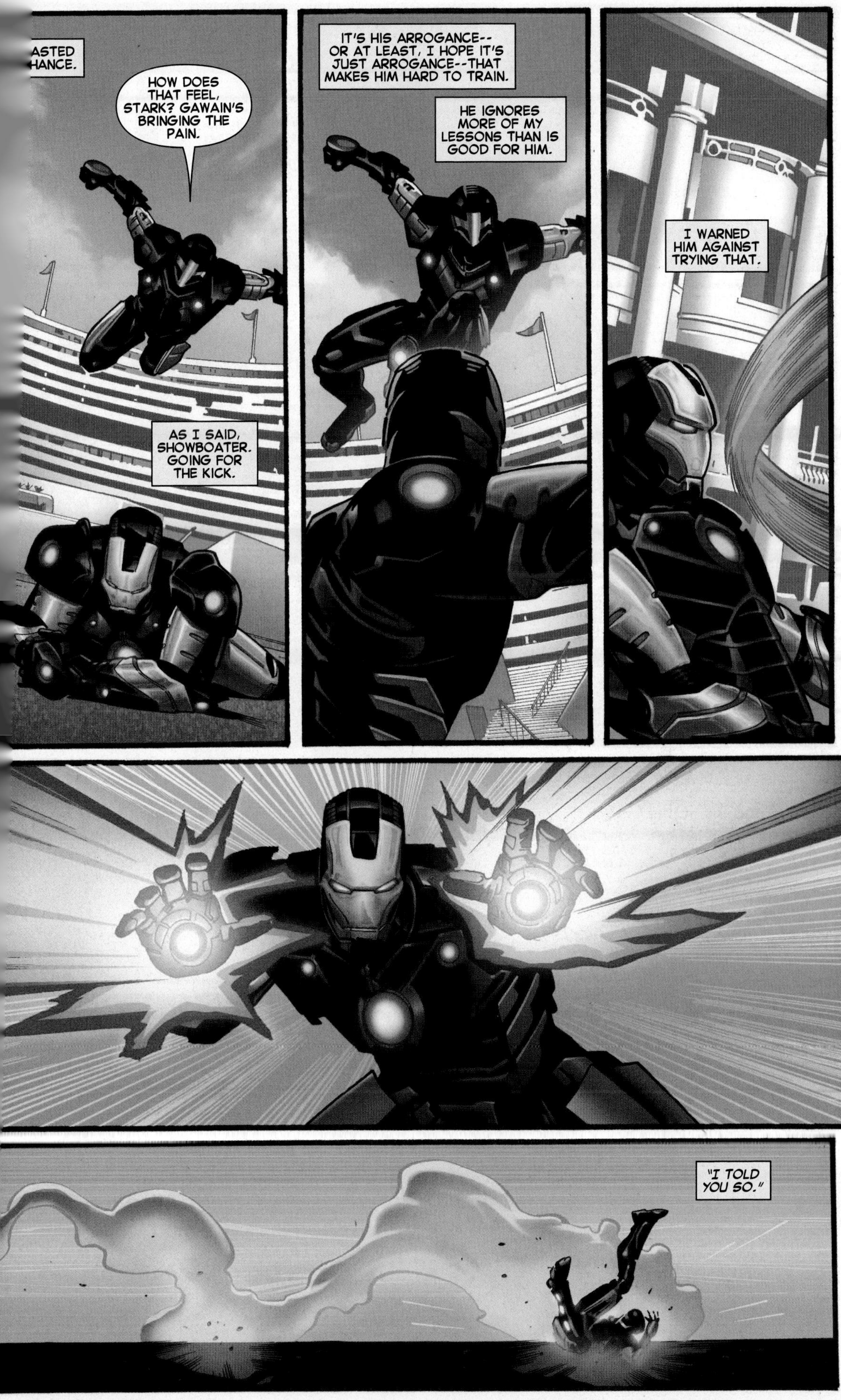

ASTED
HANCE.
HOW DOES THAT FEEL, STARK? GAWAIN'S BRINGING THE PAIN.
AS I SAID, SHOWBOATER. GOING FOR THE KICK.
IT'S HIS ARROGANCE-- OR AT LEAST, I HOPE IT'S JUST ARROGANCE--THAT MAKES HIM HARD TO TRAIN.
HE IGNORES MORE OF MY LESSONS THAN IS GOOD FOR HIM.
I WARNED HIM AGAINST TRYING THAT.
"I TOLD YOU SO."

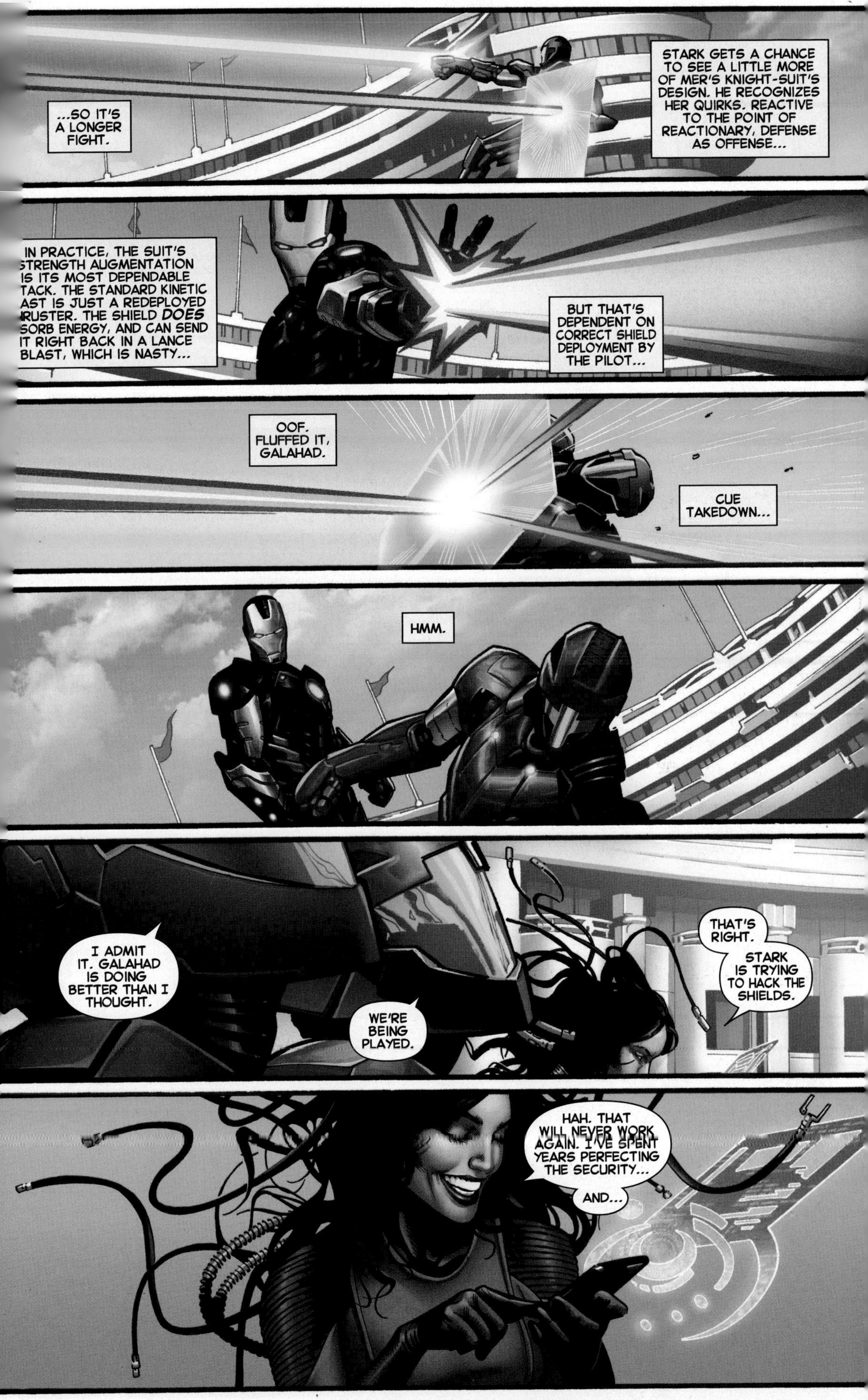
...SO IT'S A LONGER FIGHT.
STARK GETS A CHANCE TO SEE A LITTLE MORE OF MER'S KNIGHT-SUIT'S DESIGN. HE RECOGNIZES HER QUIRKS. REACTIVE TO THE POINT OF REACTIONARY, DEFENSE AS OFFENSE...
IN PRACTICE, THE SUIT'S STRENGTH AUGMENTATION IS ITS MOST DEPENDABLE TACK. THE STANDARD KINETIC AST IS JUST A REDEPLOYED RUSTER. THE SHIELD *DOES* SORB ENERGY, AND CAN SEND IT RIGHT BACK IN A LANCE BLAST, WHICH IS NASTY...
BUT THAT'S DEPENDENT ON CORRECT SHIELD DEPLOYMENT BY THE PILOT...
OOF. FLUFFED IT, GALAHAD.
CUE TAKEDOWN...
HMM.
I ADMIT IT. GALAHAD IS DOING BETTER THAN I THOUGHT.
WE'RE BEING PLAYED.
THAT'S RIGHT.
STARK IS TRYING TO HACK THE SHIELDS.
HAH. THAT WILL NEVER WORK AGAIN. I'VE SPENT YEARS PERFECTING THE SECURITY...
AND...

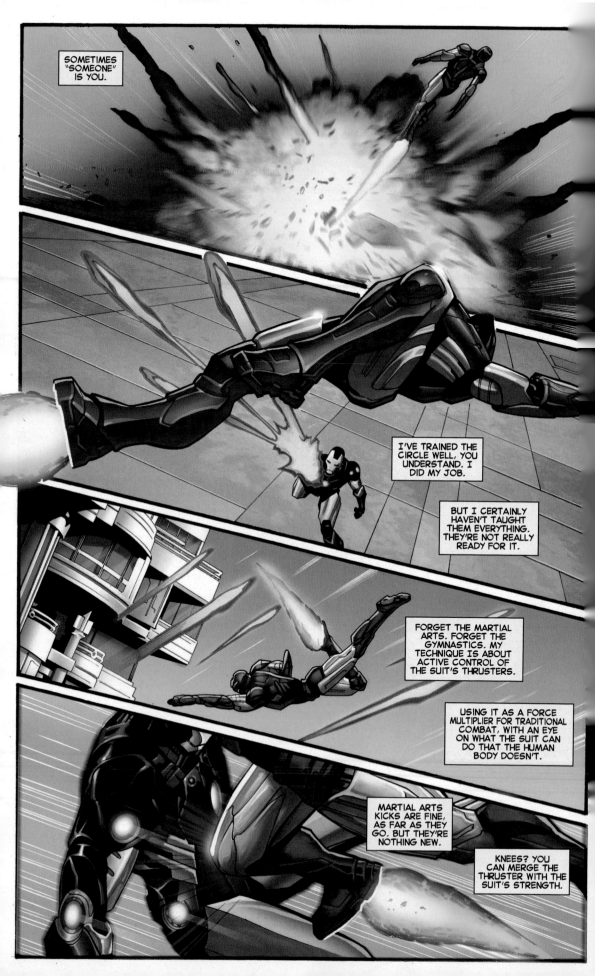

MY SYSTEM REGISTERS HALF A DOZEN TARGET LOCKS...WHICH IS ABOUT HALF A DOZEN LESS THAN I'D EXPECT. HE'S UP TO SOMETHING.

HE HASN'T USED HIS LEFT REPULS--

THAT'S NOT A REPULSOR.

MERLIN! THE GRAIL!

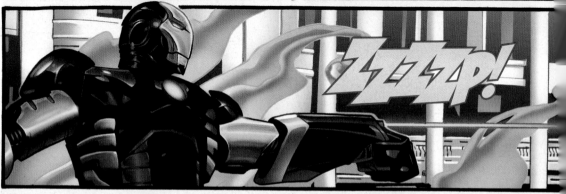

ZZZZP!

THE FORCE FIELD WAS A CUTE DESIGN. GOOD WITH KINETICS.

BUT MAKING IT LIGHT-PERMEABLE? LEAVES IT OPEN TO ALL KIND OF LASERS. ESPECIALLY A HIGH-INTENSITY X-RAY.

SHOULD HAVE WIDENED THE RANGE OF PROTECTION RATHER THAN GOING SO FAR INTO THAT OVER-ENGINEERED ANTI-HACKING BUILD.

NOT AGAINNOT AGAINNOT AGAIN.

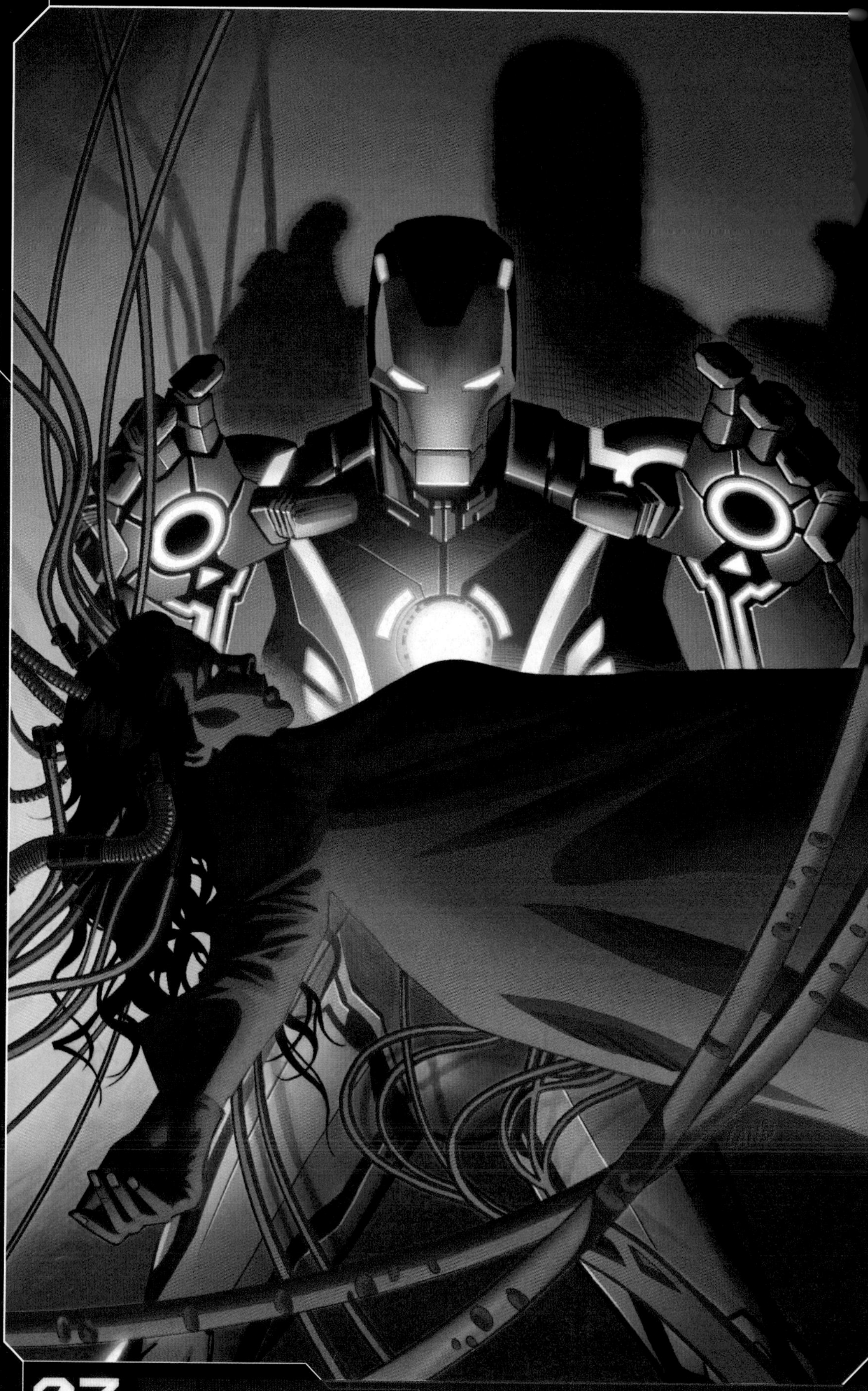

03 IT MAKES US STRONGER

TONY. I *REALLY* DON'T UNDERSTAND WHAT YOU'RE DOING NOW...

ISN'T IT OBVIOUS, FUTURE CEO-OF-THE-YEAR PEPPER POTTS? I'M PREPARING GRILLED CHEESE ON TOAST... IN A MICROWAVE.

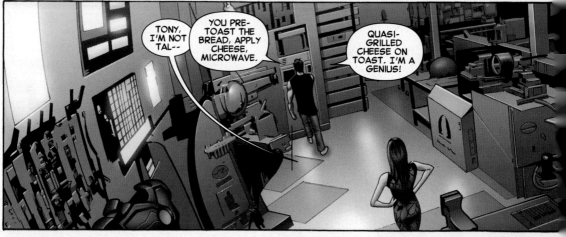

TONY, I'M NOT TAL--

YOU PRE-TOAST THE BREAD, APPLY CHEESE, MICROWAVE.

QUASI-GRILLED CHEESE ON TOAST. I'M A GENIUS!

TONY! BE SERIOUS! I'M TALKING ABOUT--

I'M A MAN OF SCIENCE, PEPPER. DON'T STAND IN THE WAY OF SCIENCE.

IT MAY NOT BE RIGHT. IT MAY DEFY ALL NATURAL LAW, BUT I'M GOING TO DO IT ANYWAY.

AFTER WHAT I DID FOR THE MILITARY, CAN YOU HONESTLY SAY THIS IS ANY WORSE? DO NOT JUDGE ME, POTTS.

I *MEANT* WHAT ARE YOU DOING WITH ALL THE NEW MODULAR SUITS?

YOUR LAST ARMOR WAS BASED ON *LIQUID* TECH AND *SMART* METALS. ISN'T THIS A STEP BACK?

OH, *THAT.*

I COULD CREATE ALMOST ANYTHING WITH THE LIQUID TECH...BUT A *SPECIALIZED* TOOL WORKS BETTER AT ITS *SPECIALIST* TASK.

I COULD MORPH A REPULSOR CANNON, SURE... BUT A ONE-PURPOSE UNIT UPS THE KICK.

THIS IS SWAPPING FLEXIBILITY FOR EFFECTIVENESS.

THIS IS ABOUT MAKING CHOICES AND LIVING WITH THEM.

SO WHEN I CHASE DOWN THE COLOMBIAN EXTREMIS SIGNAL, I HAVE TO *PLAN* MY APPROACH...

IS THAT THE EXTREMIS ENHANCILE THAT DISAPPEARED?

NO, IT *DIED.* MAYA'S DIGITAL CARE PACKAGE FROM BEYOND THE GRAVE EXPLAINED SHE KEYED DATA INTO THE SIGNAL. THE ENHANCILE FLATLINED.

THAT *MAY* IMPLY THEY TRANS- FORMED THE SUBJECT INTO SOMETHING THAT DIDN'T SURVIVE.

IF THEY'RE BEING *OVER- AMBITIOUS* WITH EXTREMIS, THAT'S ALL KINDS OF WORRY. WHO CAN TELL HOW LONG THE NEW SIGNAL WILL LAST?

IT'S THE MANSION OF A BUSINESSMAN. ONE JUAN CARLOS VALENCIA.

S.H.I.E.L.D. SAY HE'S A DRUG CAPO. THOSE S.H.I.E.L.D. GUYS ARE SO *SCURRILOUS* WITH THEIR GOSSIP.

SO--HOW DO I PLAY THIS?

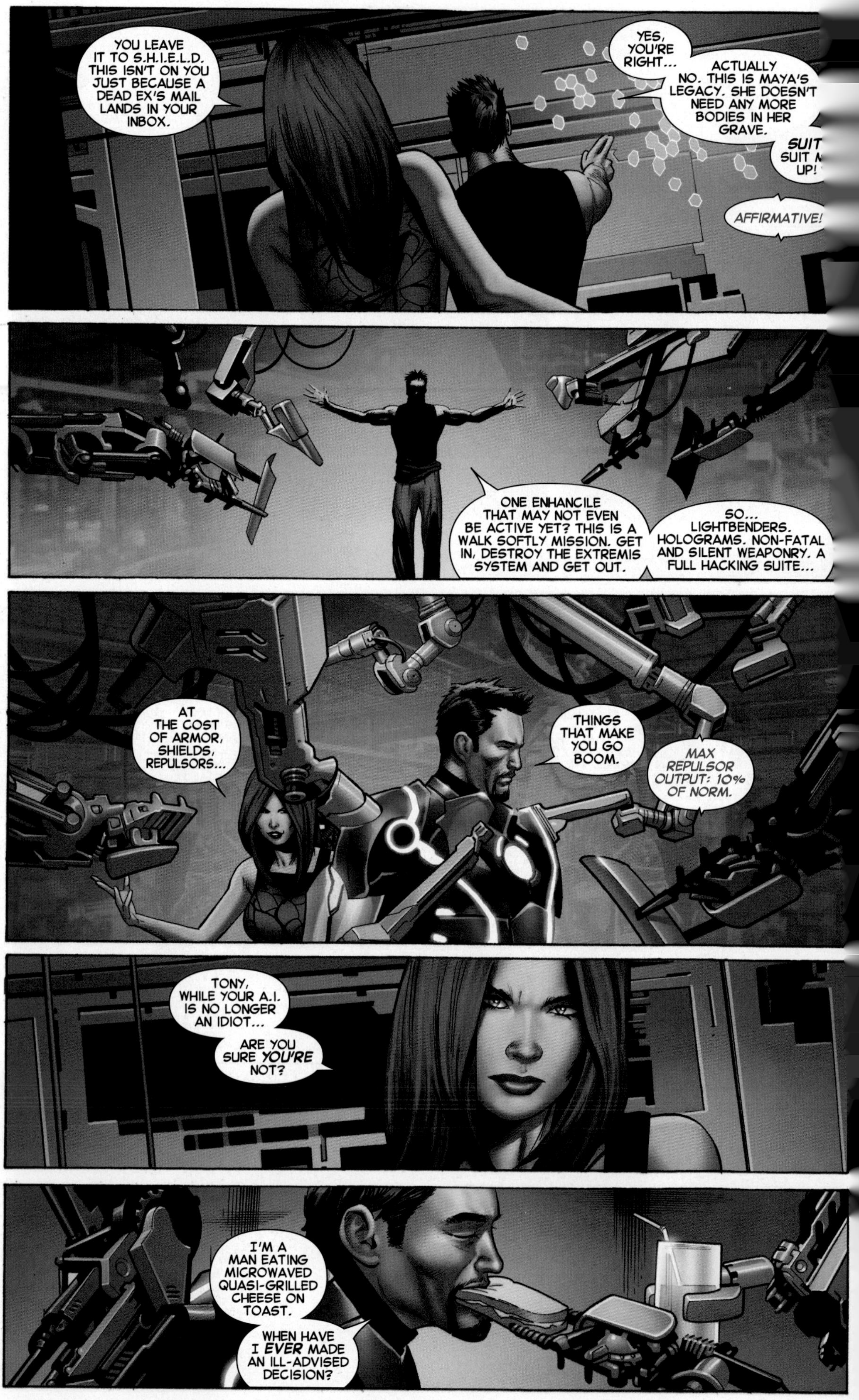
YOU LEAVE IT TO S.H.I.E.L.D. THIS ISN'T ON YOU JUST BECAUSE A DEAD EX'S MAIL LANDS IN YOUR INBOX.
YES, YOU'RE RIGHT...
ACTUALLY NO. THIS IS MAYA'S LEGACY. SHE DOESN'T NEED ANY MORE BODIES IN HER GRAVE.
SUIT
SUIT M
UP!
AFFIRMATIVE!
ONE ENHANCILE THAT MAY NOT EVEN BE ACTIVE YET? THIS IS A WALK SOFTLY MISSION. GET IN, DESTROY THE EXTREMIS SYSTEM AND GET OUT.
SO... LIGHTBENDERS. HOLOGRAMS. NON-FATAL AND SILENT WEAPONRY. A FULL HACKING SUITE...
AT THE COST OF ARMOR, SHIELDS, REPULSORS...
THINGS THAT MAKE YOU GO BOOM.
MAX REPULSOR OUTPUT: 10% OF NORM.
TONY, WHILE YOUR A.I. IS NO LONGER AN IDIOT...
ARE YOU SURE YOU'RE NOT?
I'M A MAN EATING MICROWAVED QUASI-GRILLED CHEESE ON TOAST.
WHEN HAVE I EVER MADE AN ILL-ADVISED DECISION?

OKAY.

DOCTOR DOOM IS D.J.-ING IN LATVERIA.

NO, THAT'S A SUPERSTAR DOOMBOT.

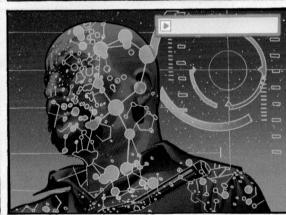

HOLOGRAM ACTIVE.

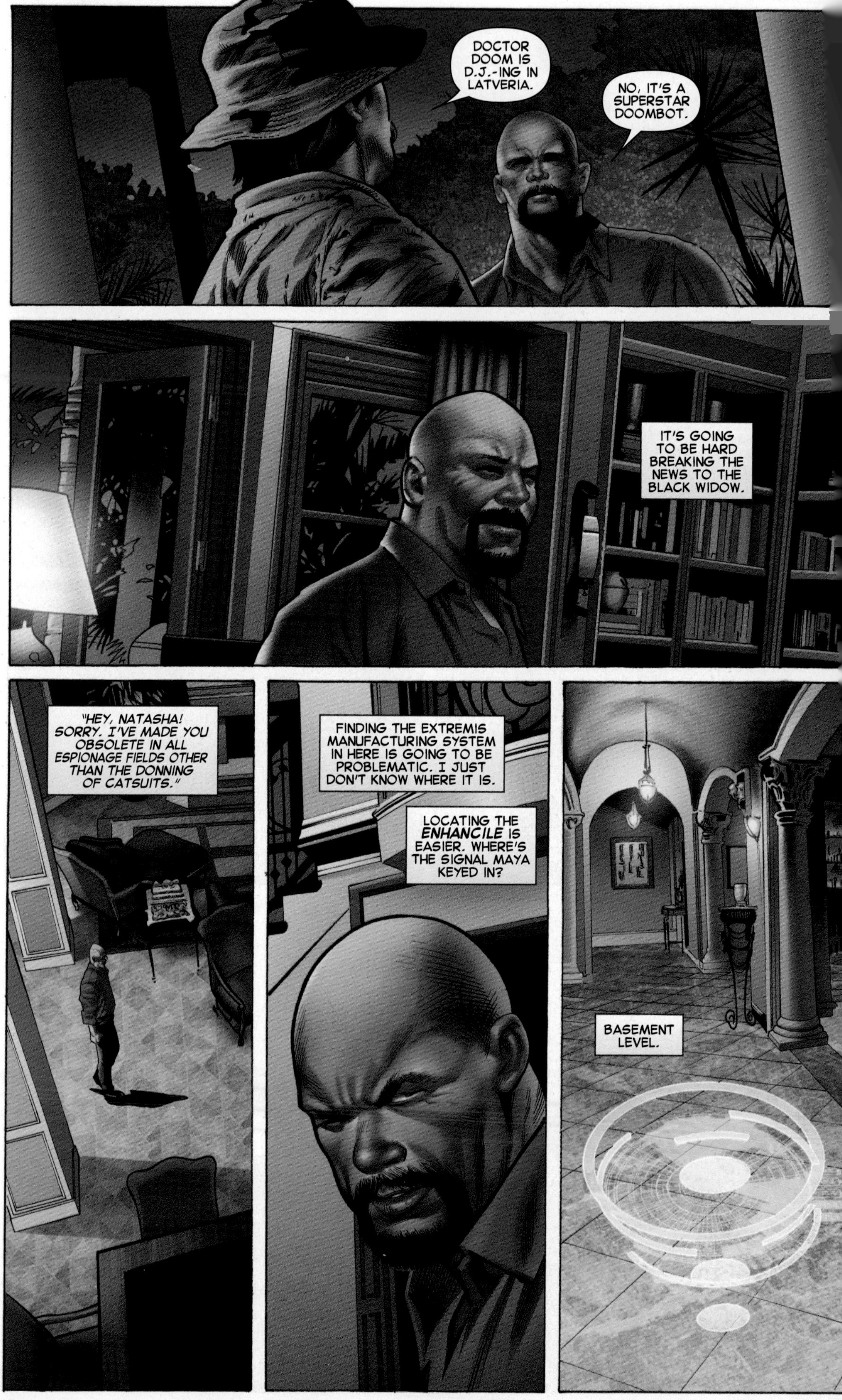
DOCTOR DOOM IS D.J.-ING IN LATVERIA.
NO, IT'S A SUPERSTAR DOOMBOT.
IT'S GOING TO BE HARD BREAKING THE NEWS TO THE BLACK WIDOW.
"HEY, NATASHA! SORRY. I'VE MADE YOU OBSOLETE IN ALL ESPIONAGE FIELDS OTHER THAN THE DONNING OF CATSUITS."
FINDING THE EXTREMIS MANUFACTURING SYSTEM IN HERE IS GOING TO BE PROBLEMATIC. I JUST DON'T KNOW WHERE IT IS.
LOCATING THE ENHANCILE IS EASIER. WHERE'S THE SIGNAL MAYA KEYED IN?
BASEMENT LEVEL.

CROSS-REFERENCE SIGNAL WITH ORBITAL SATELLITE SCANS...

GIVE ME THE BEST ROUTE.

AFFIRMATIVE.

THANK YOU.

LABORATORIES? HMM.

THE ENHANCILE'S INSIDE. EXPENSIVE LOCK. VERY NICE.

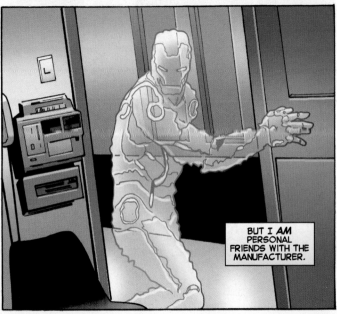

BUT I AM PERSONAL FRIENDS WITH THE MANUFACTURER.

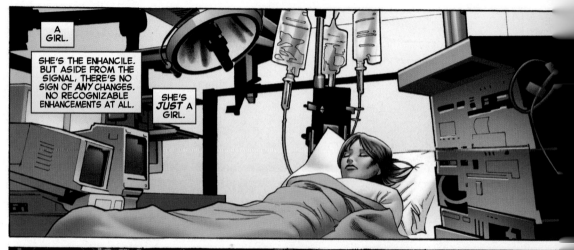

A GIRL.

SHE'S THE ENHANCILE. BUT ASIDE FROM THE SIGNAL, THERE'S NO SIGN OF *ANY* CHANGES. NO RECOGNIZABLE ENHANCEMENTS AT ALL.

SHE'S *JUST* A GIRL.

SHE'S A VICTIM. SHE HAS TO BE. THEY'RE RUNNING SOME KIND OF EXPERIMENT.

TIME TO TAKE A CHANCE...

I'M IRON MAN. I'M HERE TO SAVE YOU.

DO YOU REMEMBER WHERE THEY PERFORMED THE OPERATION?

GUARDS!

SORRY, NATASHA.

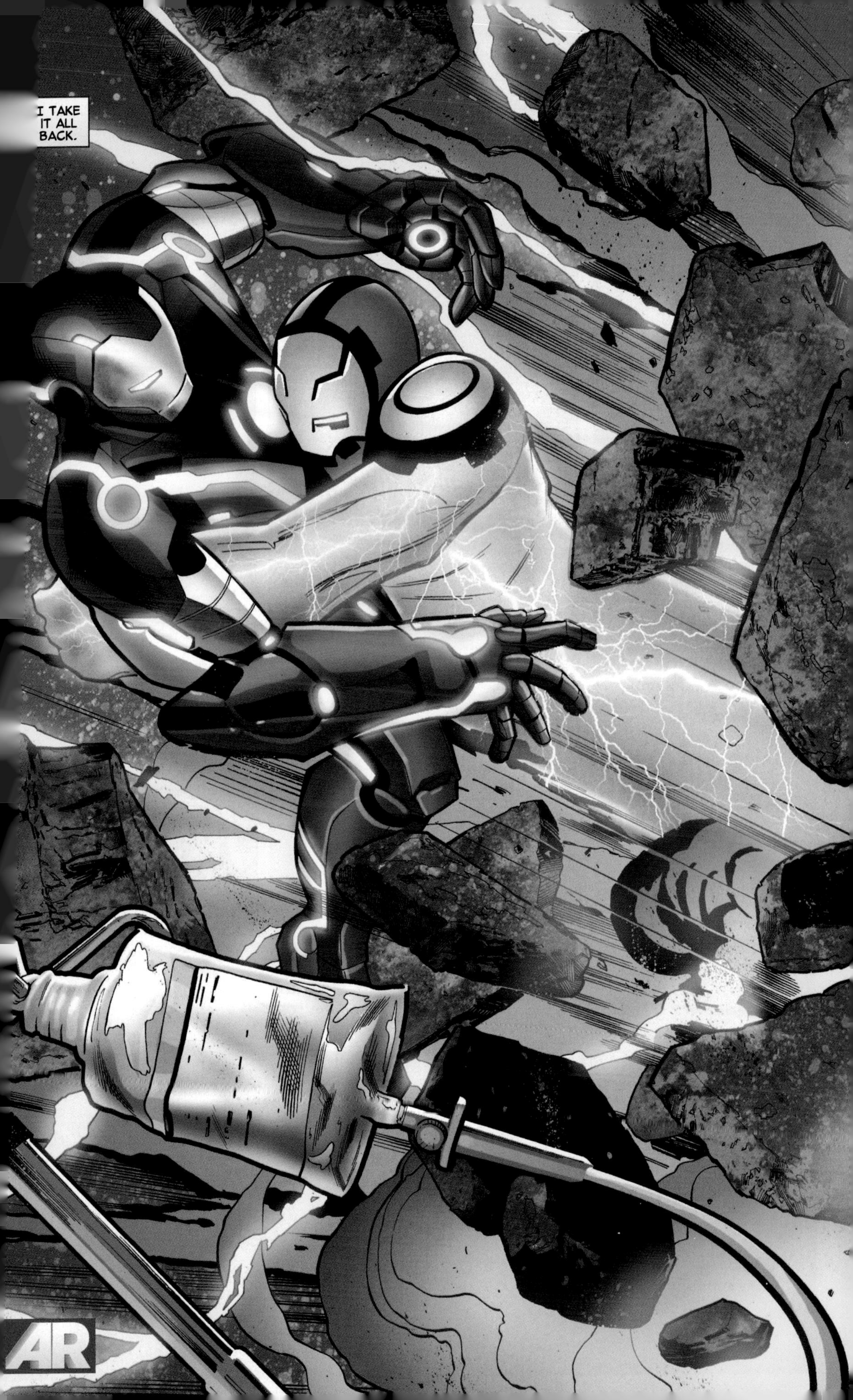
I TAKE IT ALL BACK.
AR

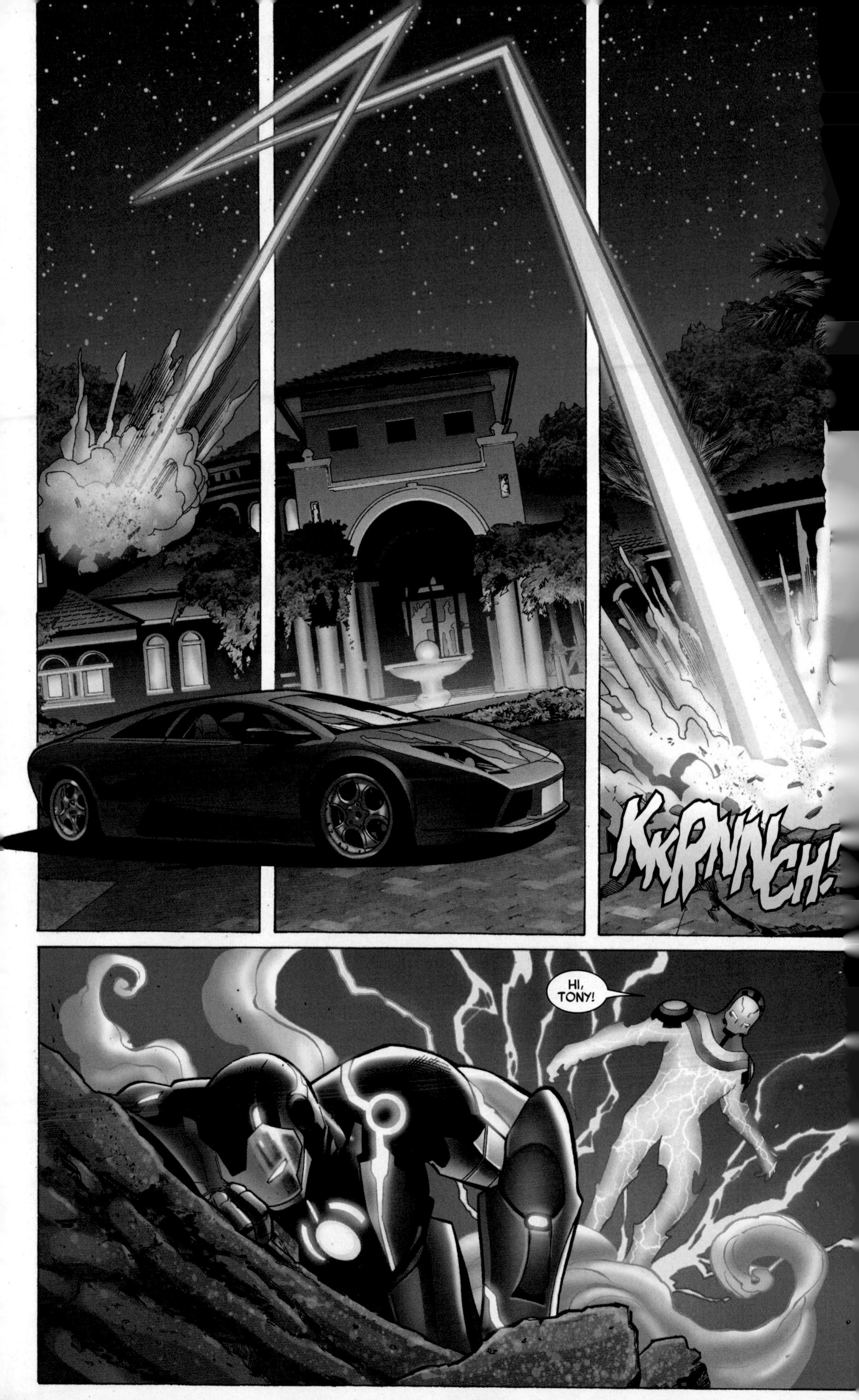
KKRNNCH!
HI, TONY!

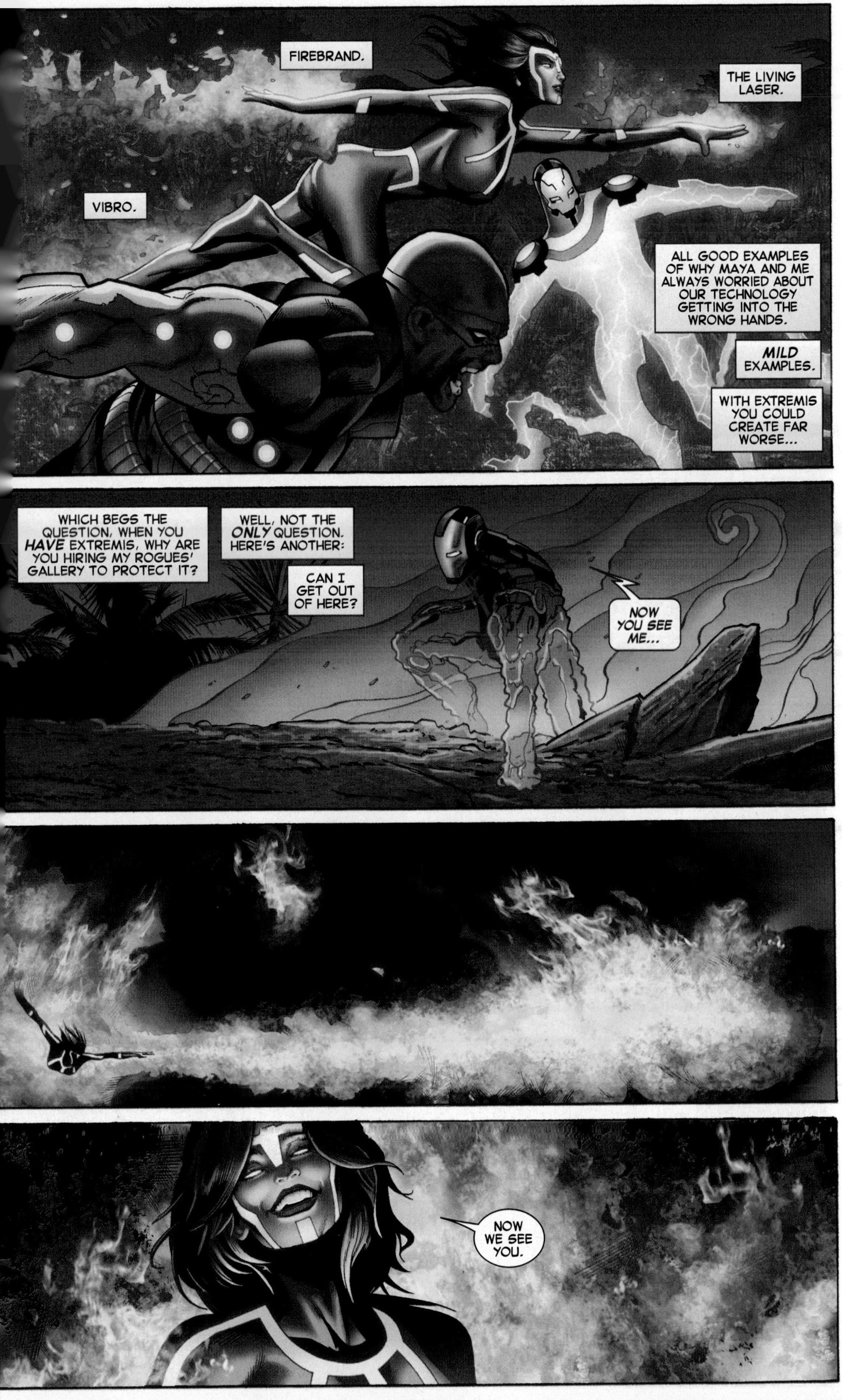

FIREBRAND.
THE LIVING LASER.
VIBRO.
ALL GOOD EXAMPLES OF WHY MAYA AND ME ALWAYS WORRIED ABOUT OUR TECHNOLOGY GETTING INTO THE WRONG HANDS.
MILD EXAMPLES.
WITH EXTREMIS YOU COULD CREATE FAR WORSE...
WHICH BEGS THE QUESTION, WHEN YOU HAVE EXTREMIS, WHY ARE YOU HIRING MY ROGUES' GALLERY TO PROTECT IT?
WELL, NOT THE ONLY QUESTION. HERE'S ANOTHER:
CAN I GET OUT OF HERE?
NOW YOU SEE ME...
NOW WE SEE YOU.

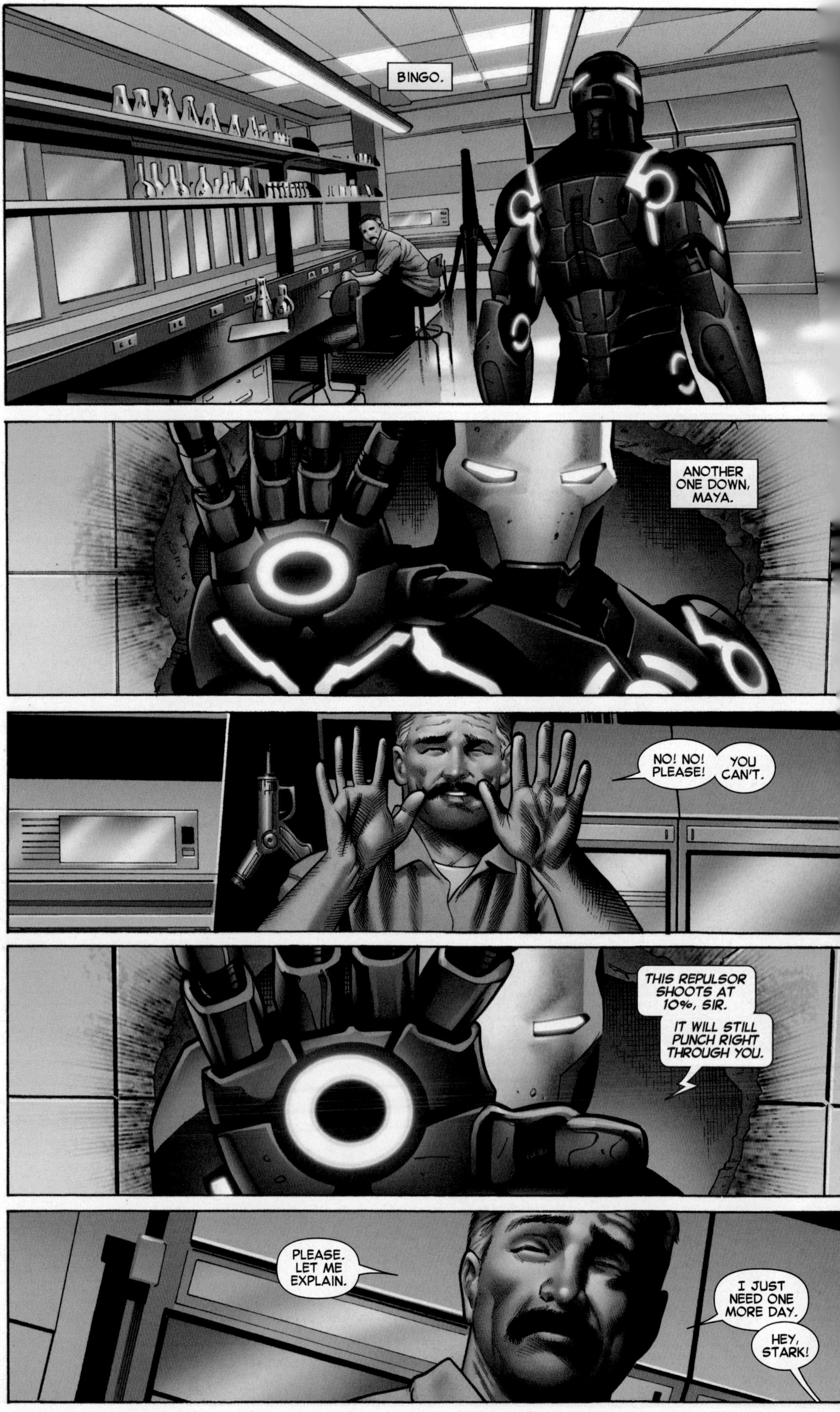
BINGO.
ANOTHER ONE DOWN, MAYA.
NO! NO! PLEASE!
YOU CAN'T.
THIS REPULSOR SHOOTS AT 10%, SIR.
IT WILL STILL PUNCH RIGHT THROUGH YOU.
PLEASE. LET ME EXPLAIN.
I JUST NEED ONE MORE DAY.
HEY, STARK!

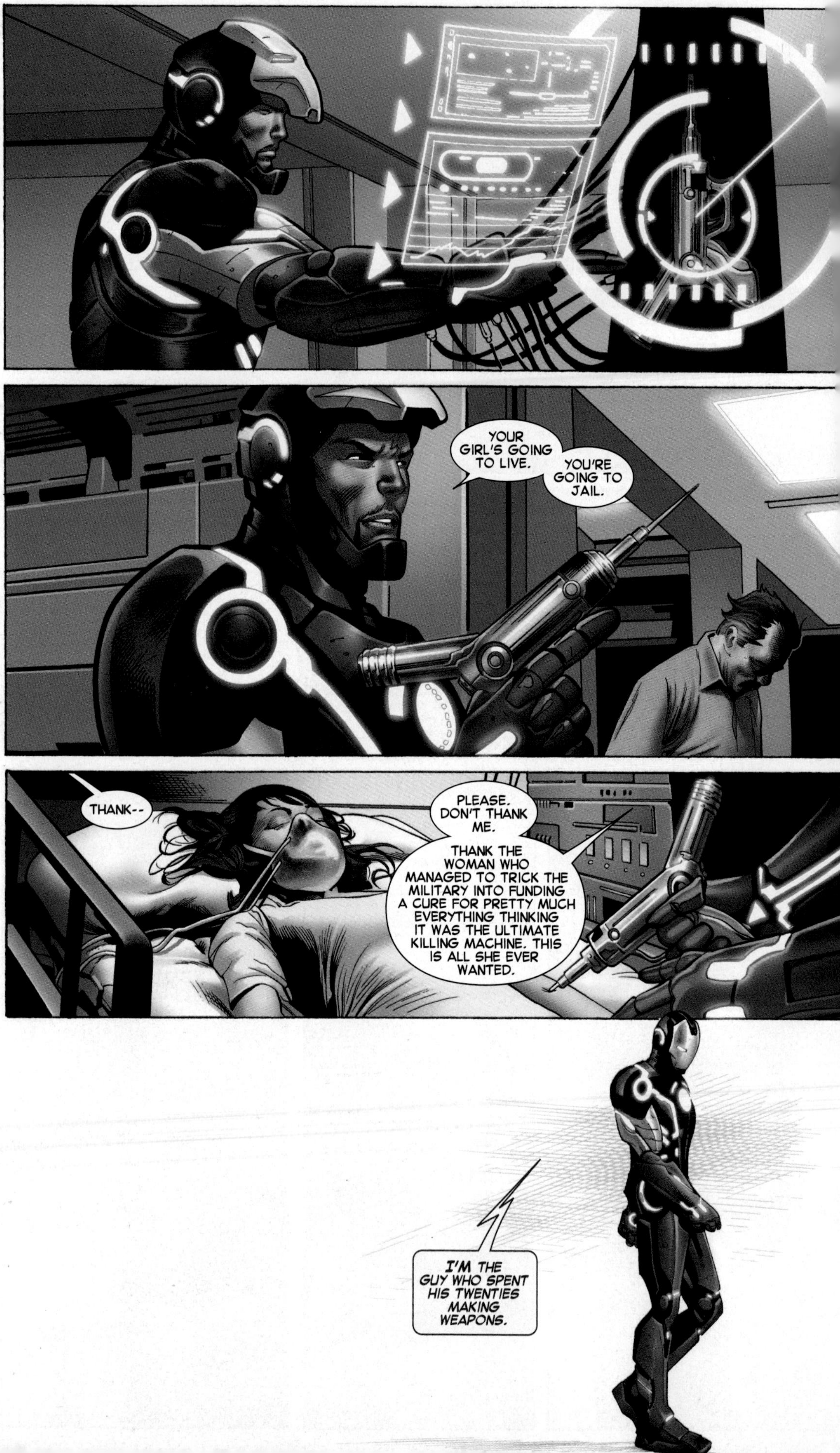
YOUR GIRL'S GOING TO LIVE.
YOU'RE GOING TO JAIL.
THANK--
PLEASE. DON'T THANK ME.
THANK THE WOMAN WHO MANAGED TO TRICK THE MILITARY INTO FUNDING A CURE FOR PRETTY MUCH EVERYTHING THINKING IT WAS THE ULTIMATE KILLING MACHINE. THIS IS ALL SHE EVER WANTED.
I'M THE GUY WHO SPENT HIS TWENTIES MAKING WEAPONS.

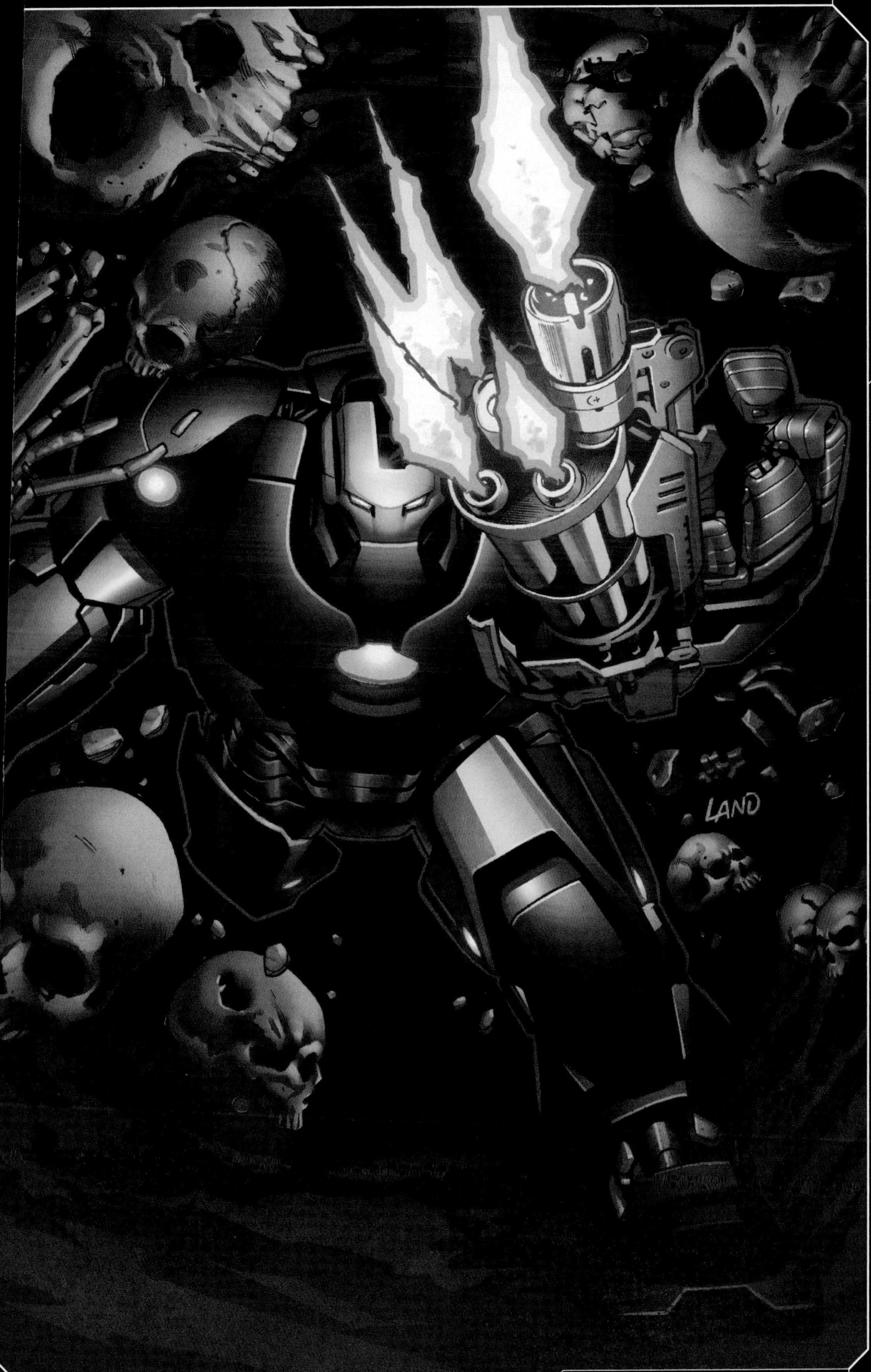
LAND

FEAR OF THE VOID 04

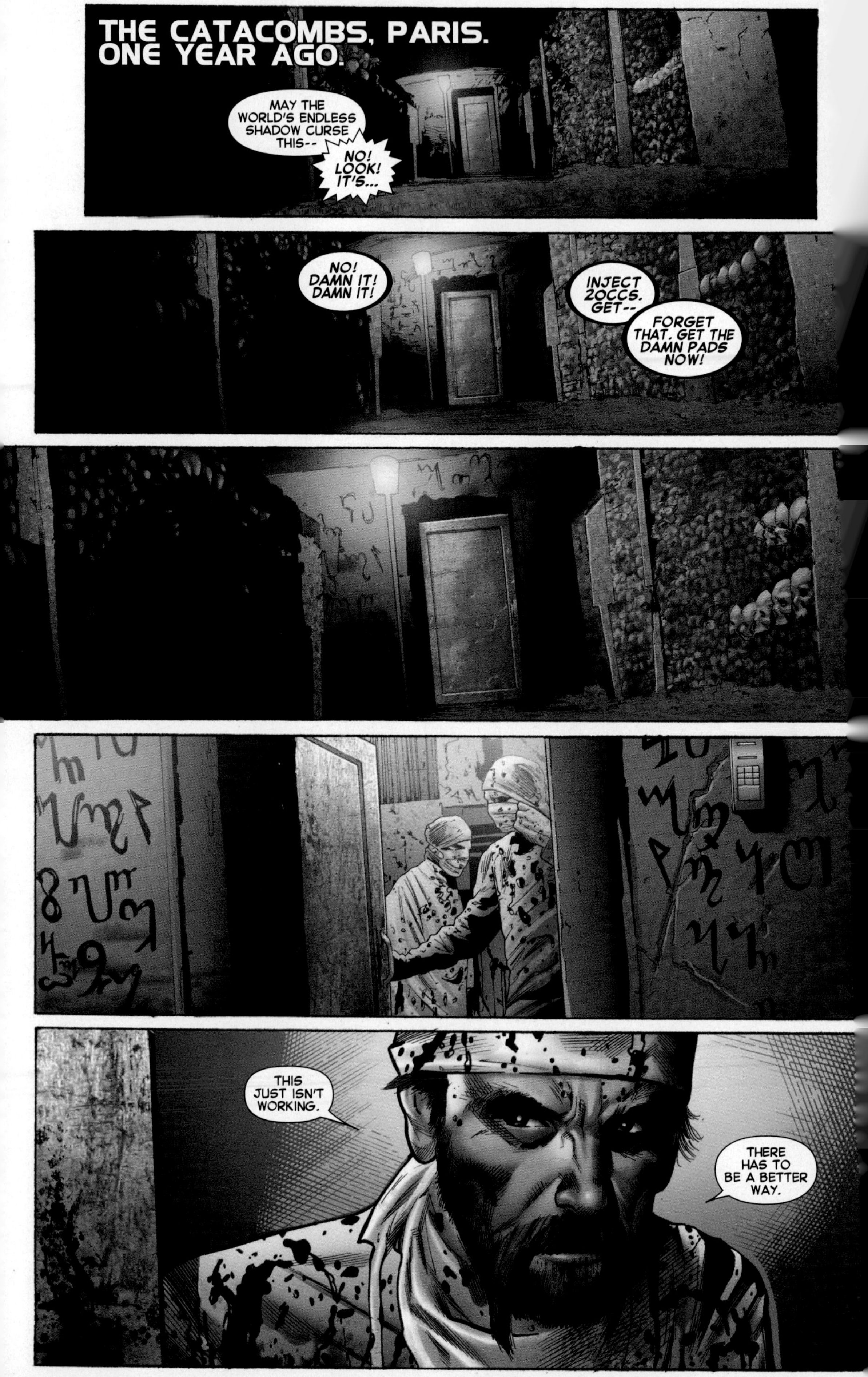
THE CATACOMBS, PARIS. ONE YEAR AGO.
MAY THE WORLD'S ENDLESS SHADOW CURSE THIS--
NO! LOOK! IT'S...
NO! DAMN IT! DAMN IT!
INJECT 20CCS. GET--
FORGET THAT. GET THE DAMN PADS NOW!
THIS JUST ISN'T WORKING.
THERE HAS TO BE A BETTER WAY.

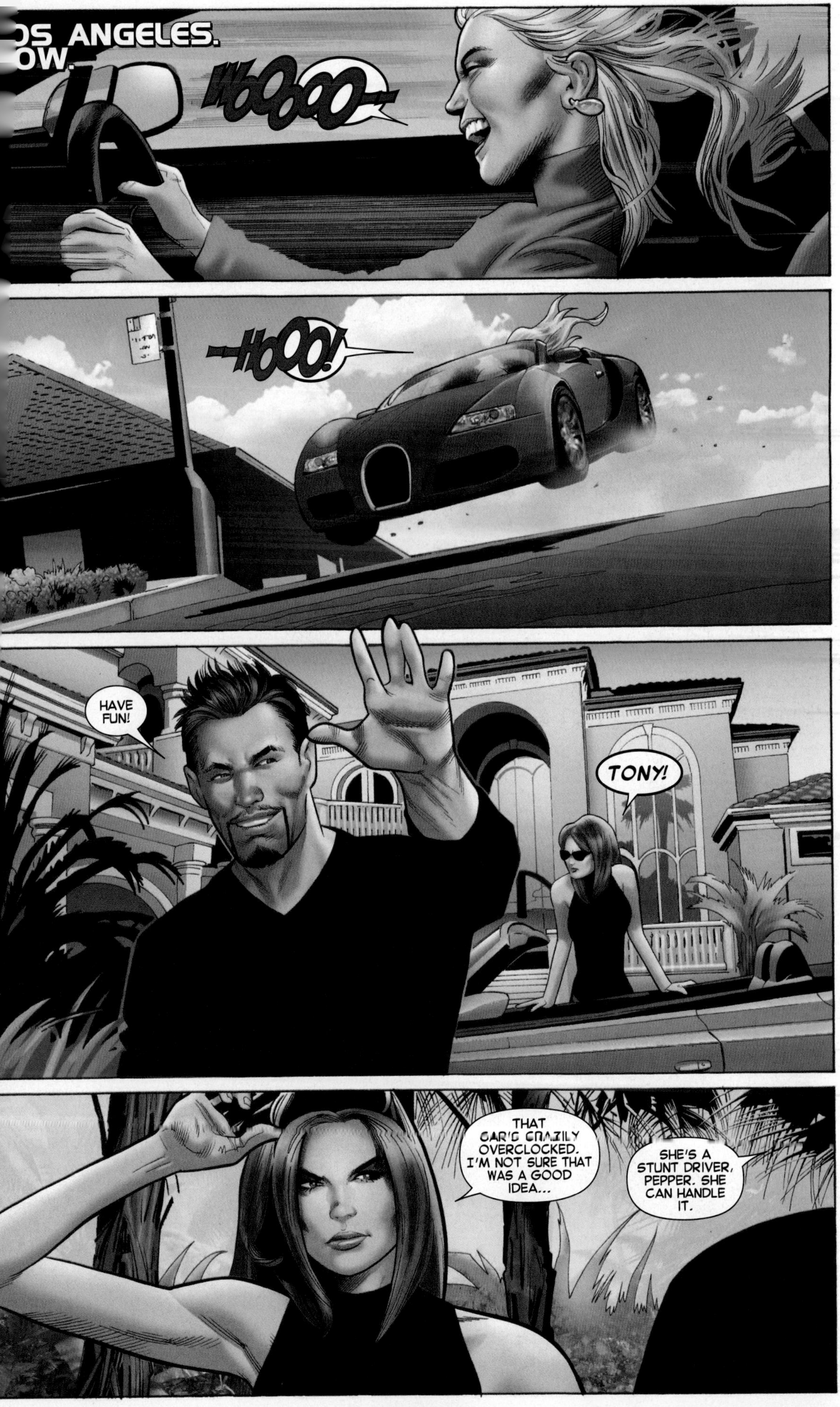

OS ANGELES.
OW.
WOOOOO--
--HOOO!
HAVE FUN!
TONY!
THAT CAR'S CRAZILY OVERCLOCKED. I'M NOT SURE THAT WAS A GOOD IDEA...
SHE'S A STUNT DRIVER, PEPPER. SHE CAN HANDLE IT.

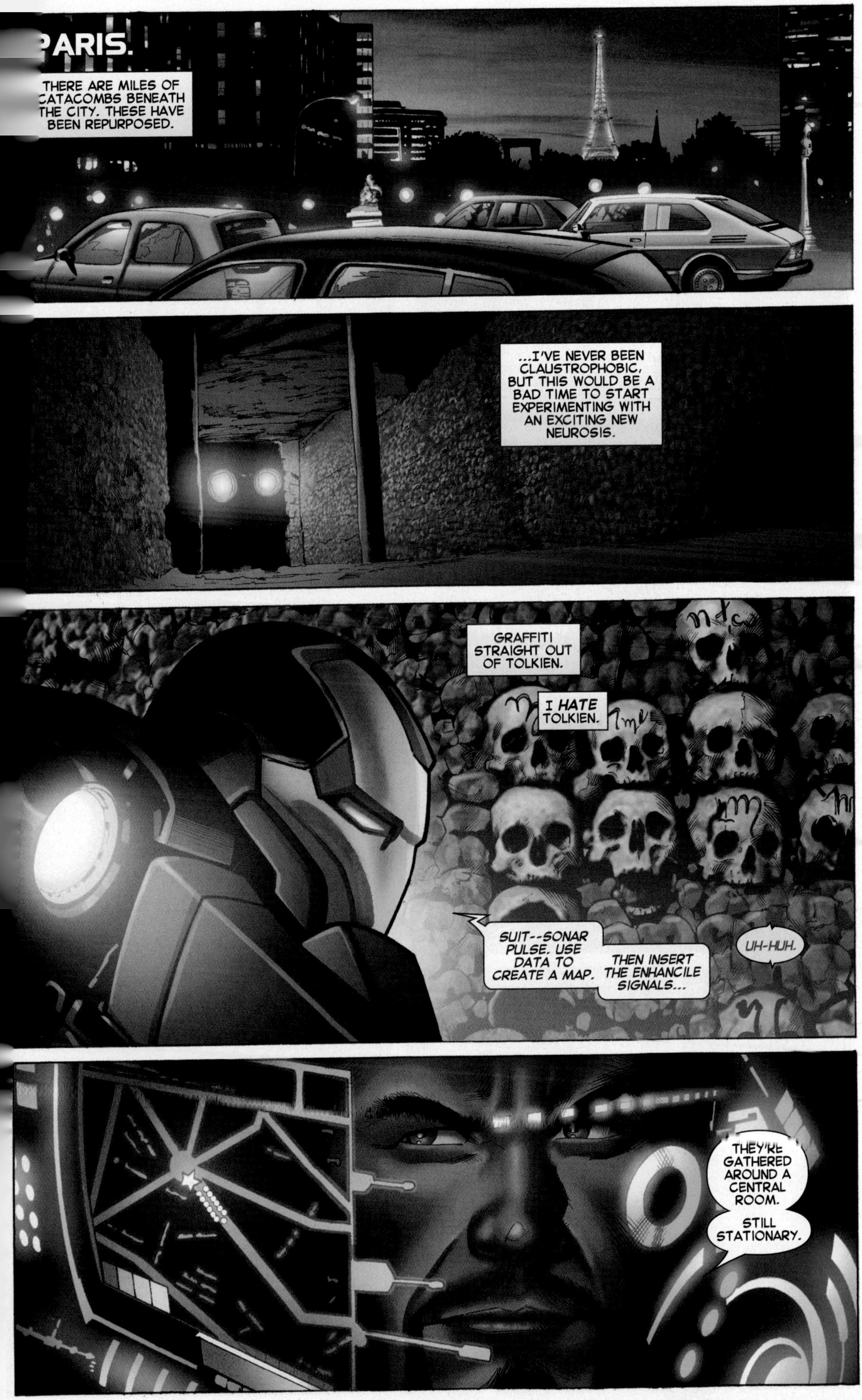
PARIS.
THERE ARE MILES OF CATACOMBS BENEATH THE CITY. THESE HAVE BEEN REPURPOSED.
...I'VE NEVER BEEN CLAUSTROPHOBIC, BUT THIS WOULD BE A BAD TIME TO START EXPERIMENTING WITH AN EXCITING NEW NEUROSIS.
GRAFFITI STRAIGHT OUT OF TOLKIEN.
I HATE TOLKIEN.
SUIT--SONAR PULSE. USE DATA TO CREATE A MAP.
THEN INSERT THE ENHANCILE SIGNALS...
UH-HUH.
THEY'RE GATHERED AROUND A CENTRAL ROOM.
STILL STATIONARY.

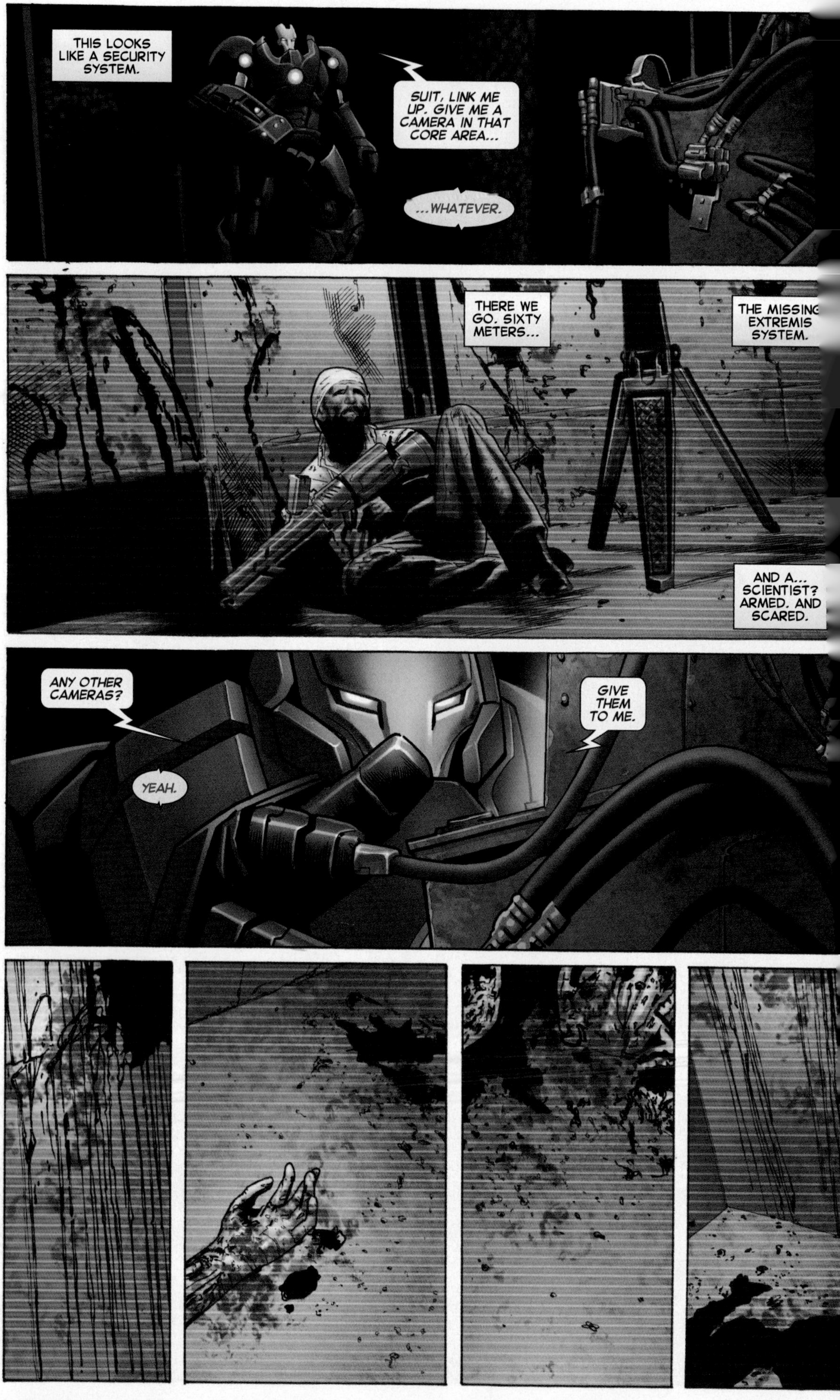
THIS LOOKS LIKE A SECURITY SYSTEM.
SUIT, LINK ME UP. GIVE ME A CAMERA IN THAT CORE AREA...
...WHATEVER.
THERE WE GO. SIXTY METERS...
THE MISSING EXTREMIS SYSTEM.
AND A... SCIENTIST? ARMED. AND SCARED.
ANY OTHER CAMERAS?
YEAH.
GIVE THEM TO ME.

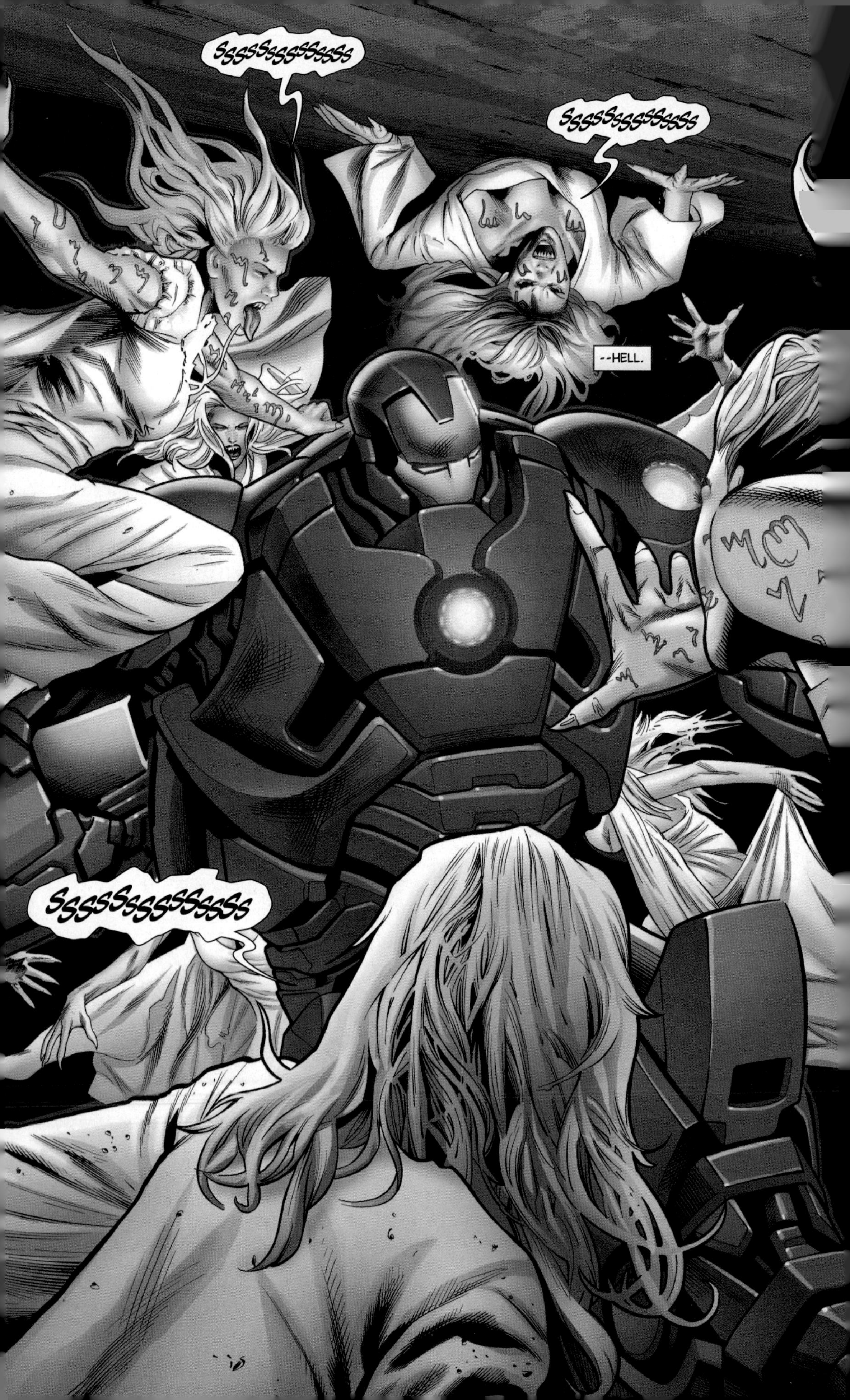
SsssSssssSssss
SsssSssssSsssss
--HELL.
SssssSsssSsssss

HELL!

I COULD FIGHT *A HULK* IN THIS SUIT.

BUT NOT THIRTEEN.

Sssssssssssss

NO.

GET IN HERE.

QUICKLY!

KKKRRR KK KK!

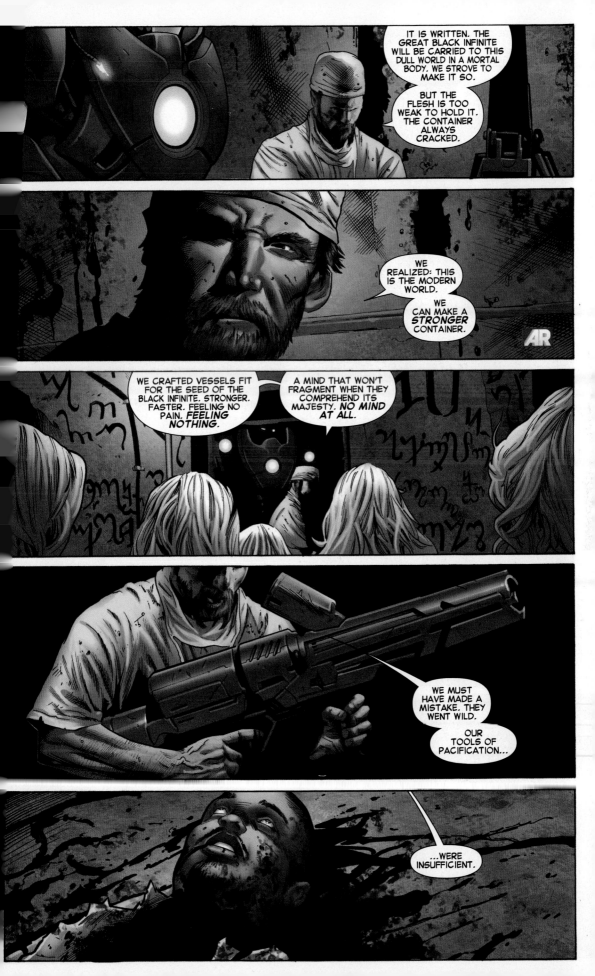

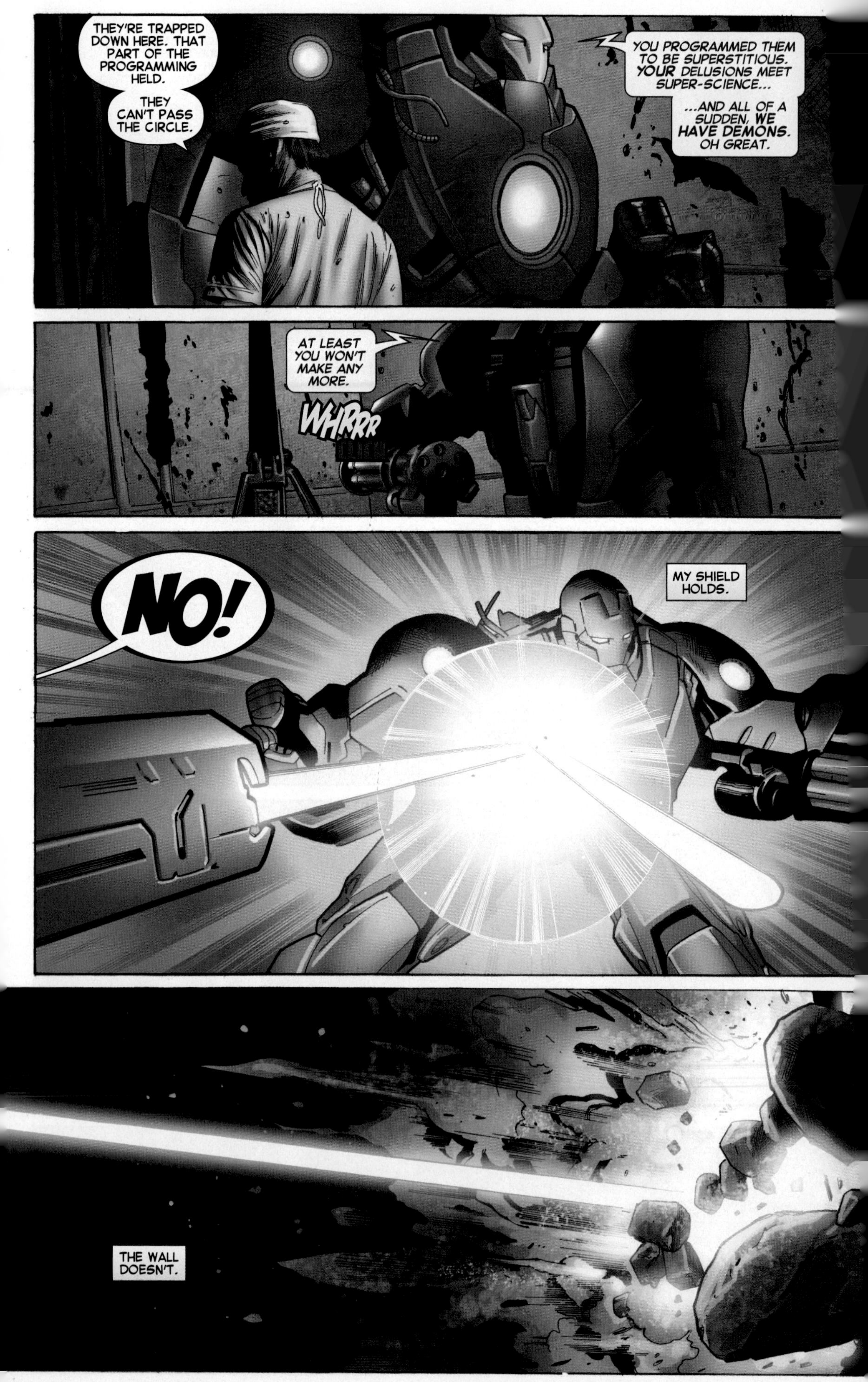
THEY'RE TRAPPED DOWN HERE. THAT PART OF THE PROGRAMMING HELD.
THEY CAN'T PASS THE CIRCLE.
YOU PROGRAMMED THEM TO BE SUPERSTITIOUS. YOUR DELUSIONS MEET SUPER-SCIENCE...
...AND ALL OF A SUDDEN, WE HAVE DEMONS. OH GREAT.
AT LEAST YOU WON'T MAKE ANY MORE.
WHRRR
NO!
MY SHIELD HOLDS.
THE WALL DOESN'T.

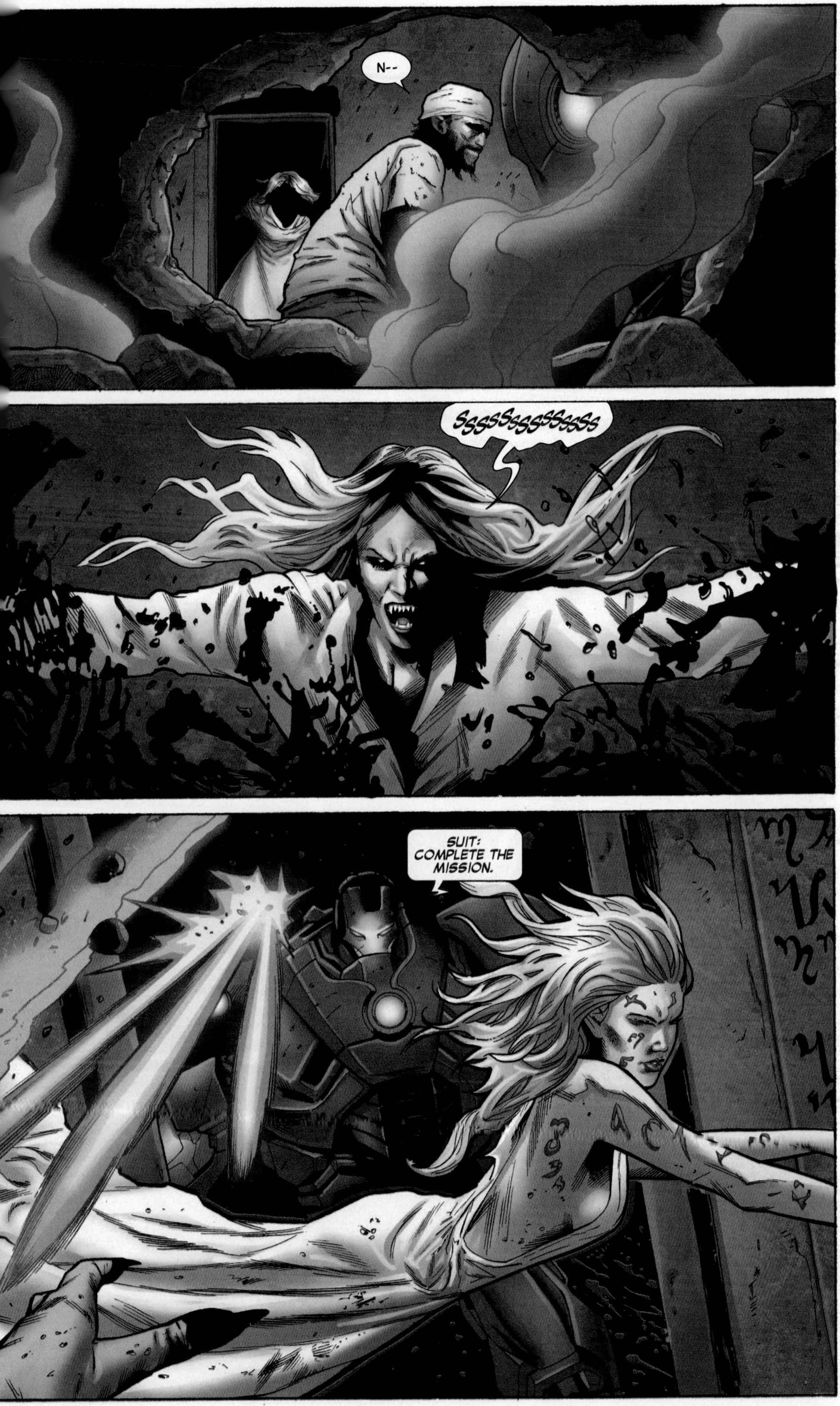
N--
SsssSssssSsssss
SUIT: COMPLETE THE MISSION.

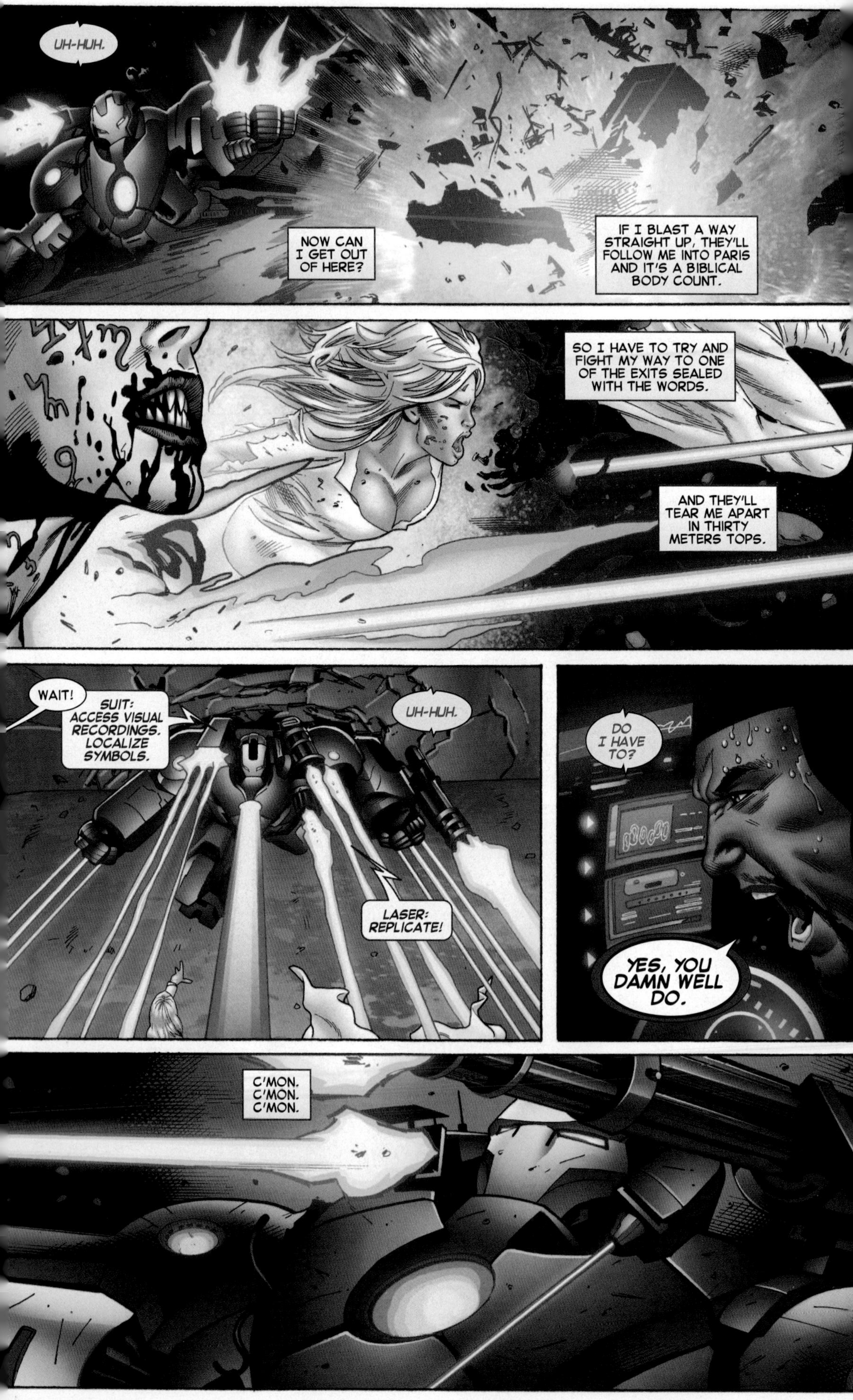
UH-HUH.
NOW CAN I GET OUT OF HERE?
IF I BLAST A WAY STRAIGHT UP, THEY'LL FOLLOW ME INTO PARIS AND IT'S A BIBLICAL BODY COUNT.
SO I HAVE TO TRY AND FIGHT MY WAY TO ONE OF THE EXITS SEALED WITH THE WORDS.
AND THEY'LL TEAR ME APART IN THIRTY METERS TOPS.
WAIT!
SUIT: ACCESS VISUAL RECORDINGS. LOCALIZE SYMBOLS.
UH-HUH.
LASER: REPLICATE!
DO I HAVE TO?
YES, YOU DAMN WELL DO.
C'MON. C'MON. C'MON.

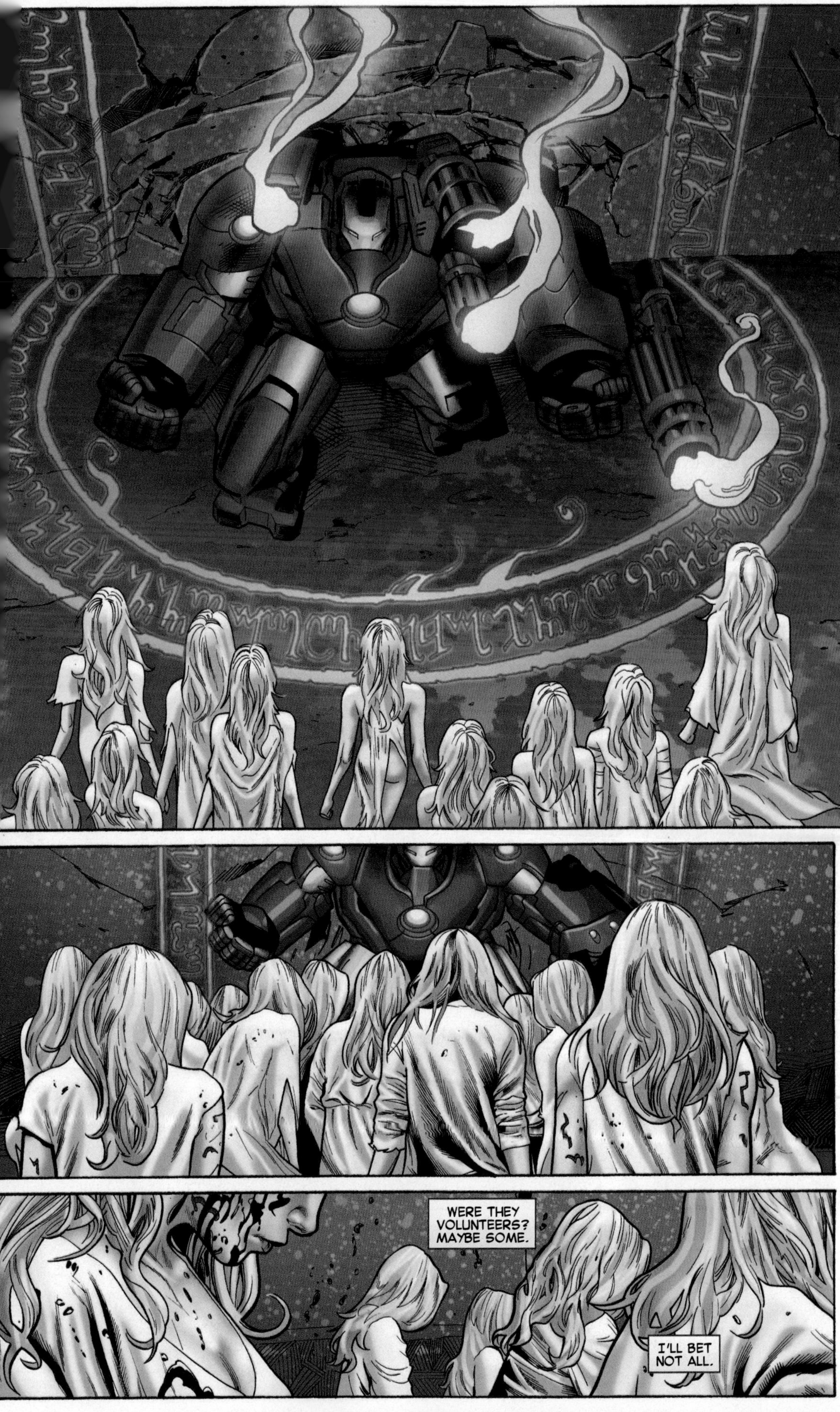
WERE THEY VOLUNTEERS? MAYBE SOME.
I'LL BET NOT ALL.

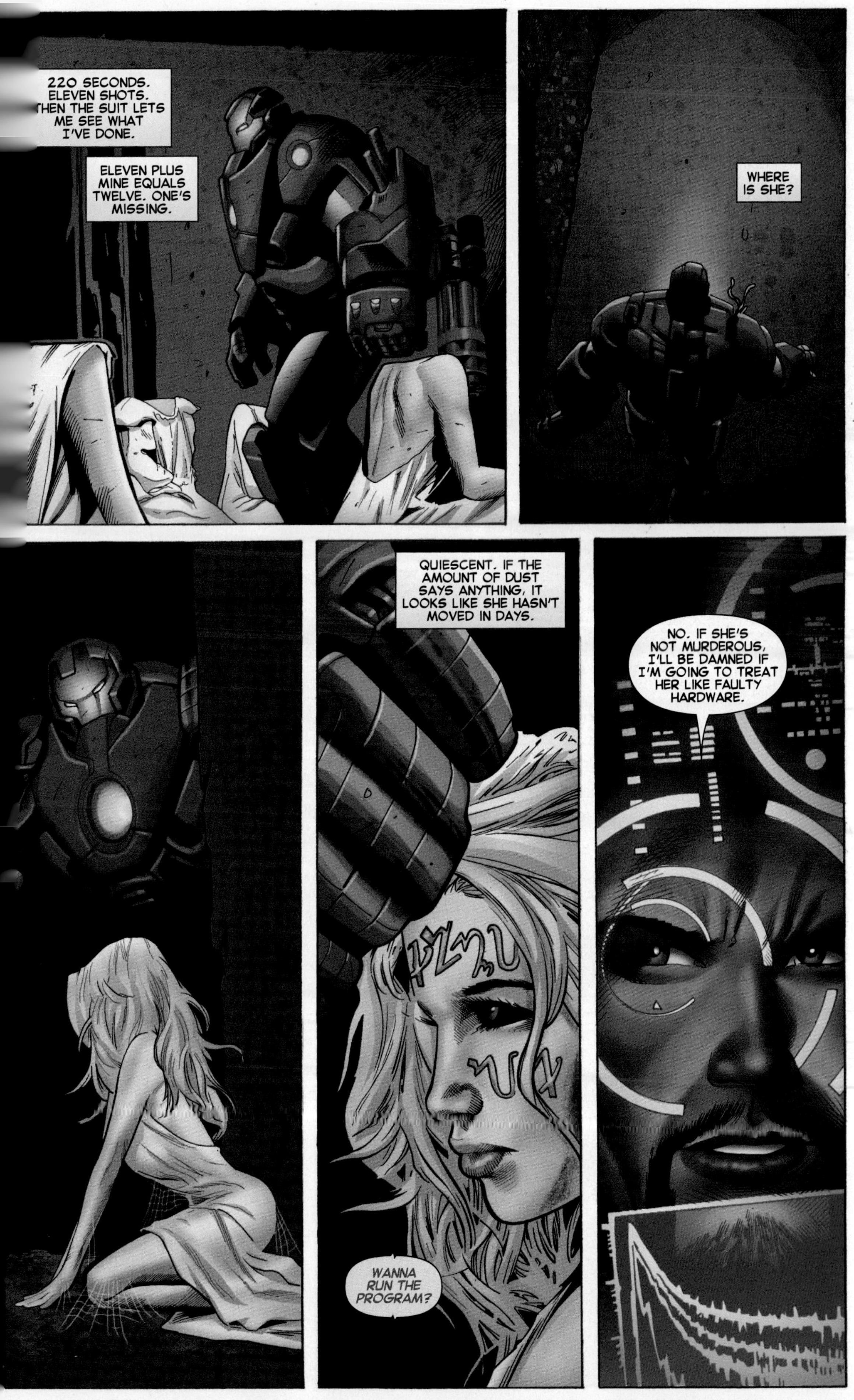
220 SECONDS. ELEVEN SHOTS. THEN THE SUIT LETS ME SEE WHAT I'VE DONE.
ELEVEN PLUS MINE EQUALS TWELVE. ONE'S MISSING.
WHERE IS SHE?
QUIESCENT. IF THE AMOUNT OF DUST SAYS ANYTHING, IT LOOKS LIKE SHE HASN'T MOVED IN DAYS.
WANNA RUN THE PROGRAM?
NO. IF SHE'S NOT MURDEROUS, I'LL BE DAMNED IF I'M GOING TO TREAT HER LIKE FAULTY HARDWARE.

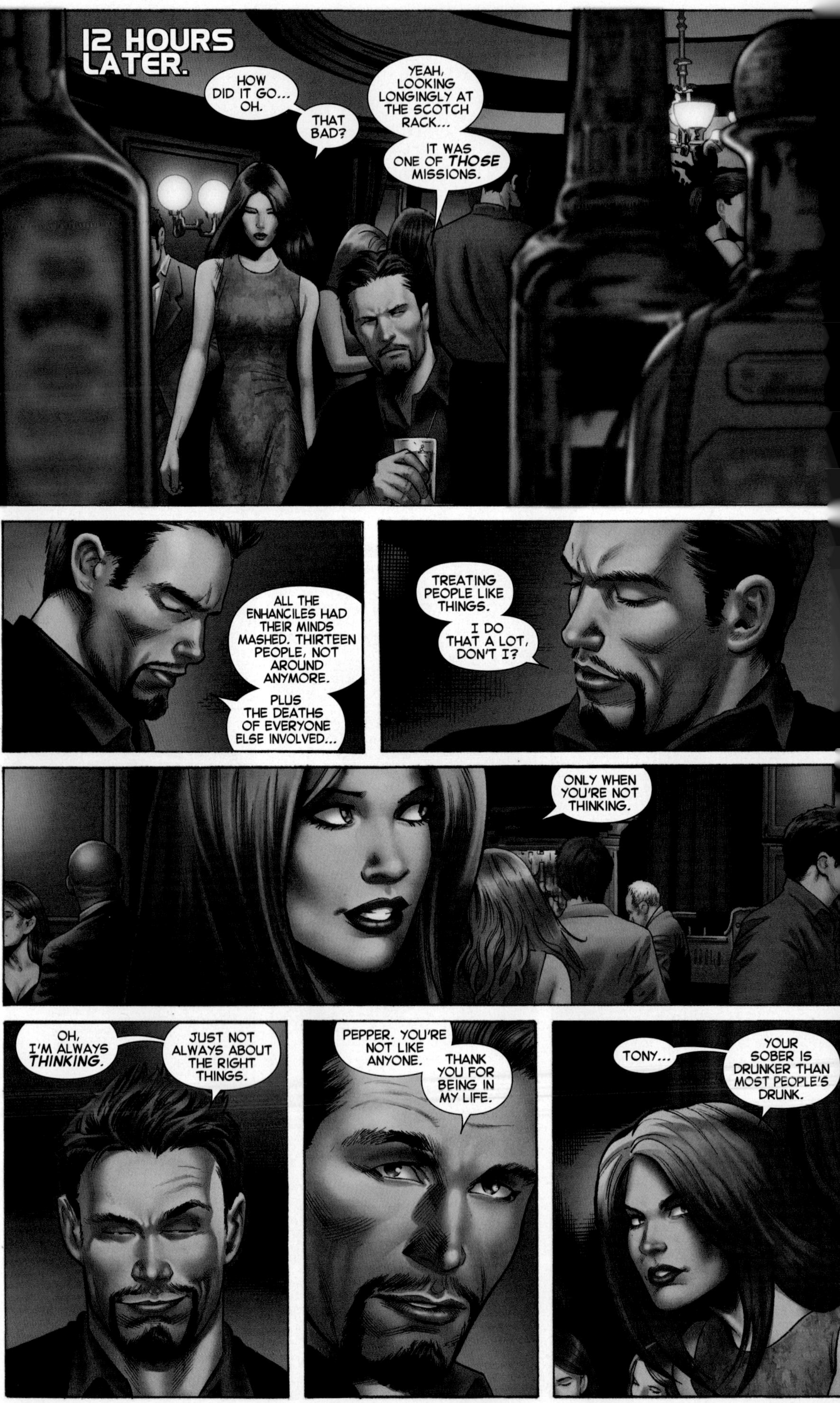
12 HOURS LATER.
HOW DID IT GO... OH.
THAT BAD?
YEAH, LOOKING LONGINGLY AT THE SCOTCH RACK...
IT WAS ONE OF *THOSE* MISSIONS.
ALL THE ENHANCILES HAD THEIR MINDS MASHED. THIRTEEN PEOPLE, NOT AROUND ANYMORE.
PLUS THE DEATHS OF EVERYONE ELSE INVOLVED...
TREATING PEOPLE LIKE THINGS.
I DO THAT A LOT, DON'T I?
ONLY WHEN YOU'RE NOT THINKING.
OH, I'M ALWAYS *THINKING.*
JUST NOT ALWAYS ABOUT THE RIGHT THINGS.
PEPPER. YOU'RE NOT LIKE ANYONE.
THANK YOU FOR BEING IN MY LIFE.
TONY...
YOUR SOBER IS DRUNKER THAN MOST PEOPLE'S DRUNK.

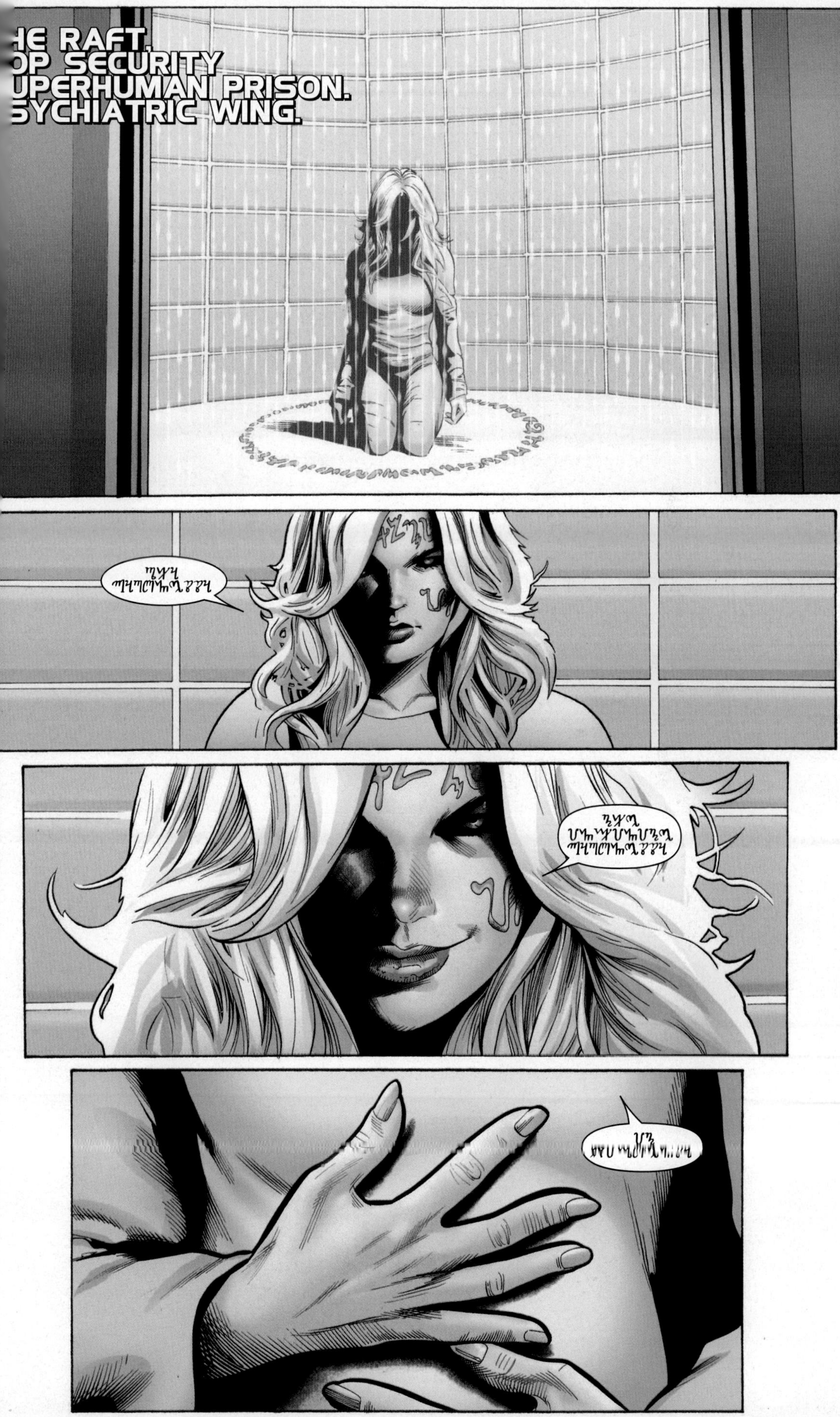
HE RAFT.
OP SECURITY
UPERHUMAN PRISON.
SYCHIATRIC WING.

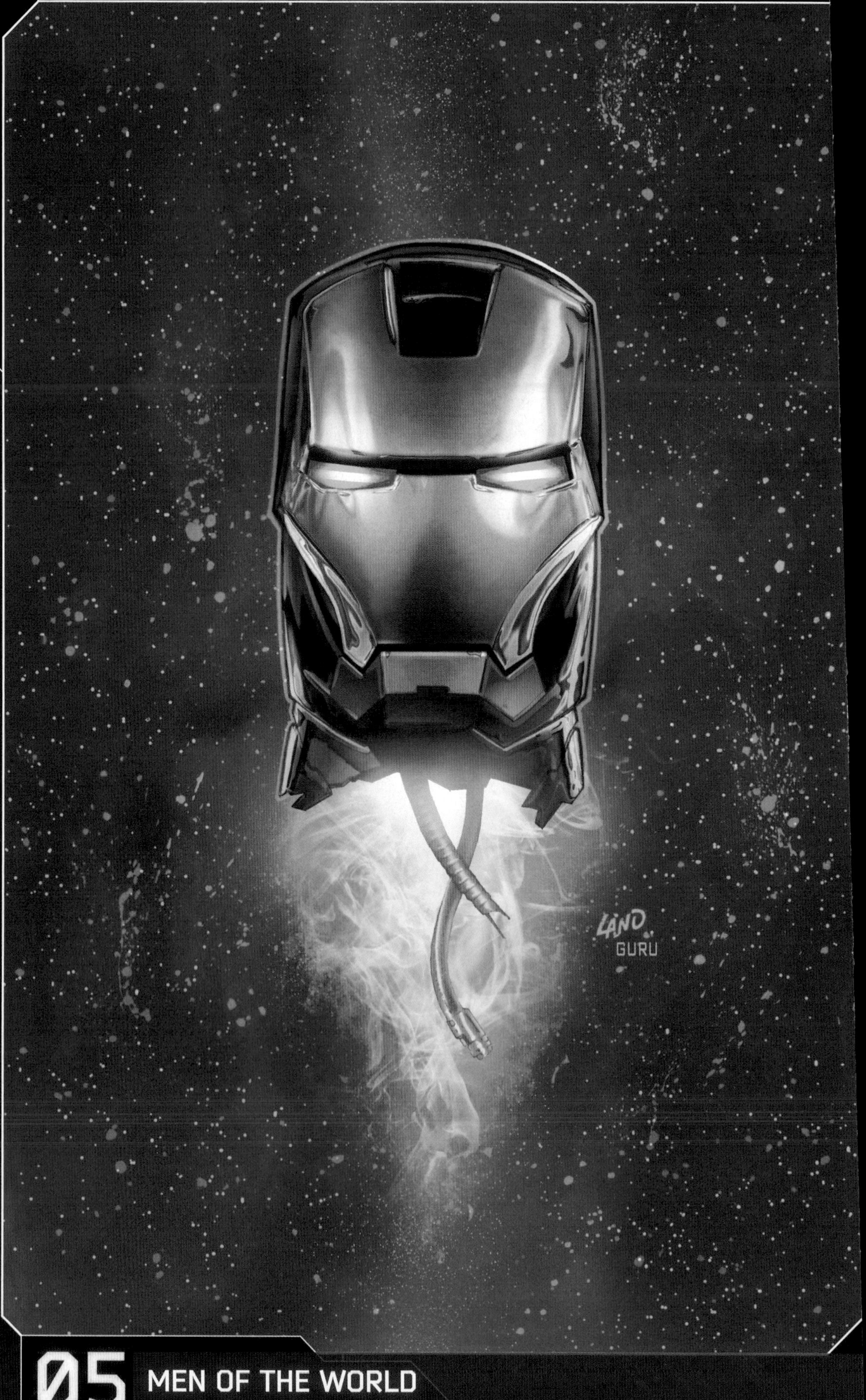
LAND
GURU

05 MEN OF THE WORLD

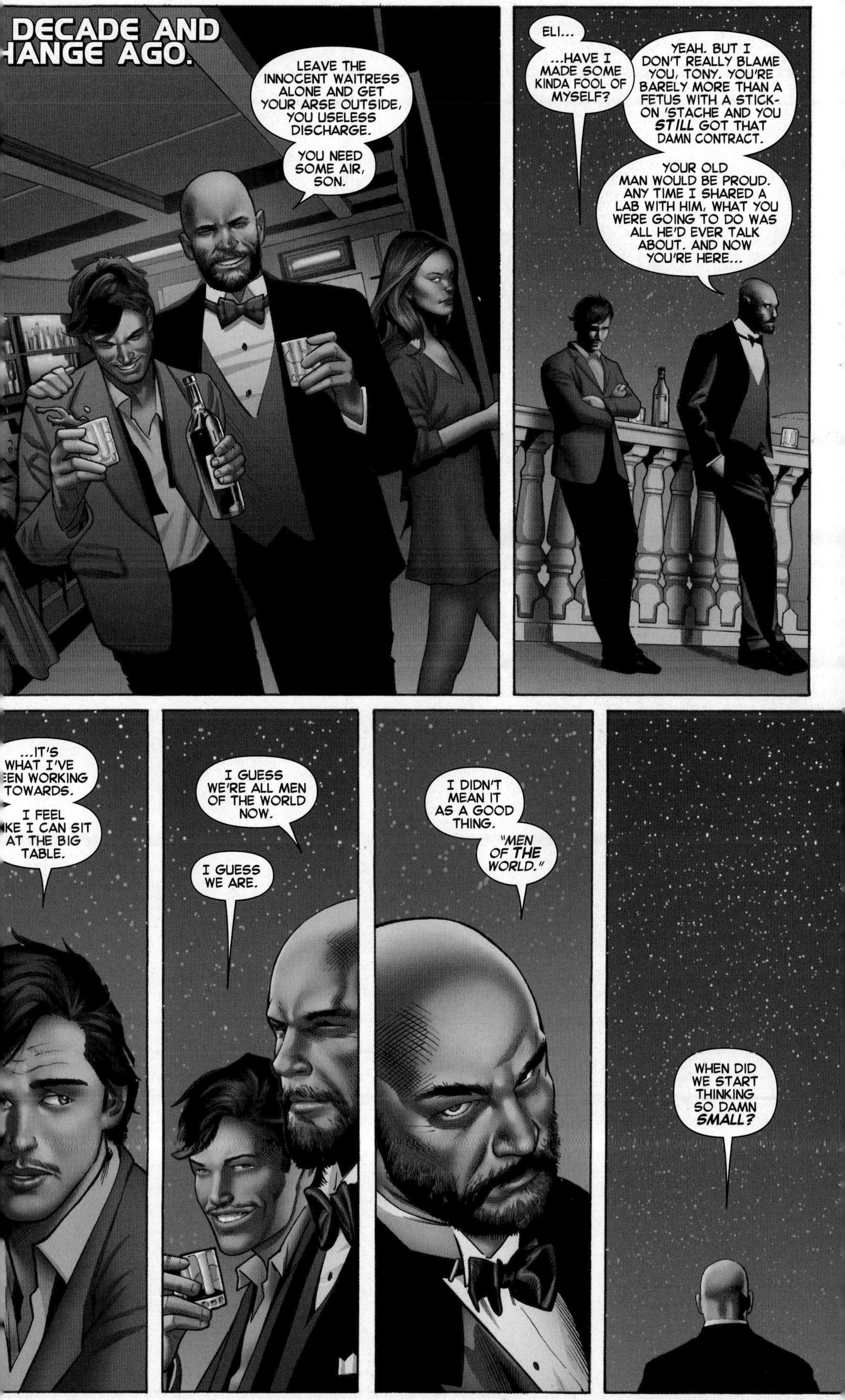
DECADE AND
HANGE AGO.
LEAVE THE INNOCENT WAITRESS ALONE AND GET YOUR ARSE OUTSIDE, YOU USELESS DISCHARGE.
YOU NEED SOME AIR, SON.
ELI...
...HAVE I MADE SOME KINDA FOOL OF MYSELF?
YEAH. BUT I DON'T REALLY BLAME YOU, TONY. YOU'RE BARELY MORE THAN A FETUS WITH A STICK-ON 'STACHE AND YOU STILL GOT THAT DAMN CONTRACT.
YOUR OLD MAN WOULD BE PROUD. ANY TIME I SHARED A LAB WITH HIM, WHAT YOU WERE GOING TO DO WAS ALL HE'D EVER TALK ABOUT. AND NOW YOU'RE HERE...
...IT'S WHAT I'VE EEN WORKING TOWARDS.
I FEEL KE I CAN SIT AT THE BIG TABLE.
I GUESS WE'RE ALL MEN OF THE WORLD NOW.
I GUESS WE ARE.
I DIDN'T MEAN IT AS A GOOD THING.
"MEN OF THE WORLD."
WHEN DID WE START THINKING SO DAMN SMALL?

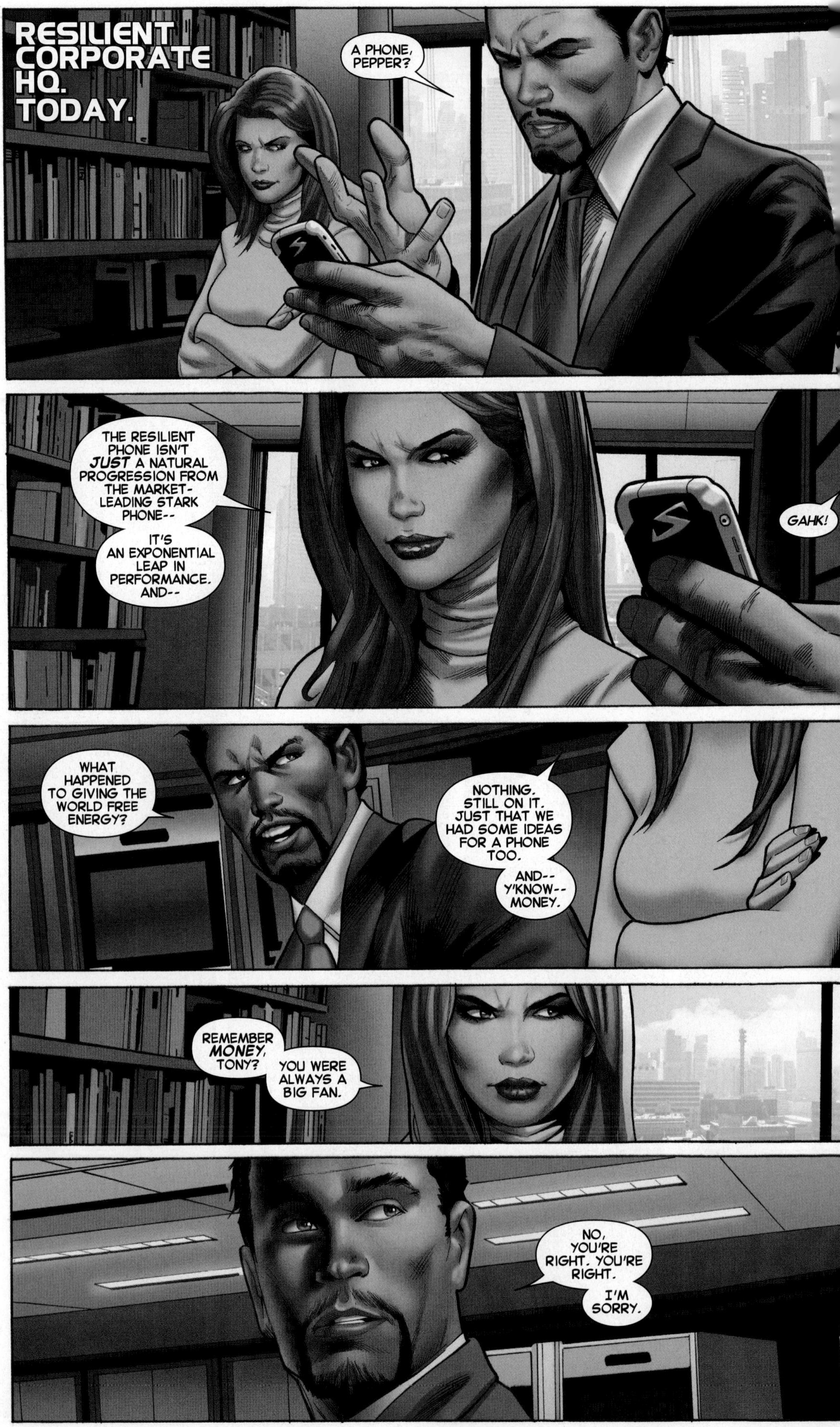
RESILIENT CORPORATE HQ. TODAY.
A PHONE, PEPPER?
THE RESILIENT PHONE ISN'T JUST A NATURAL PROGRESSION FROM THE MARKET-LEADING STARK PHONE--
IT'S AN EXPONENTIAL LEAP IN PERFORMANCE. AND--
GAHK!
WHAT HAPPENED TO GIVING THE WORLD FREE ENERGY?
NOTHING. STILL ON IT. JUST THAT WE HAD SOME IDEAS FOR A PHONE TOO.
AND-- Y'KNOW-- MONEY.
REMEMBER MONEY, TONY?
YOU WERE ALWAYS A BIG FAN.
NO, YOU'RE RIGHT. YOU'RE RIGHT.
I'M SORRY.

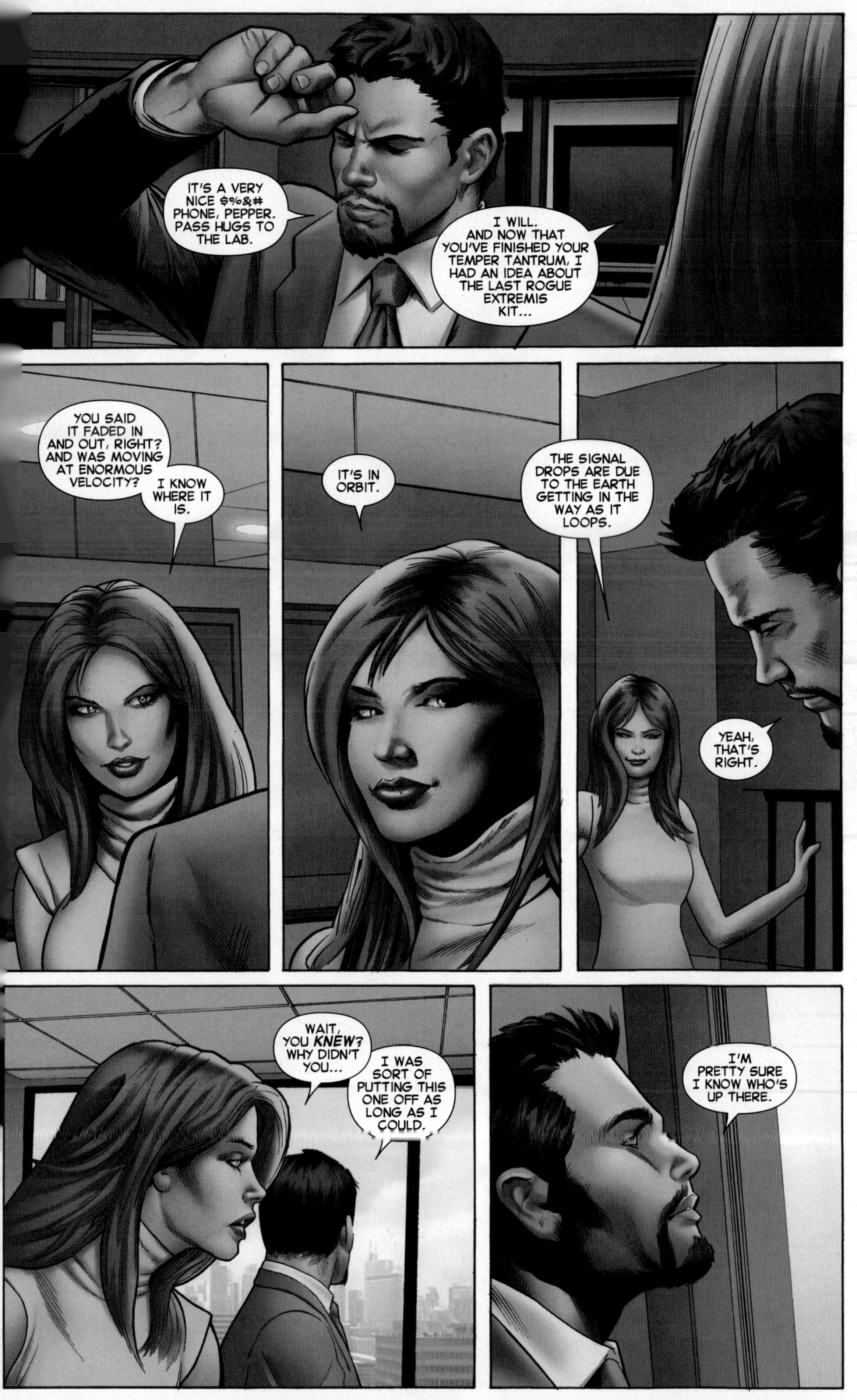
IT'S A VERY NICE $%&# PHONE, PEPPER. PASS HUGS TO THE LAB.
I WILL. AND NOW THAT YOU'VE FINISHED YOUR TEMPER TANTRUM, I HAD AN IDEA ABOUT THE LAST ROGUE EXTREMIS KIT...
YOU SAID IT FADED IN AND OUT, RIGHT? AND WAS MOVING AT ENORMOUS VELOCITY?
I KNOW WHERE IT IS.
IT'S IN ORBIT.
THE SIGNAL DROPS ARE DUE TO THE EARTH GETTING IN THE WAY AS IT LOOPS.
YEAH, THAT'S RIGHT.
WAIT, YOU KNEW? WHY DIDN'T YOU...
I WAS SORT OF PUTTING THIS ONE OFF AS LONG AS I COULD.
I'M PRETTY SURE I KNOW WHO'S UP THERE.

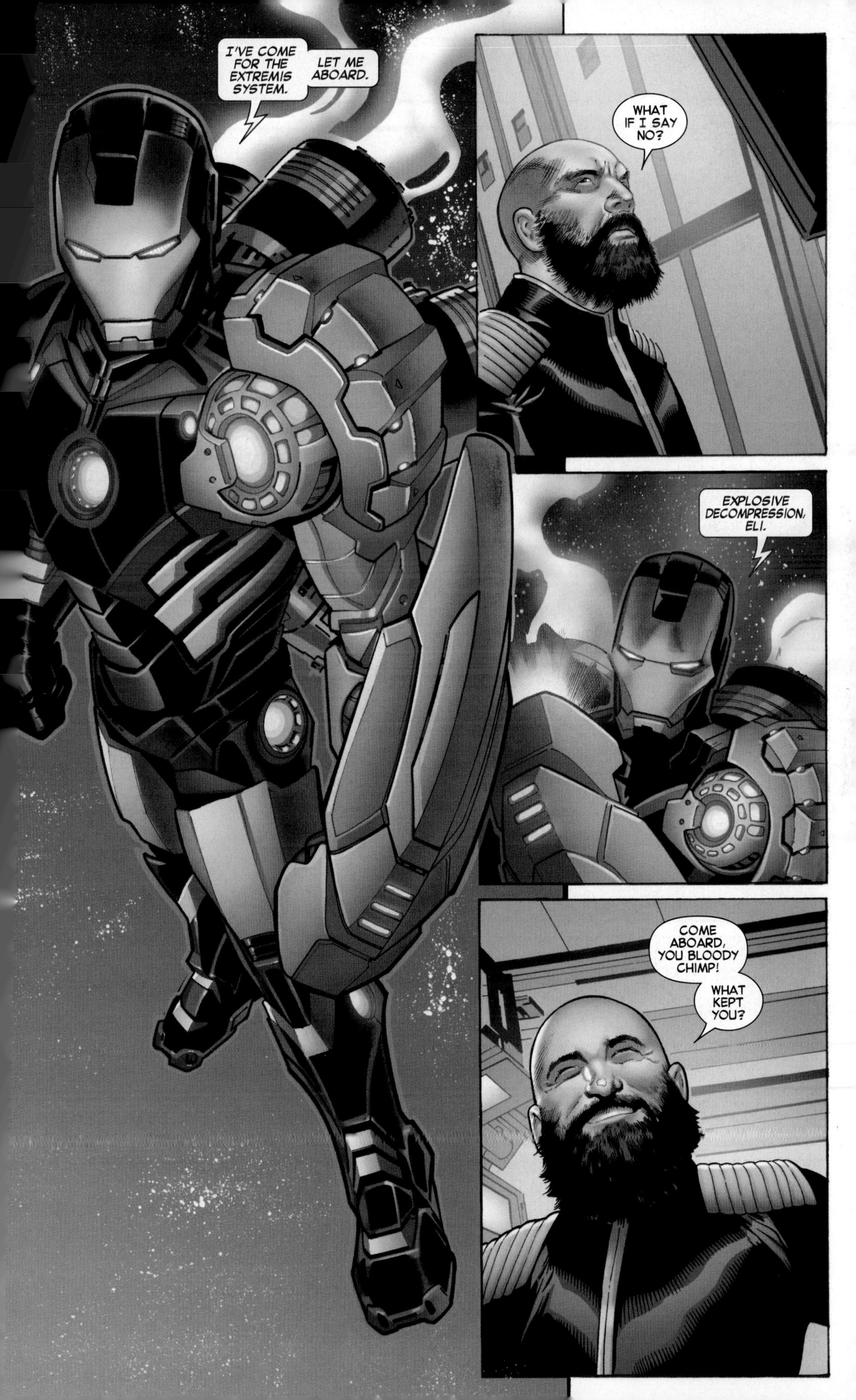
I'VE COME FOR THE EXTREMIS SYSTEM.
LET ME ABOARD.
WHAT IF I SAY NO?
EXPLOSIVE DECOMPRESSION, ELI.
COME ABOARD, YOU BLOODY CHIMP!
WHAT KEPT YOU?

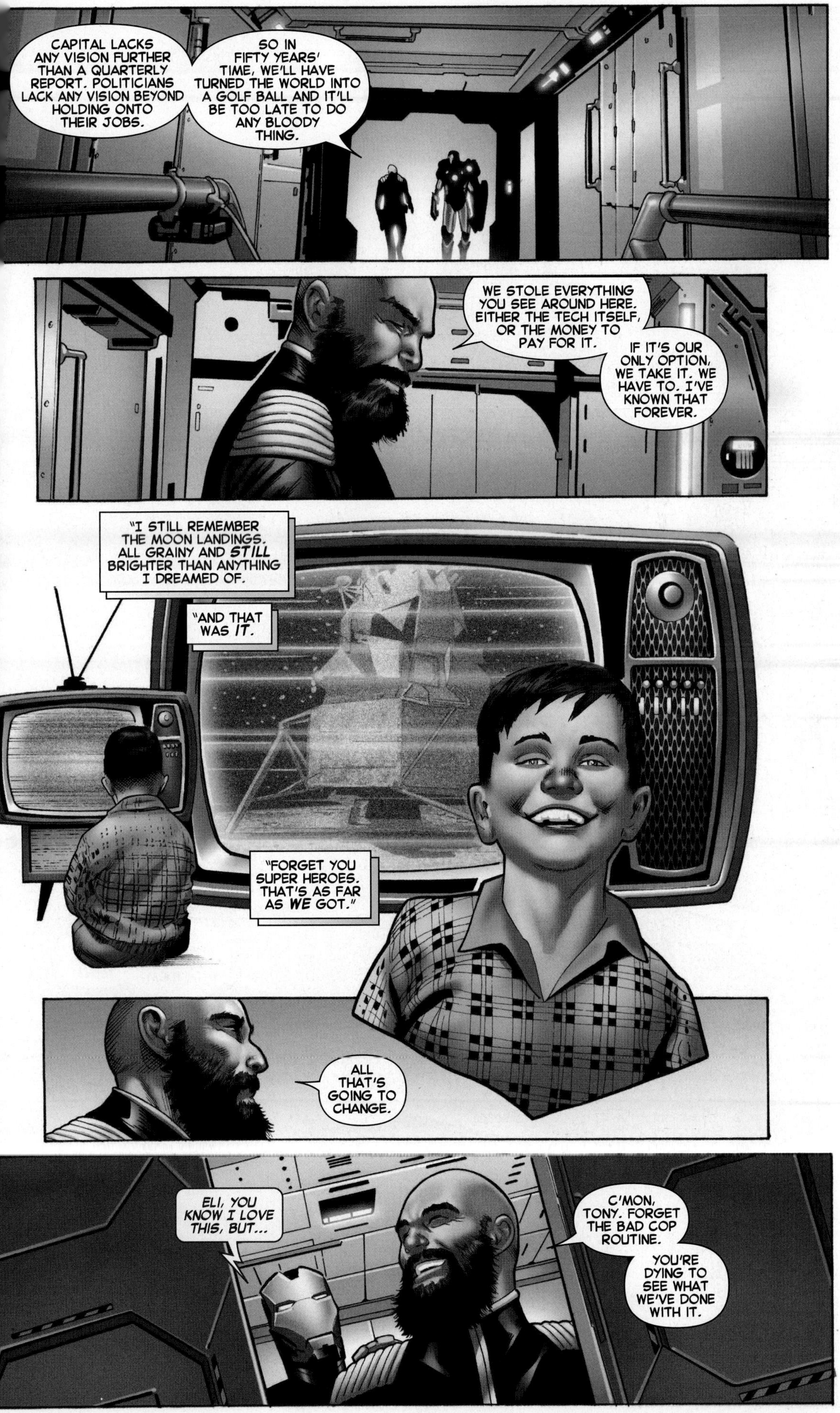
CAPITAL LACKS ANY VISION FURTHER THAN A QUARTERLY REPORT. POLITICIANS LACK ANY VISION BEYOND HOLDING ONTO THEIR JOBS.
SO IN FIFTY YEARS' TIME, WE'LL HAVE TURNED THE WORLD INTO A GOLF BALL AND IT'LL BE TOO LATE TO DO ANY BLOODY THING.
WE STOLE EVERYTHING YOU SEE AROUND HERE. EITHER THE TECH ITSELF, OR THE MONEY TO PAY FOR IT.
IF IT'S OUR ONLY OPTION, WE TAKE IT. WE HAVE TO. I'VE KNOWN THAT FOREVER.
"I STILL REMEMBER THE MOON LANDINGS. ALL GRAINY AND STILL BRIGHTER THAN ANYTHING I DREAMED OF.
"AND THAT WAS IT.
"FORGET YOU SUPER HEROES. THAT'S AS FAR AS WE GOT."
ALL THAT'S GOING TO CHANGE.
ELI, YOU KNOW I LOVE THIS, BUT...
C'MON, TONY. FORGET THE BAD COP ROUTINE.
YOU'RE DYING TO SEE WHAT WE'VE DONE WITH IT.

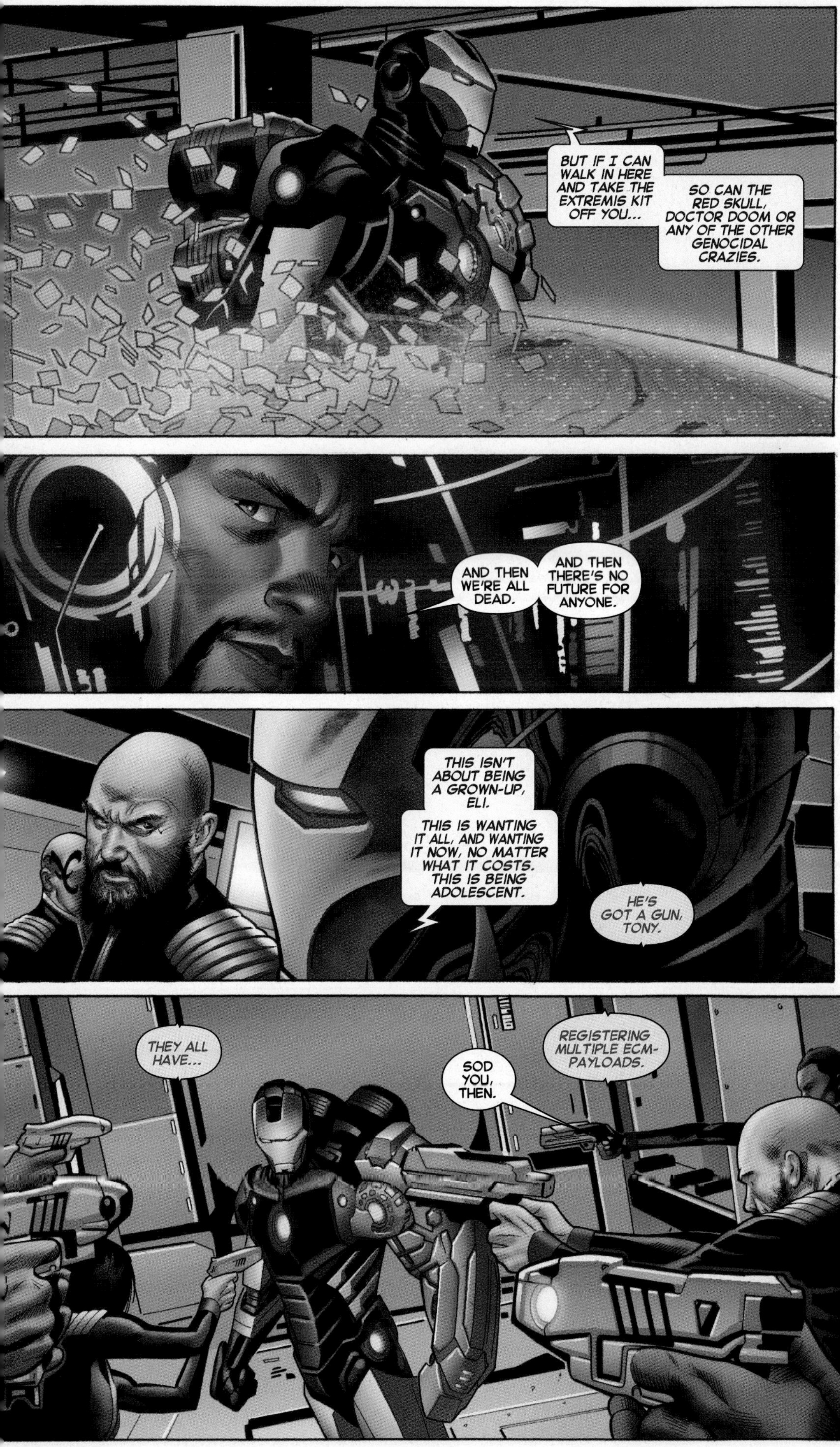
BUT IF I CAN WALK IN HERE AND TAKE THE EXTREMIS KIT OFF YOU...
SO CAN THE RED SKULL, DOCTOR DOOM OR ANY OF THE OTHER GENOCIDAL CRAZIES.
AND THEN WE'RE ALL DEAD.
AND THEN THERE'S NO FUTURE FOR ANYONE.
THIS ISN'T ABOUT BEING A GROWN-UP, ELI.
THIS IS WANTING IT ALL, AND WANTING IT NOW, NO MATTER WHAT IT COSTS. THIS IS BEING ADOLESCENT.
HE'S GOT A GUN, TONY.
THEY ALL HAVE...
SOD YOU, THEN.
REGISTERING MULTIPLE ECM-PAYLOADS.

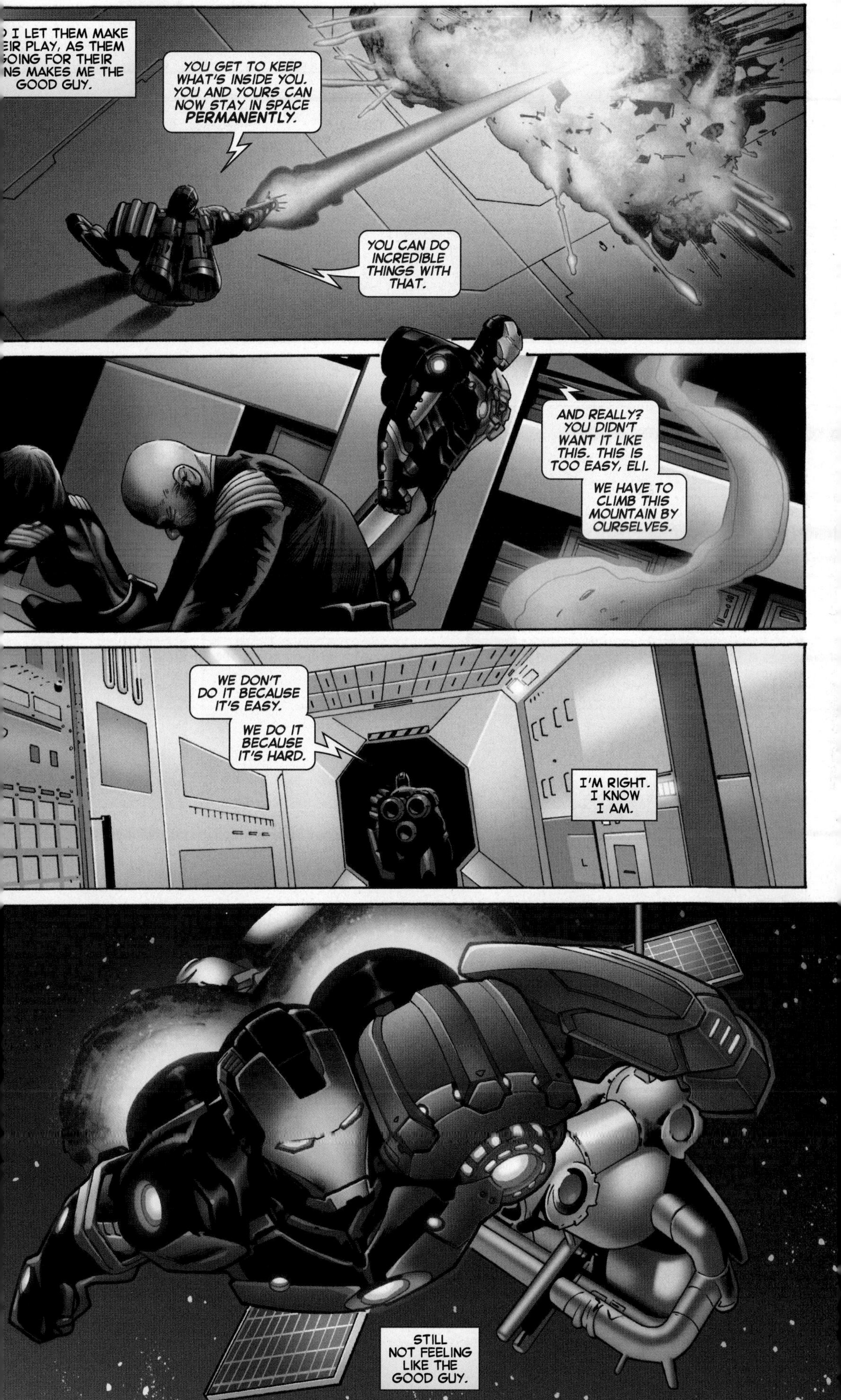

D I LET THEM MAKE EIR PLAY, AS THEM GOING FOR THEIR NS MAKES ME THE GOOD GUY.
YOU GET TO KEEP WHAT'S INSIDE YOU. YOU AND YOURS CAN NOW STAY IN SPACE PERMANENTLY.
YOU CAN DO INCREDIBLE THINGS WITH THAT.
AND REALLY? YOU DIDN'T WANT IT LIKE THIS. THIS IS TOO EASY, ELI.
WE HAVE TO CLIMB THIS MOUNTAIN BY OURSELVES.
WE DON'T DO IT BECAUSE IT'S EASY.
WE DO IT BECAUSE IT'S HARD.
I'M RIGHT. I KNOW I AM.
STILL NOT FEELING LIKE THE GOOD GUY.

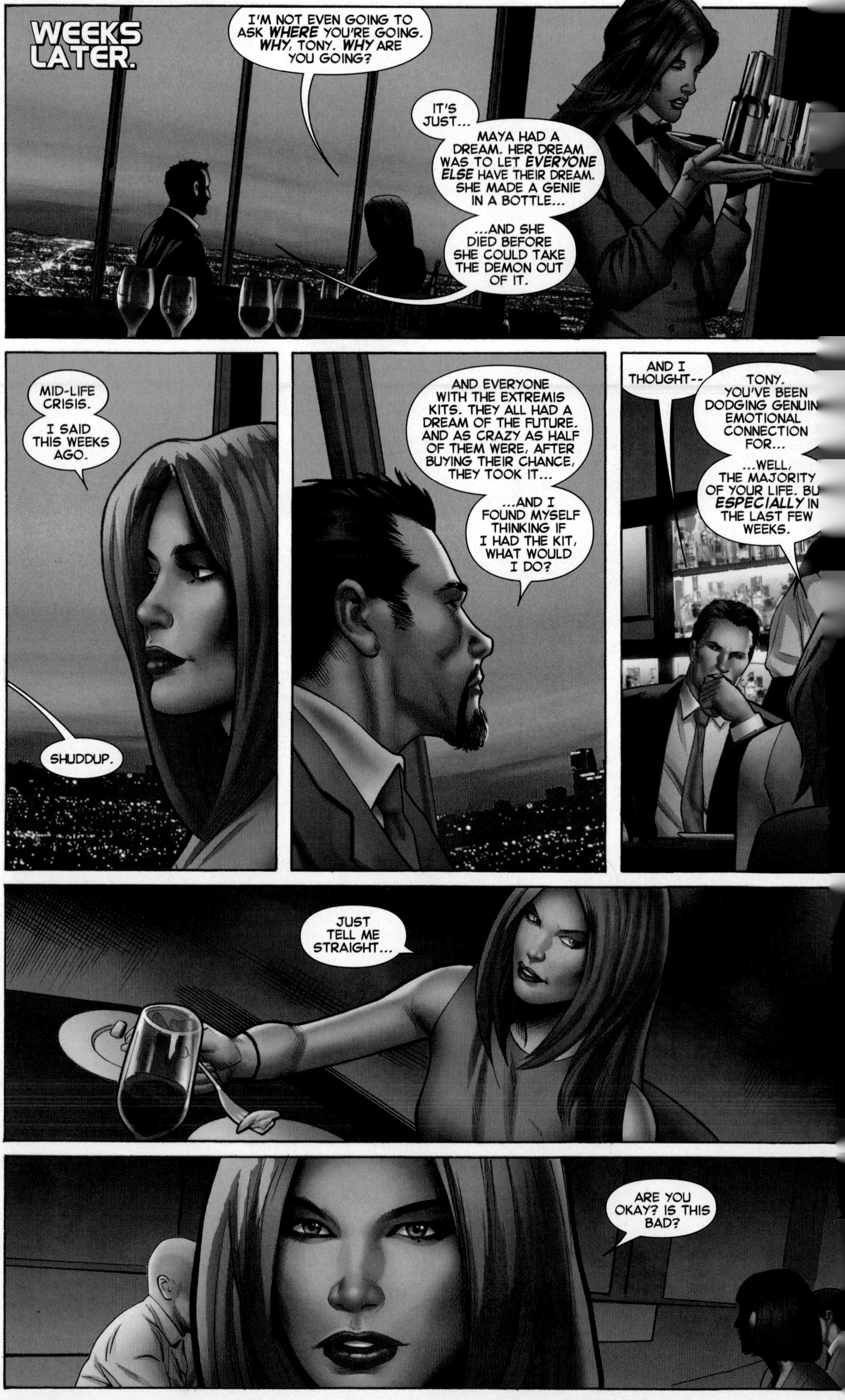
WEEKS LATER.
I'M NOT EVEN GOING TO ASK WHERE YOU'RE GOING. WHY, TONY. WHY ARE YOU GOING?
IT'S JUST...
MAYA HAD A DREAM. HER DREAM WAS TO LET EVERYONE ELSE HAVE THEIR DREAM. SHE MADE A GENIE IN A BOTTLE...
...AND SHE DIED BEFORE SHE COULD TAKE THE DEMON OUT OF IT.
MID-LIFE CRISIS.
I SAID THIS WEEKS AGO.
SHUDDUP.
AND EVERYONE WITH THE EXTREMIS KITS. THEY ALL HAD A DREAM OF THE FUTURE. AND AS CRAZY AS HALF OF THEM WERE, AFTER BUYING THEIR CHANCE, THEY TOOK IT...
...AND I FOUND MYSELF THINKING IF I HAD THE KIT, WHAT WOULD I DO?
AND I THOUGHT--
TONY. YOU'VE BEEN DODGING GENUIN EMOTIONAL CONNECTION FOR...
...WELL, THE MAJORITY OF YOUR LIFE. BU ESPECIALLY IN THE LAST FEW WEEKS.
JUST TELL ME STRAIGHT...
ARE YOU OKAY? IS THIS BAD?

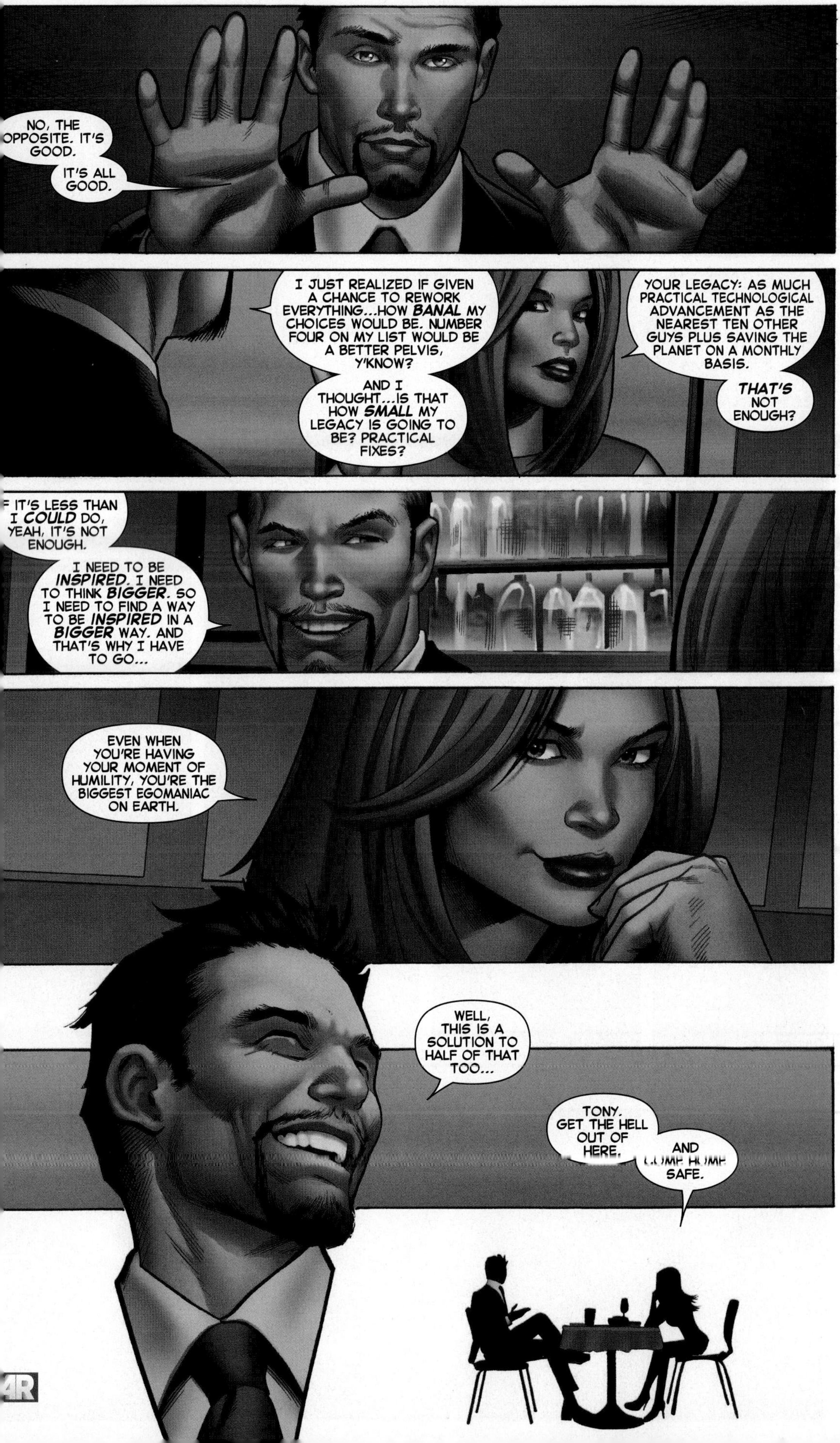
NO, THE OPPOSITE. IT'S GOOD.
IT'S ALL GOOD.
I JUST REALIZED IF GIVEN A CHANCE TO REWORK EVERYTHING...HOW BANAL MY CHOICES WOULD BE. NUMBER FOUR ON MY LIST WOULD BE A BETTER PELVIS, Y'KNOW?
AND I THOUGHT...IS THAT HOW SMALL MY LEGACY IS GOING TO BE? PRACTICAL FIXES?
YOUR LEGACY: AS MUCH PRACTICAL TECHNOLOGICAL ADVANCEMENT AS THE NEAREST TEN OTHER GUYS PLUS SAVING THE PLANET ON A MONTHLY BASIS.
THAT'S NOT ENOUGH?
F IT'S LESS THAN I COULD DO, YEAH, IT'S NOT ENOUGH.
I NEED TO BE INSPIRED. I NEED TO THINK BIGGER. SO I NEED TO FIND A WAY TO BE INSPIRED IN A BIGGER WAY. AND THAT'S WHY I HAVE TO GO...
EVEN WHEN YOU'RE HAVING YOUR MOMENT OF HUMILITY, YOU'RE THE BIGGEST EGOMANIAC ON EARTH.
WELL, THIS IS A SOLUTION TO HALF OF THAT TOO...
TONY. GET THE HELL OUT OF HERE.
AND COME HOME SAFE.

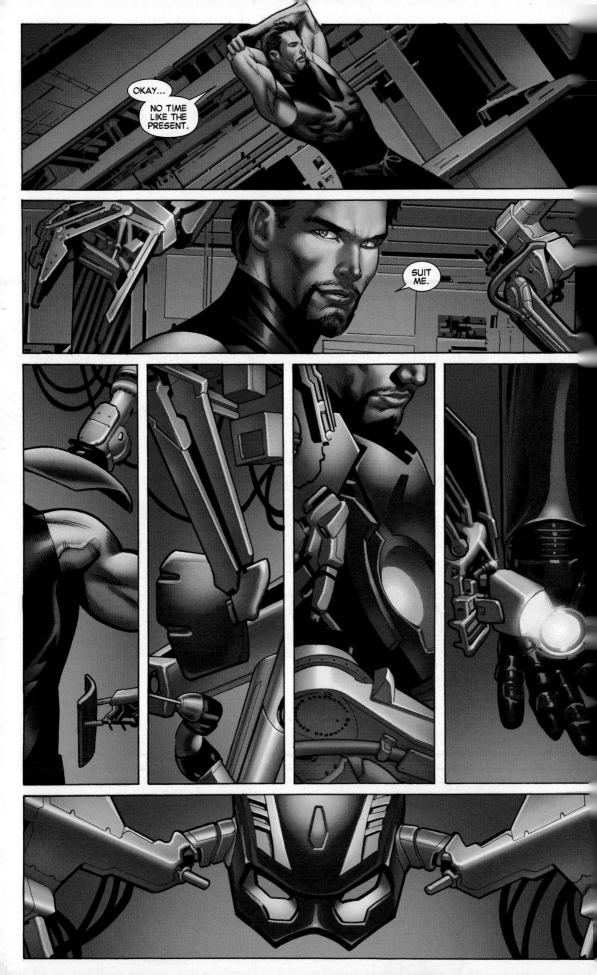

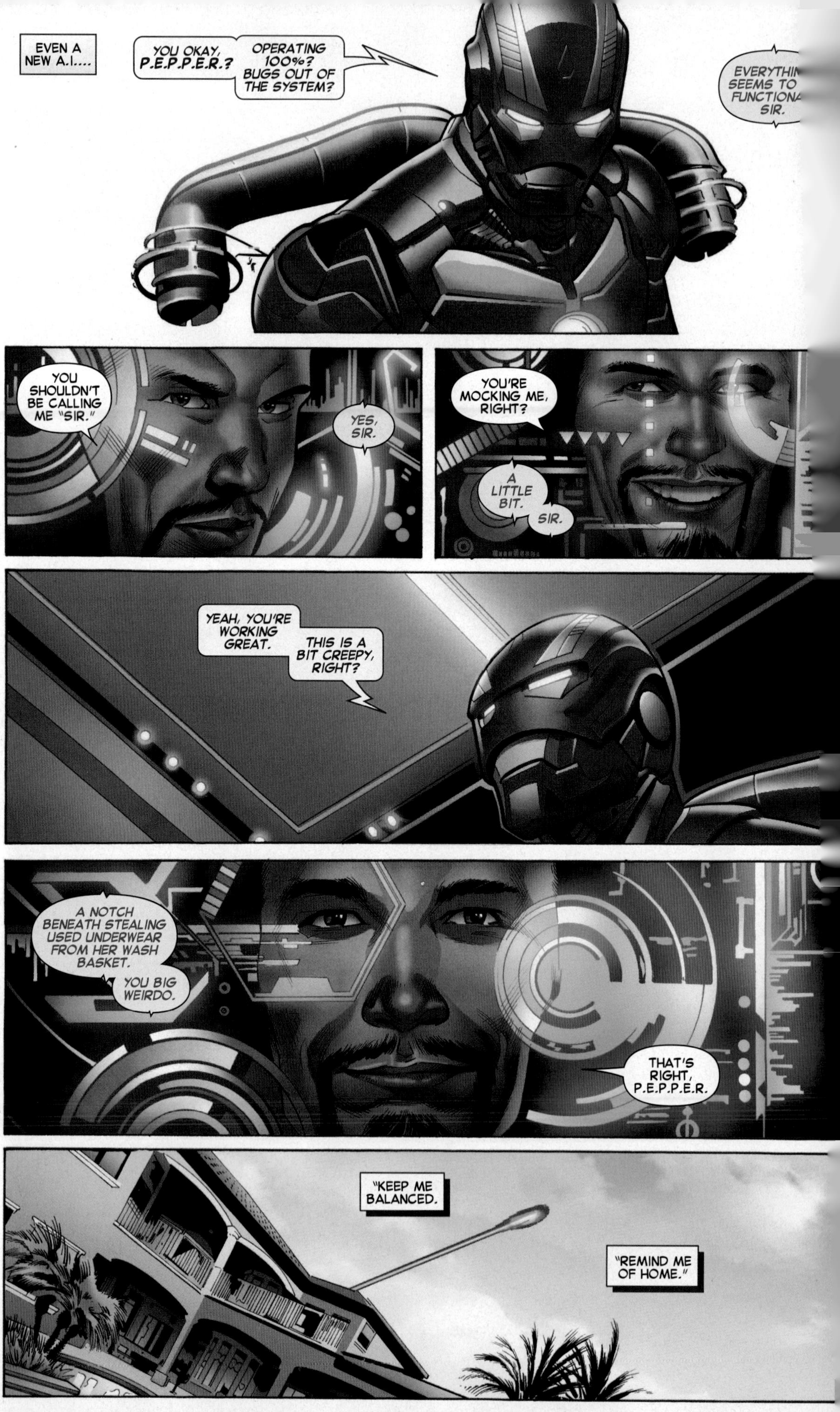
EVEN A NEW A.I....
YOU OKAY, P.E.P.P.E.R.?
OPERATING 100%? BUGS OUT OF THE SYSTEM?
EVERYTHIN SEEMS TO FUNCTIONA SIR.
YOU SHOULDN'T BE CALLING ME "SIR."
YES, SIR.
YOU'RE MOCKING ME, RIGHT?
A LITTLE BIT.
SIR.
YEAH, YOU'RE WORKING GREAT.
THIS IS A BIT CREEPY, RIGHT?
A NOTCH BENEATH STEALING USED UNDERWEAR FROM HER WASH BASKET.
YOU BIG WEIRDO.
THAT'S RIGHT, P.E.P.P.E.R.
"KEEP ME BALANCED.
"REMIND ME OF HOME."

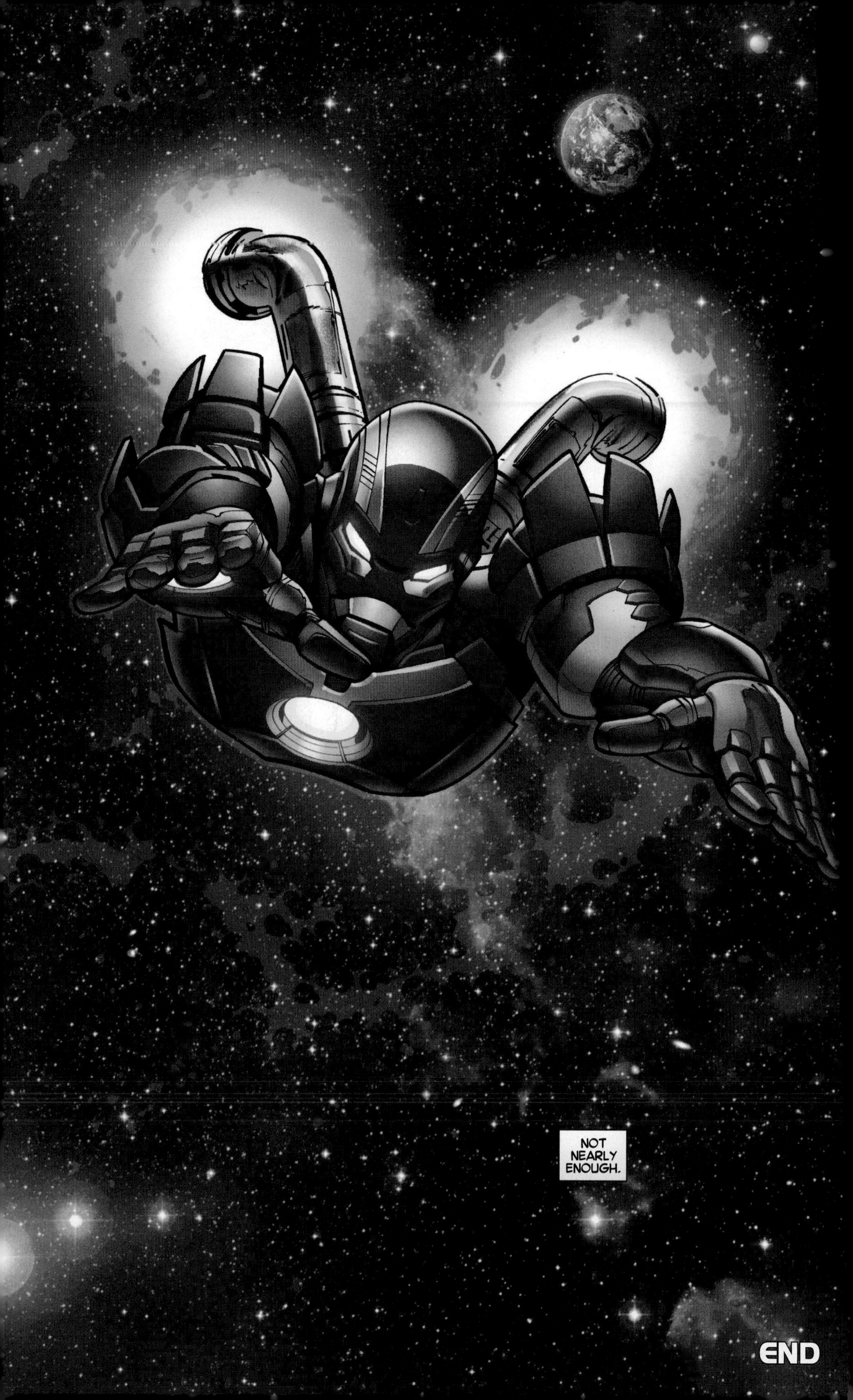
NOT NEARLY ENOUGH.
END

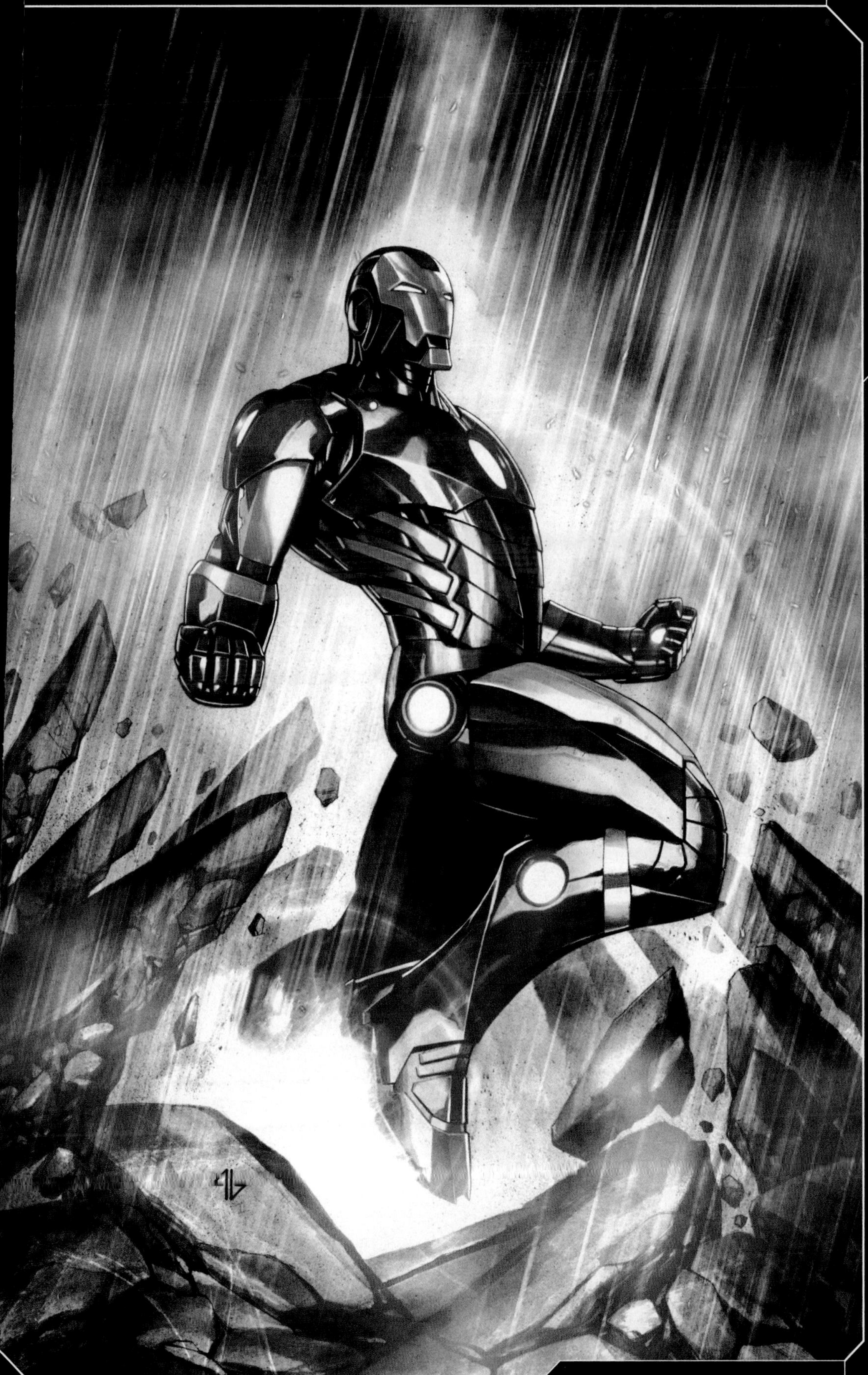

#1 **VARIANT** BY ADI GRANOV

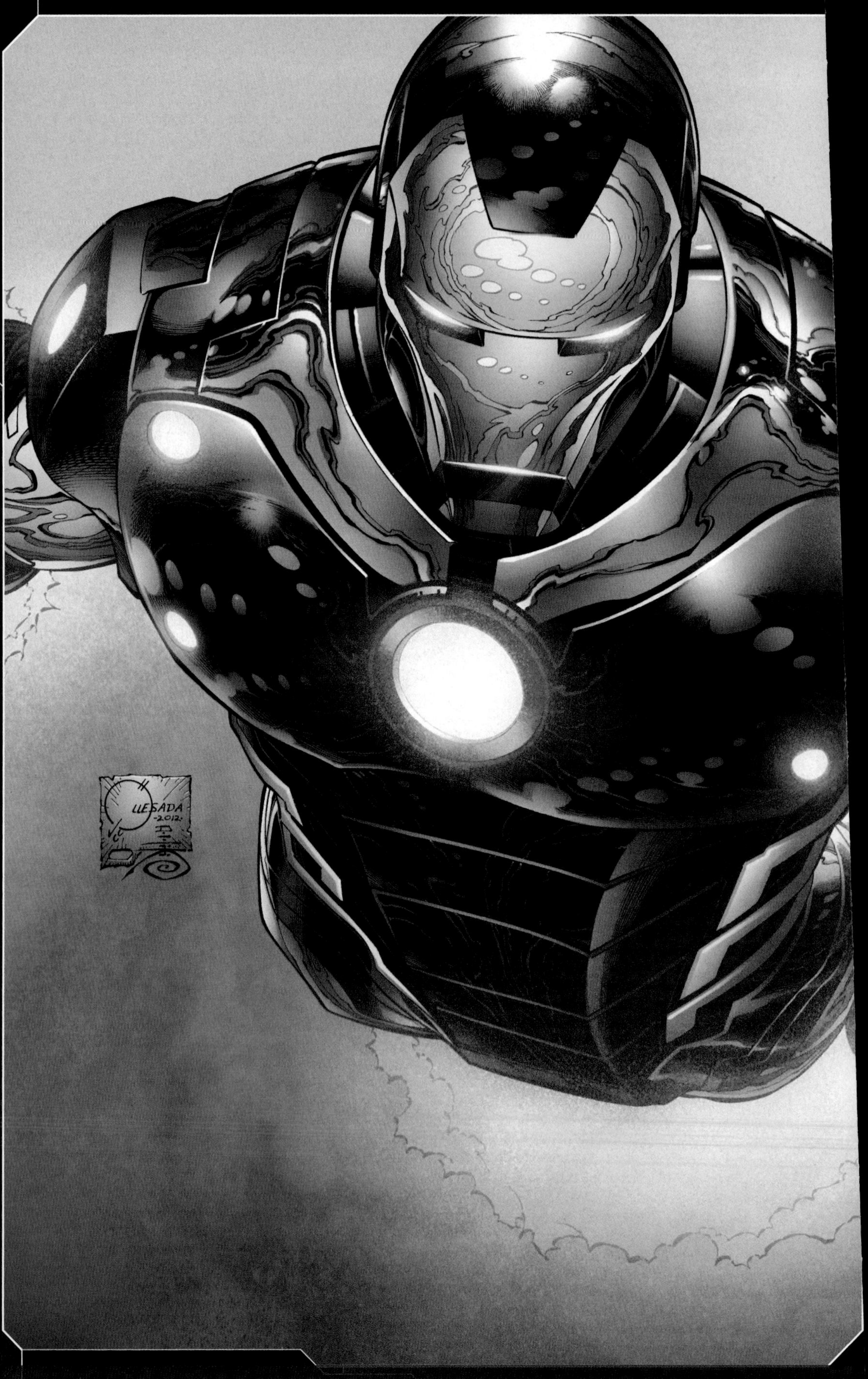

#1 VARIANT BY JOE QUESADA, DANNY MIKI & RICHARD ISANOVE

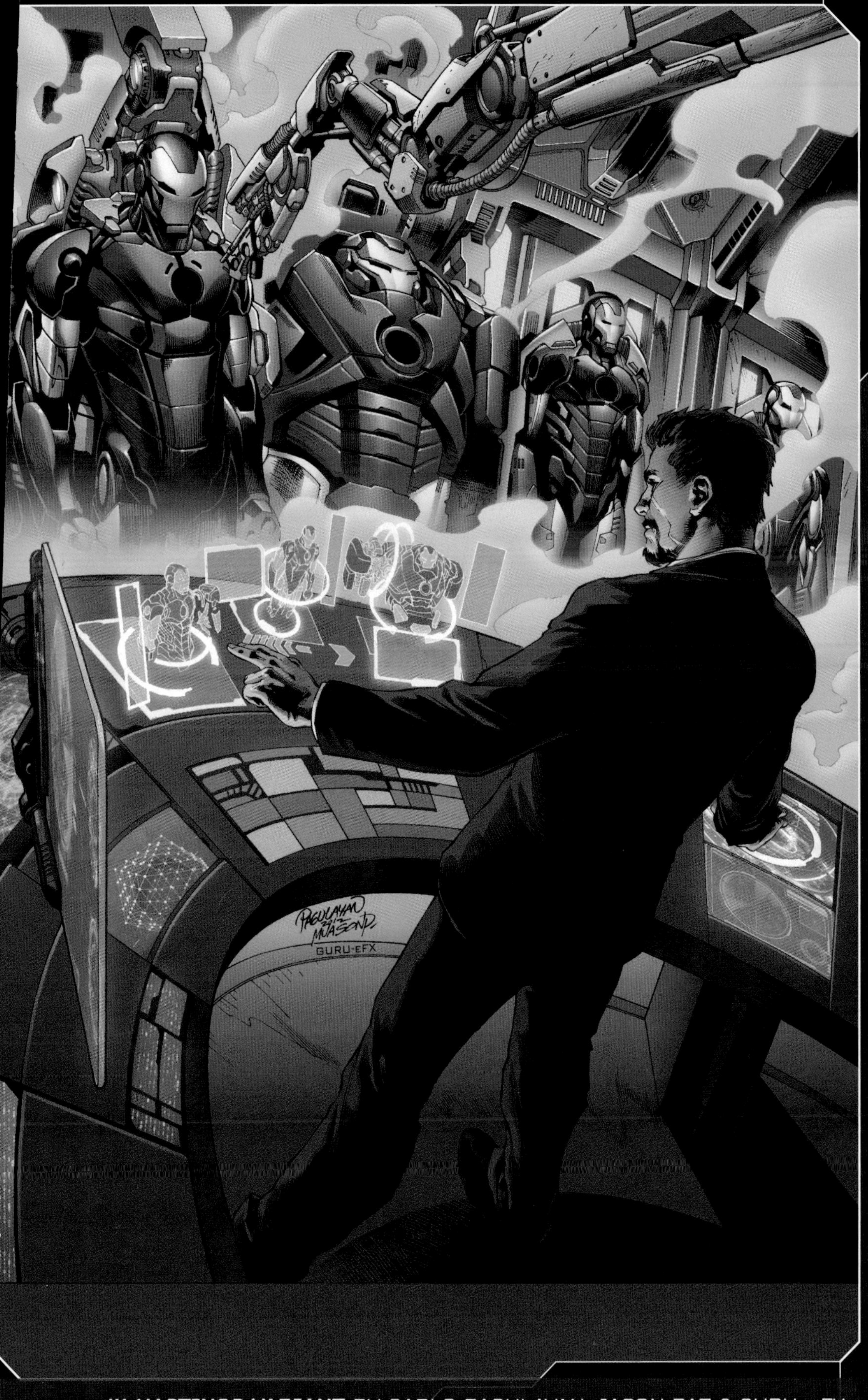
PAGULAYAN 2012 MUASONP.
GURU-eFX

#1 HASTINGS VARIANT BY CARLO PAGULAYAN, JASON PAZ & GURU-eFX

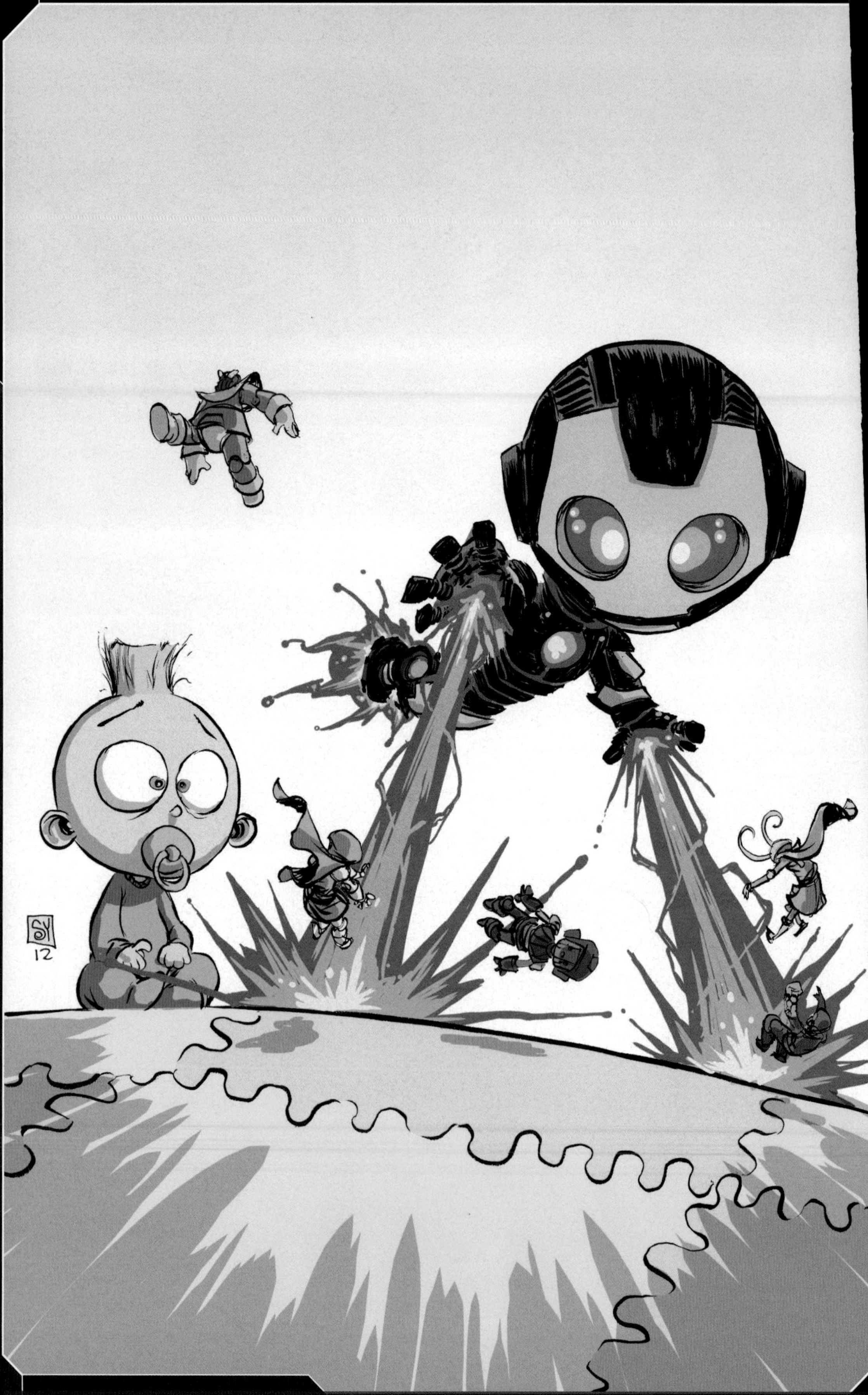
SY
12

#1 YOUNG VARIANT BY SKOTTIE YOUNG

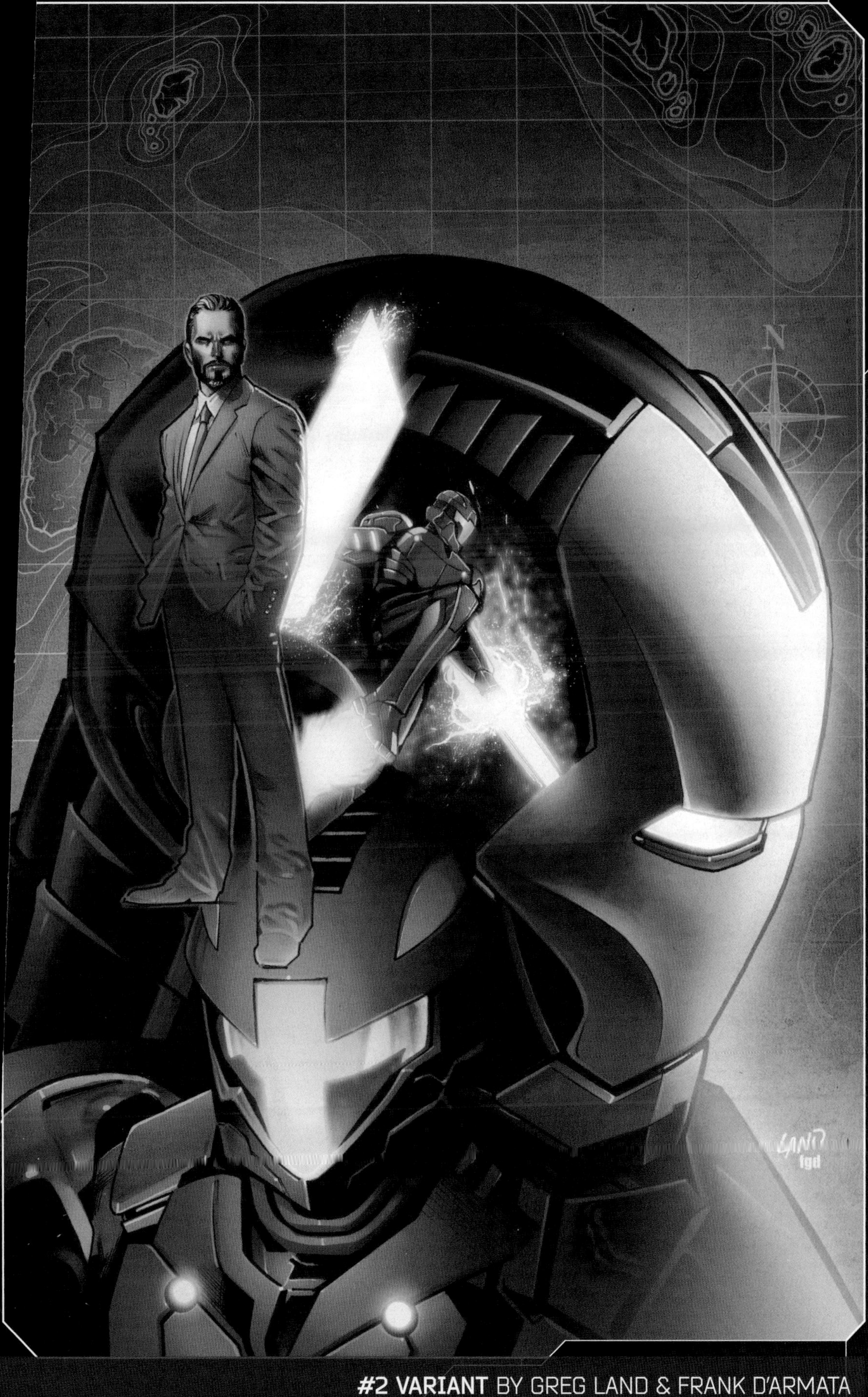

#2 VARIANT BY GREG LAND & FRANK D'ARMATA

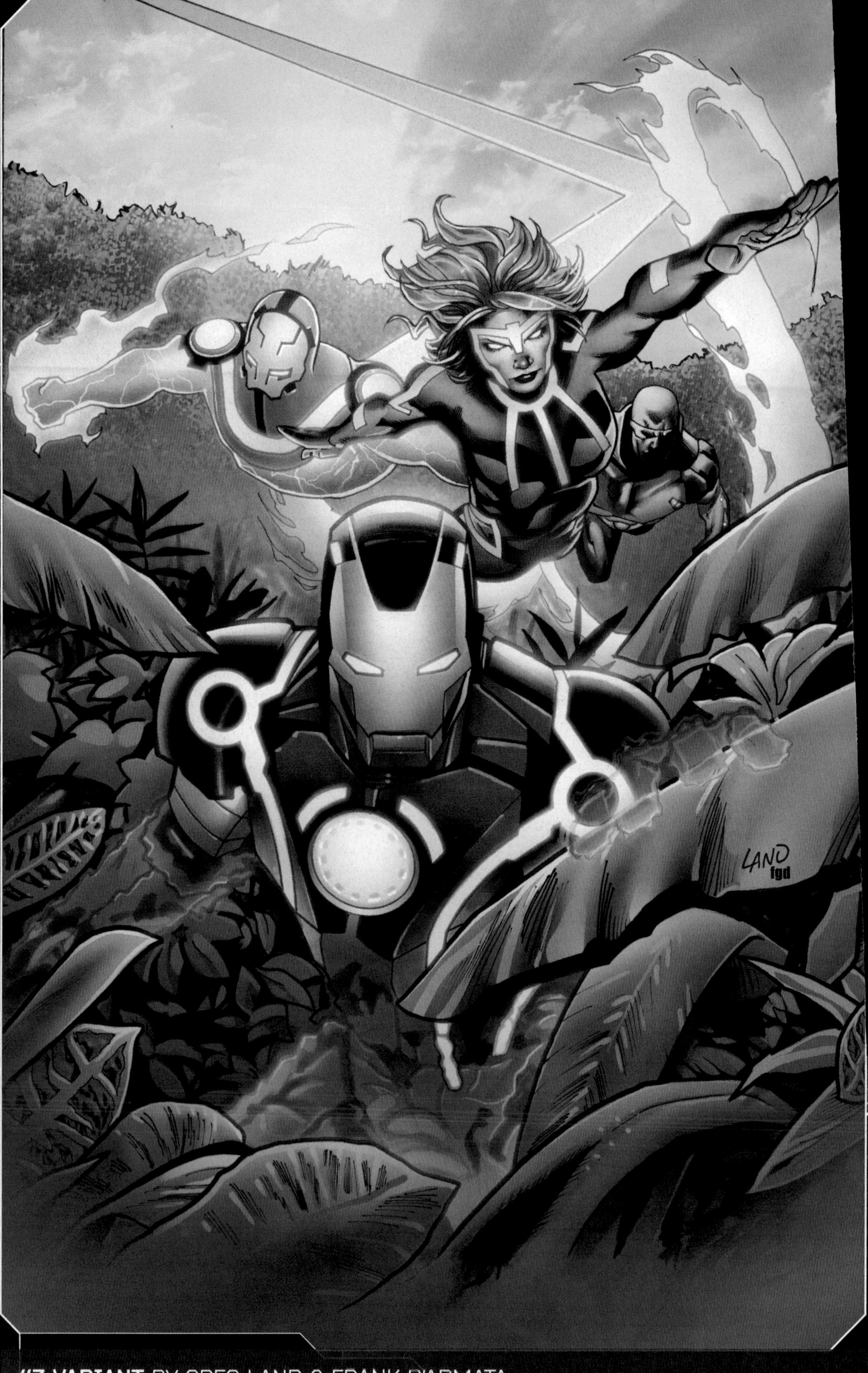
LAND
fgd

#3 VARIANT BY GREG LAND & FRANK D'ARMATA

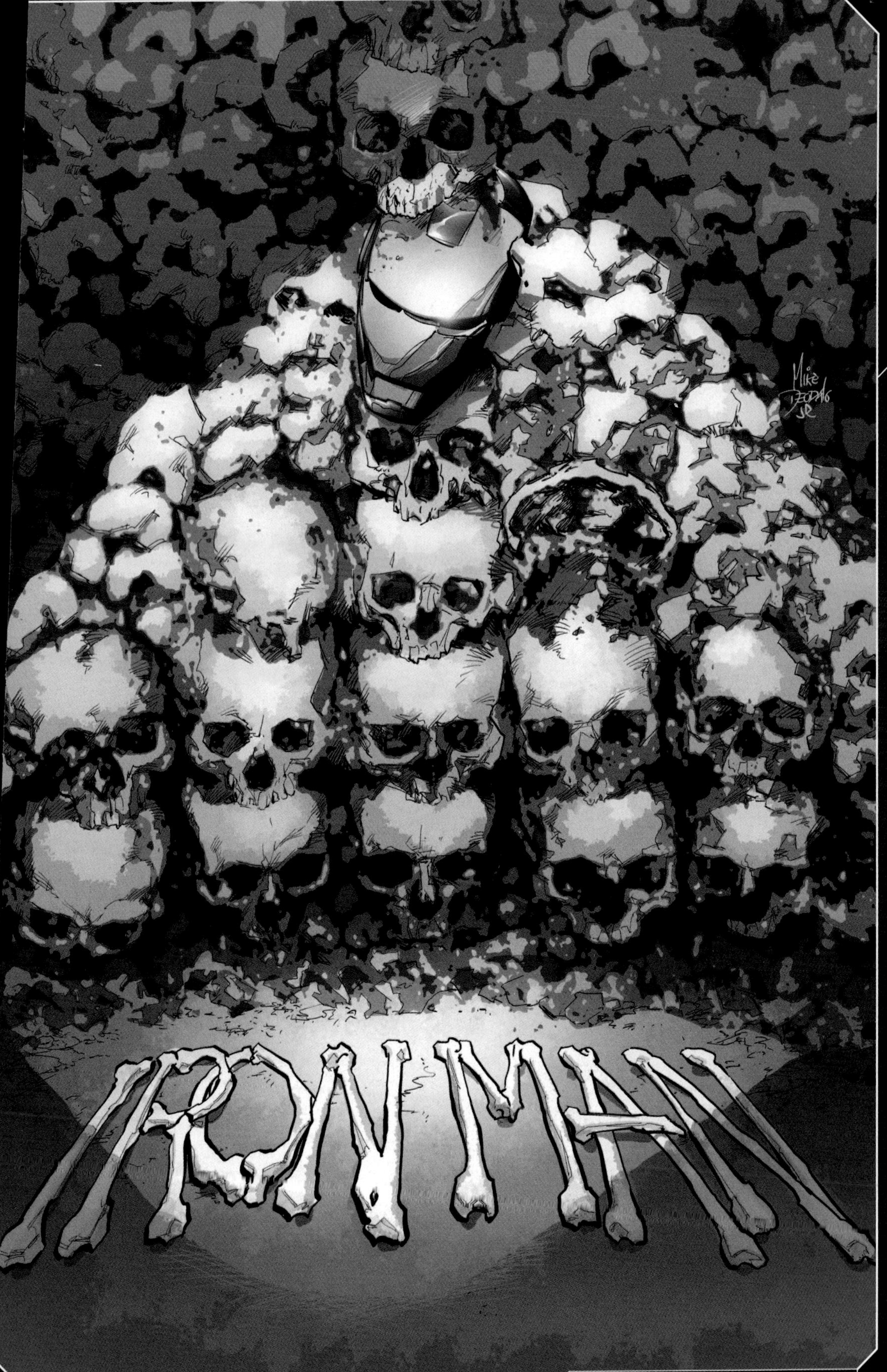
IRON MAN
Mike Deodato Jr.

#4 VARIANT BY MIKE DEODATO & RAIN BEREDO

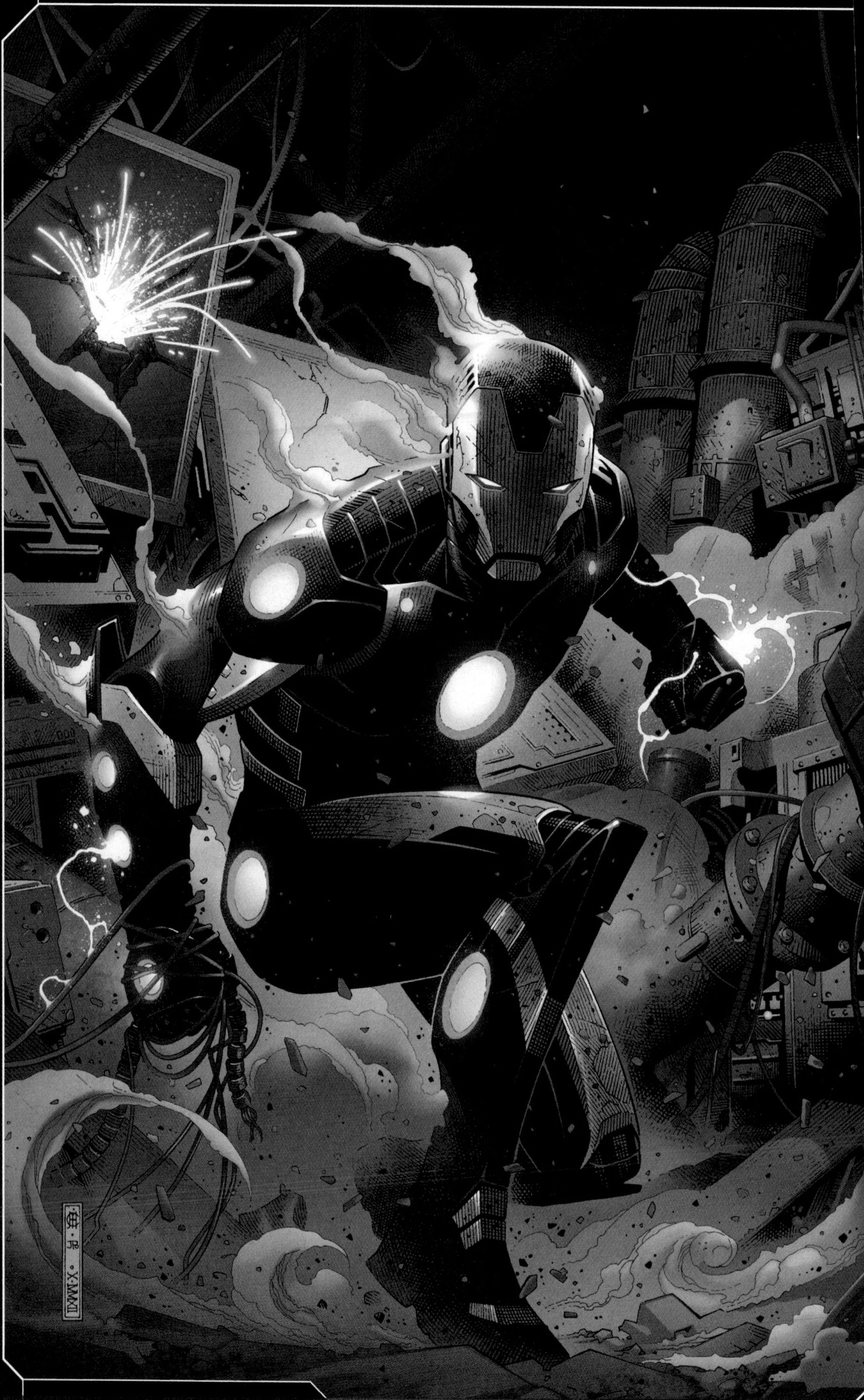

#5 VARIANT BY JIM CHEUNG & JUSTIN PONSOR

base config notes
design notes for armor
UNIVERSAL

model number MACH.01596
armor type UNIVERSAL.01

AI core coordinates extreme modularity of sub-units

$x^2 + (2)x + hi$
too high!

0.269.354%
8963.125 / 6.04

$X(6) + 23-1°$

$2 \cdot (6.3)$
$9(x x^2)$

nothing is future proof. but it's worth a shot!

$h = V_i x hi$

classic black? gold is trickier — but if you can't pull it off — who can?

984.023
986+364.03/982
148% | 32.069°
OUT 96.321°

$hi + Qu = 9x(x) + 2.1$

$3a-2i \Sigma x + fi$

**PROJECTED
VITALS MONITOR**

CORE 98.3690
EKG 96%
DMR 96.3210
OPR 068%

489.236+4897.026°
7963.012/65.120+6.217°
36.025°

000.159°
029.366°
789.023°
4+3698/89+012

★

984.023
951.369
951.147
600.796
543.198
766.124

#1 ARMOR DESIGN VARIANT BY CARLO PAGULAYAN & JARED FLETCHER

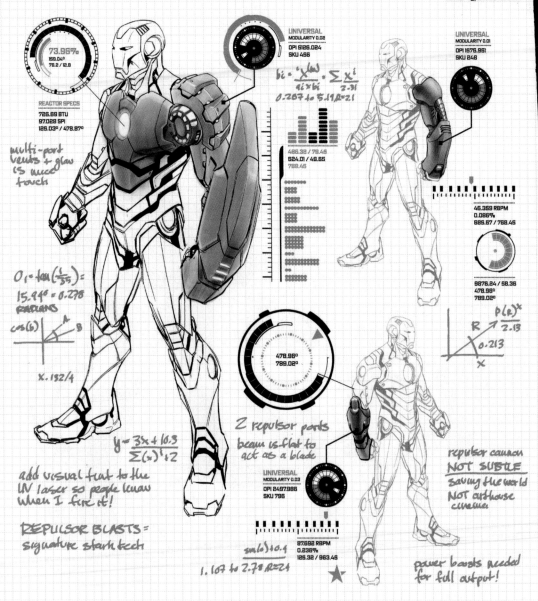

base config notes
design notes for amor
UNIVERSAL.01_03
model number MACH.01596
armor type MODULARITY

#2 ARMOR DESIGN VARIANT BY CARLO PAGULAYAN & JARED FLETCHER

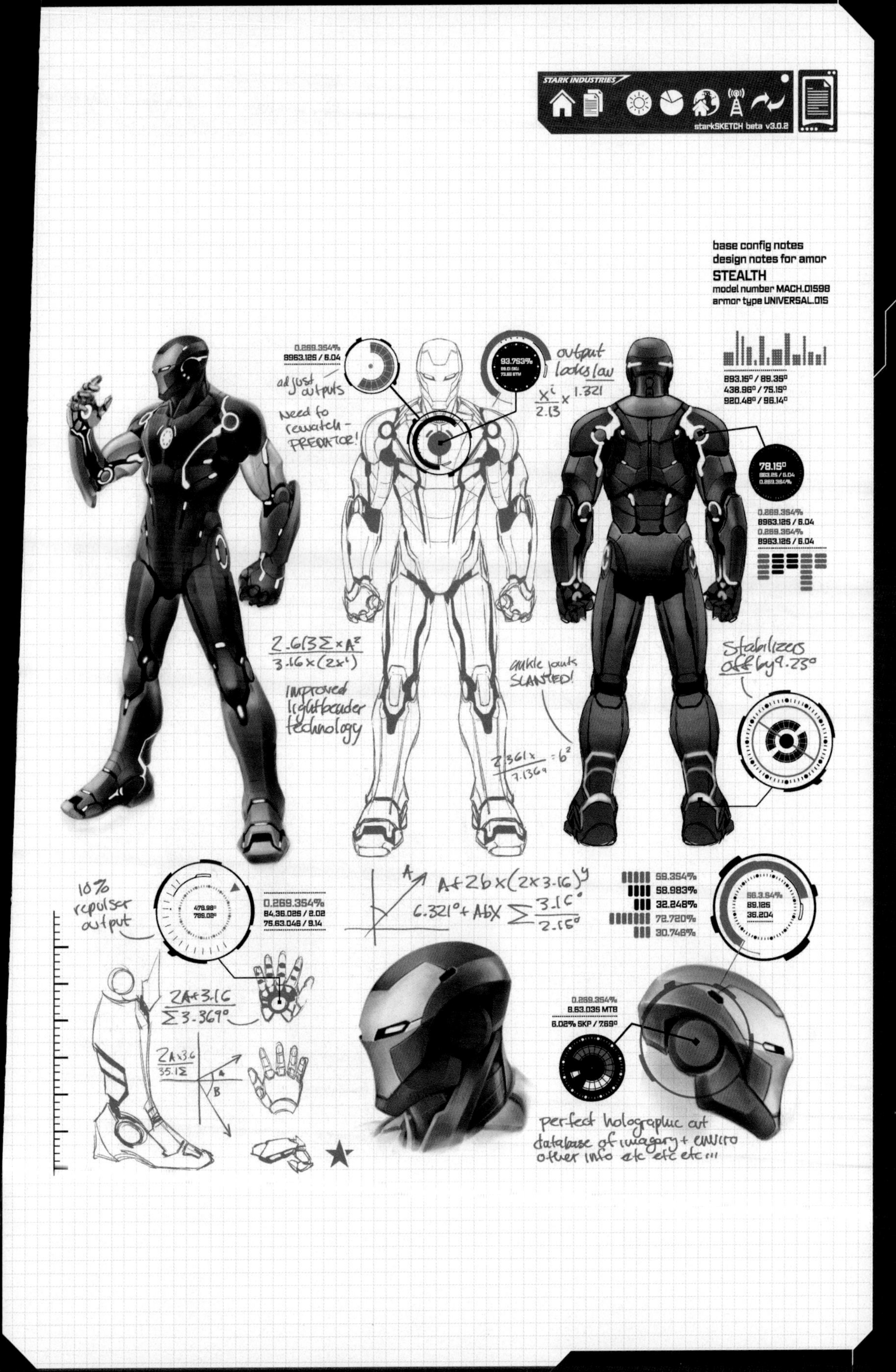
STARK INDUSTRIES
starkSKETCH beta v3.0.2
base config notes
design notes for amor
STEALTH
model number MACH.01598
armor type UNIVERSAL.015
adjust outputs
Need to rewatch - PREDATOR!
output looks low
improved lightbender technology
ankle joints SLANTED!
Stabilizers off by 9.23°
10% repulser output
perfect holographic art database of imagery + enviro other info etc etc etc...

#3 ARMOR DESIGN VARIANT BY CARLO PAGULAYAN & JARED FLETCHER

base config notes
design notes for amor
HEAVY
model number MACH.01599
armor type UNIVERSAL.01H

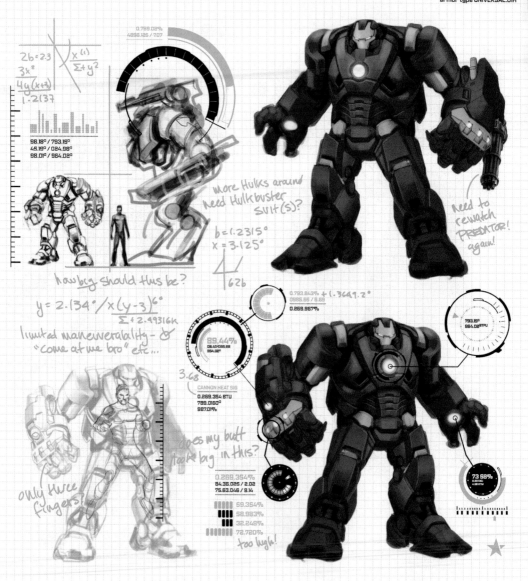

More Hulks around
Need Hulkbuster
suit(s)?

need to
rewatch
PREDATOR!
again!

$b = 1.2315°$
$x = 3.125°$

how big should this be?

$$y = 2.134° / x (y-3)^6°$$
$$\Sigma + 2.49316k$$

limited maneuverability - &
"come at me bro" etc...

does my butt
look big in this?

only three
fingers

too high!

CANNON HEAT SIG

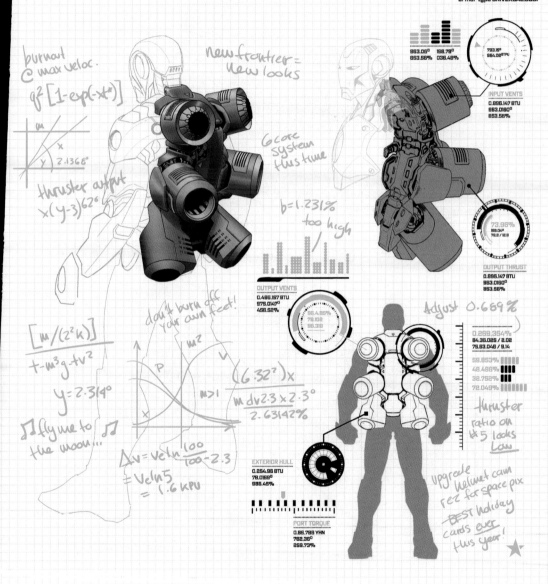

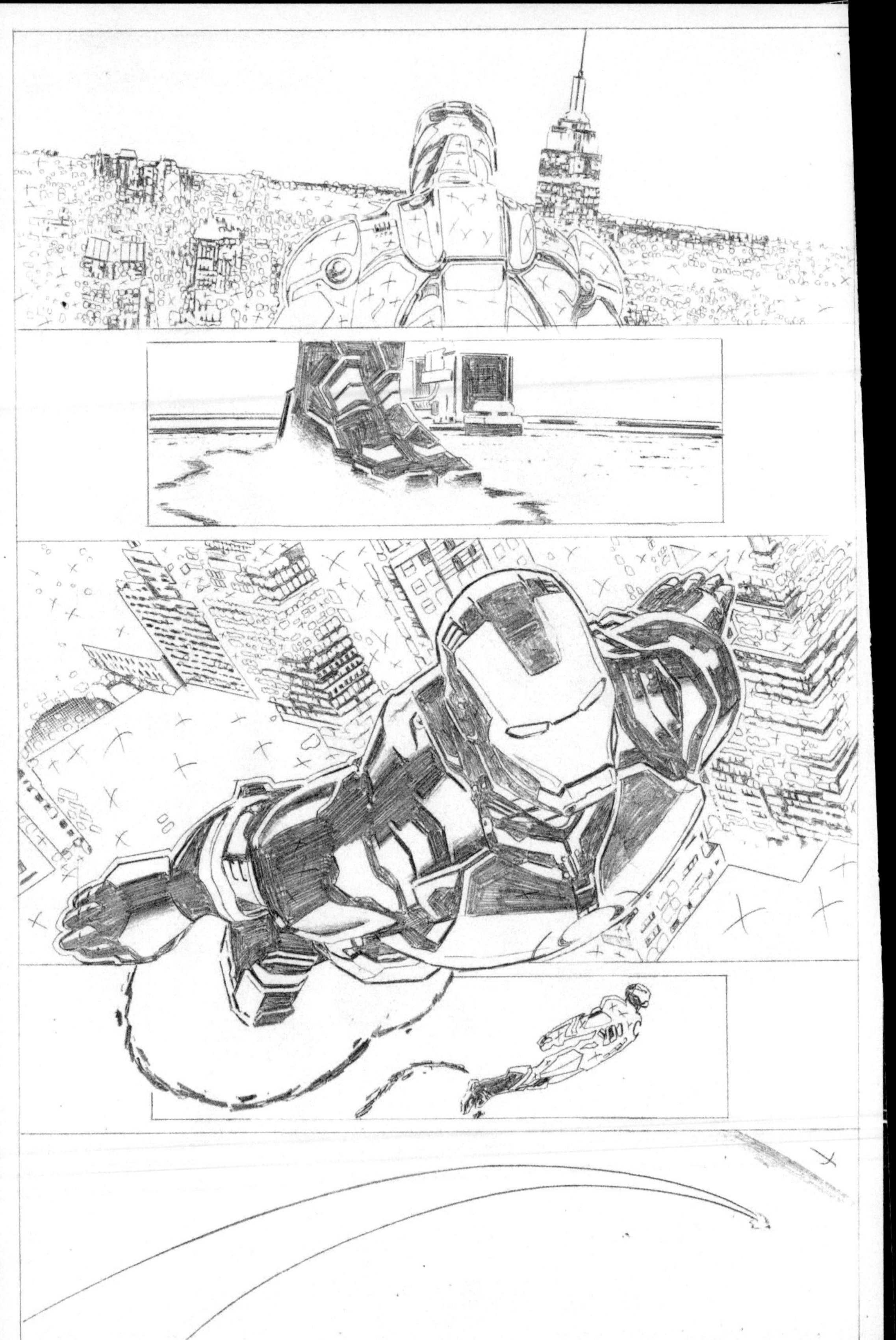

PENCILS BY GREG LAND & INKS BY JAY LEISTEN

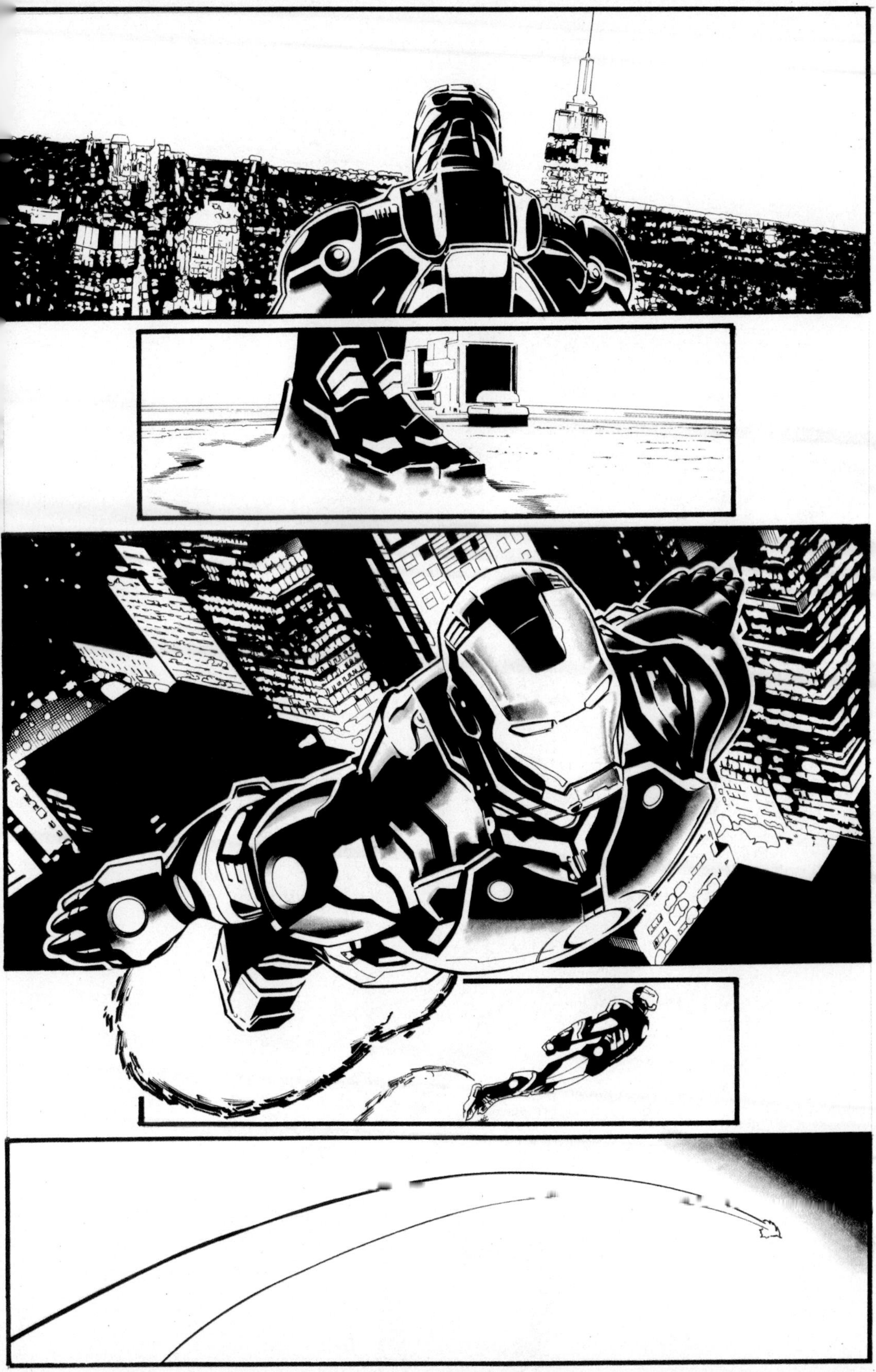

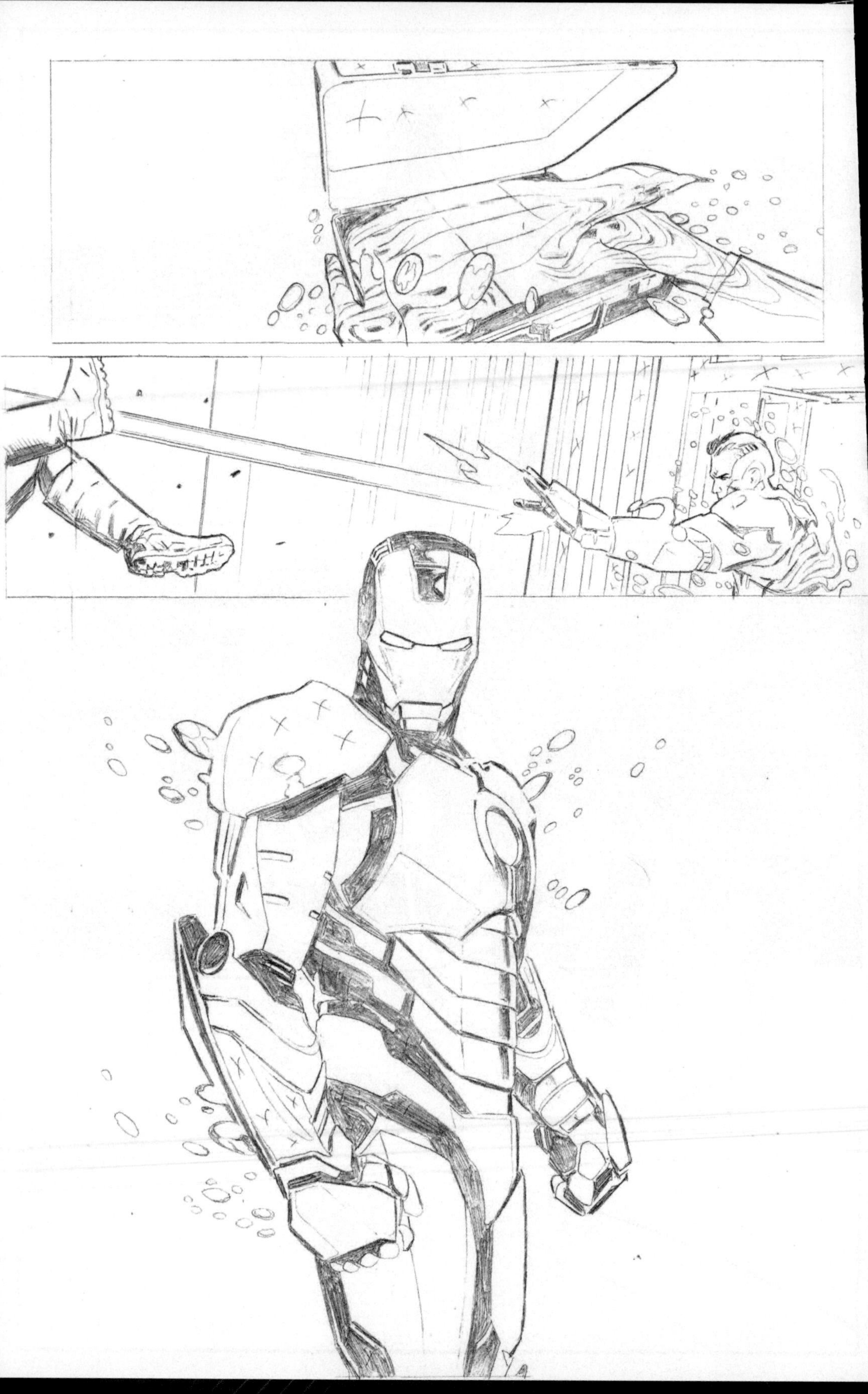

PENCILS BY GREG LAND & INKS BY JAY LEISTEN

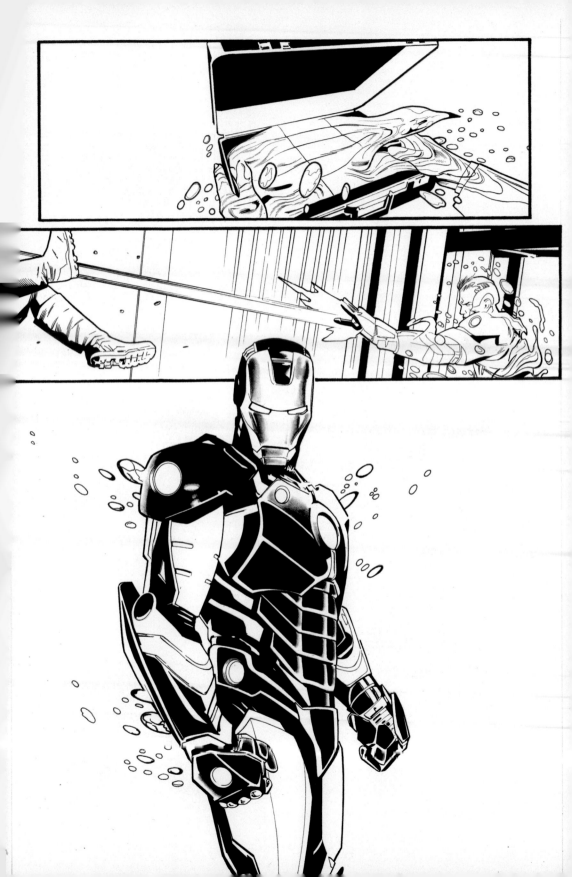

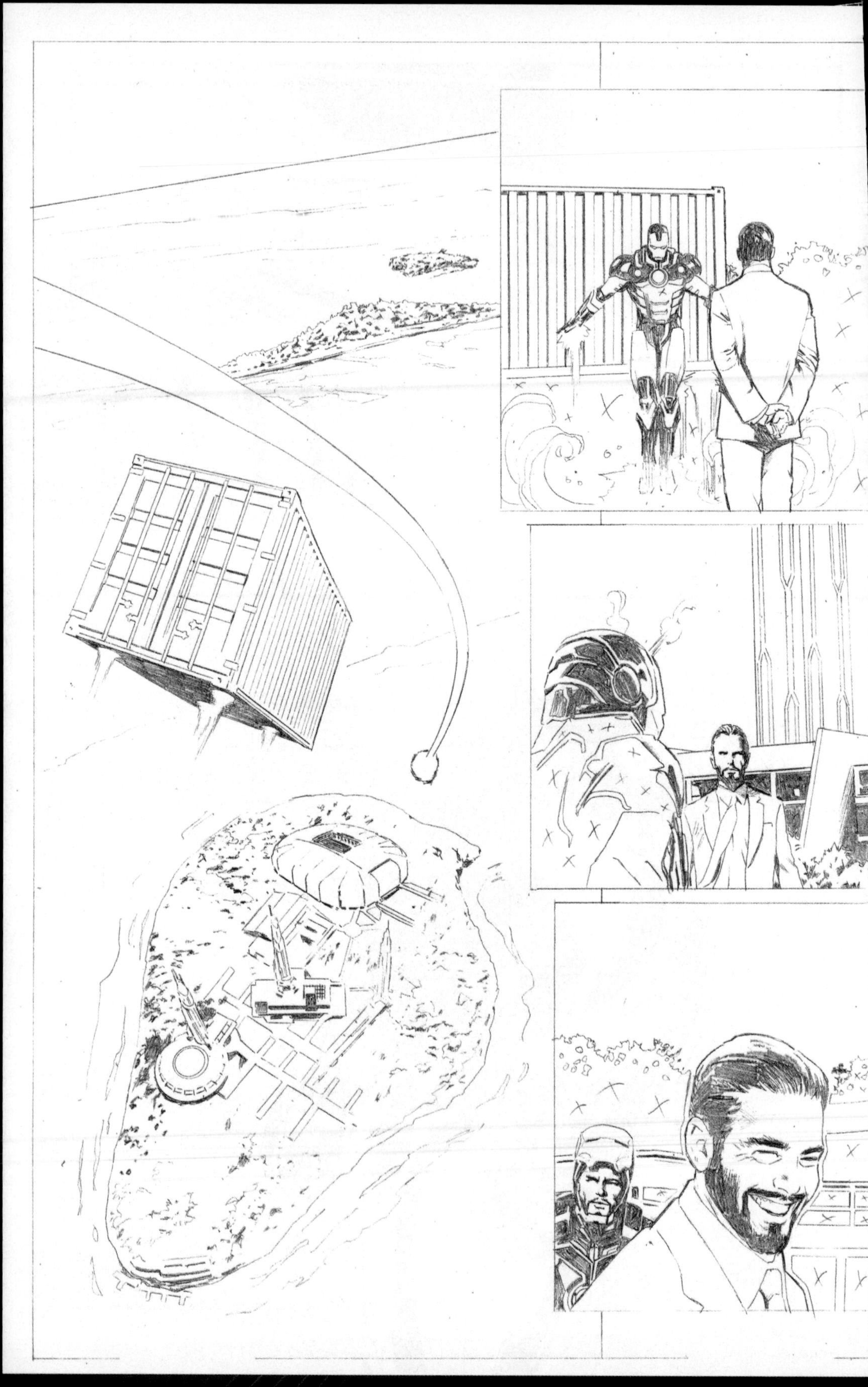

PENCILS BY GREG LAND & INKS BY JAY LEISTEN

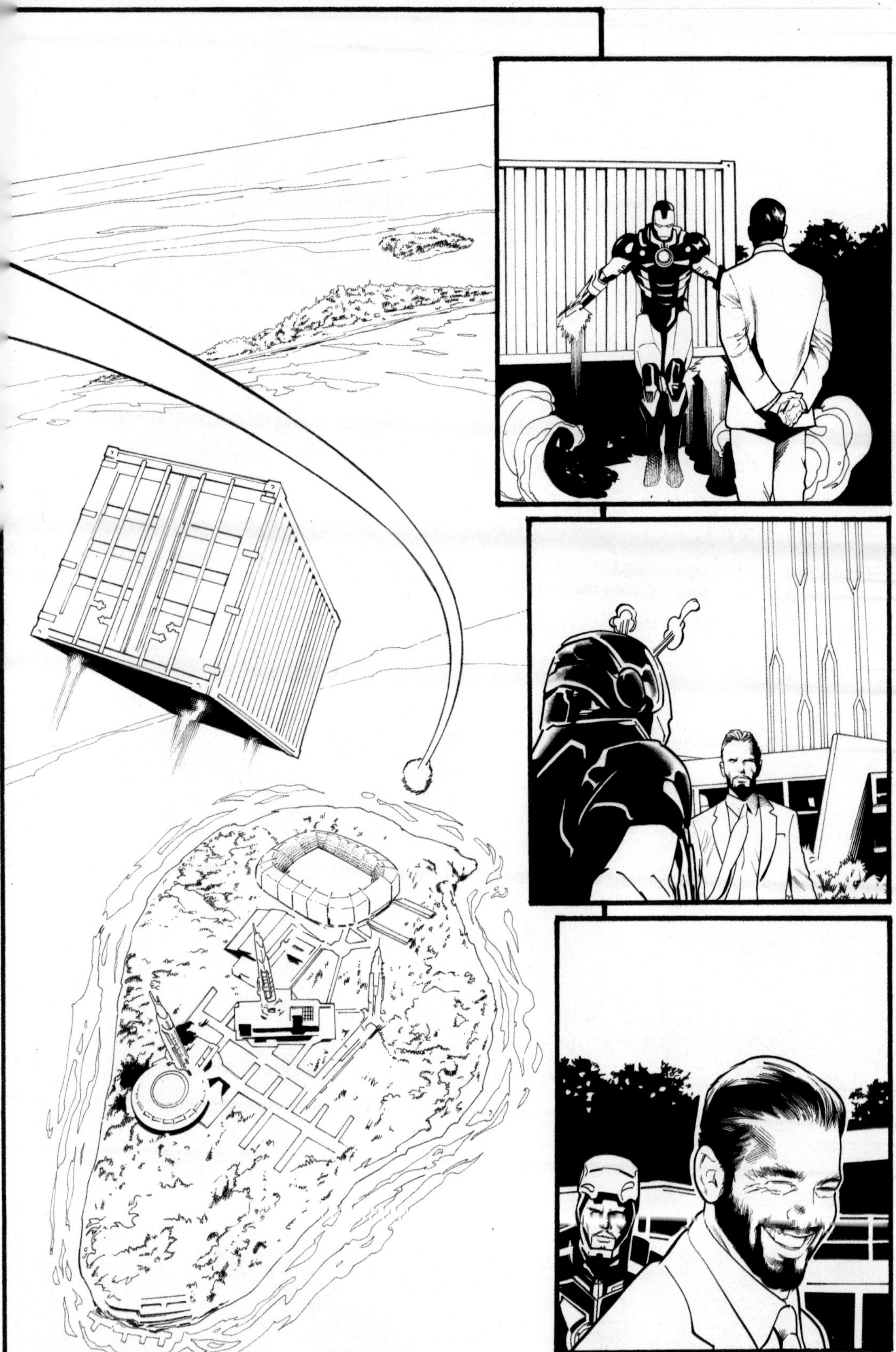

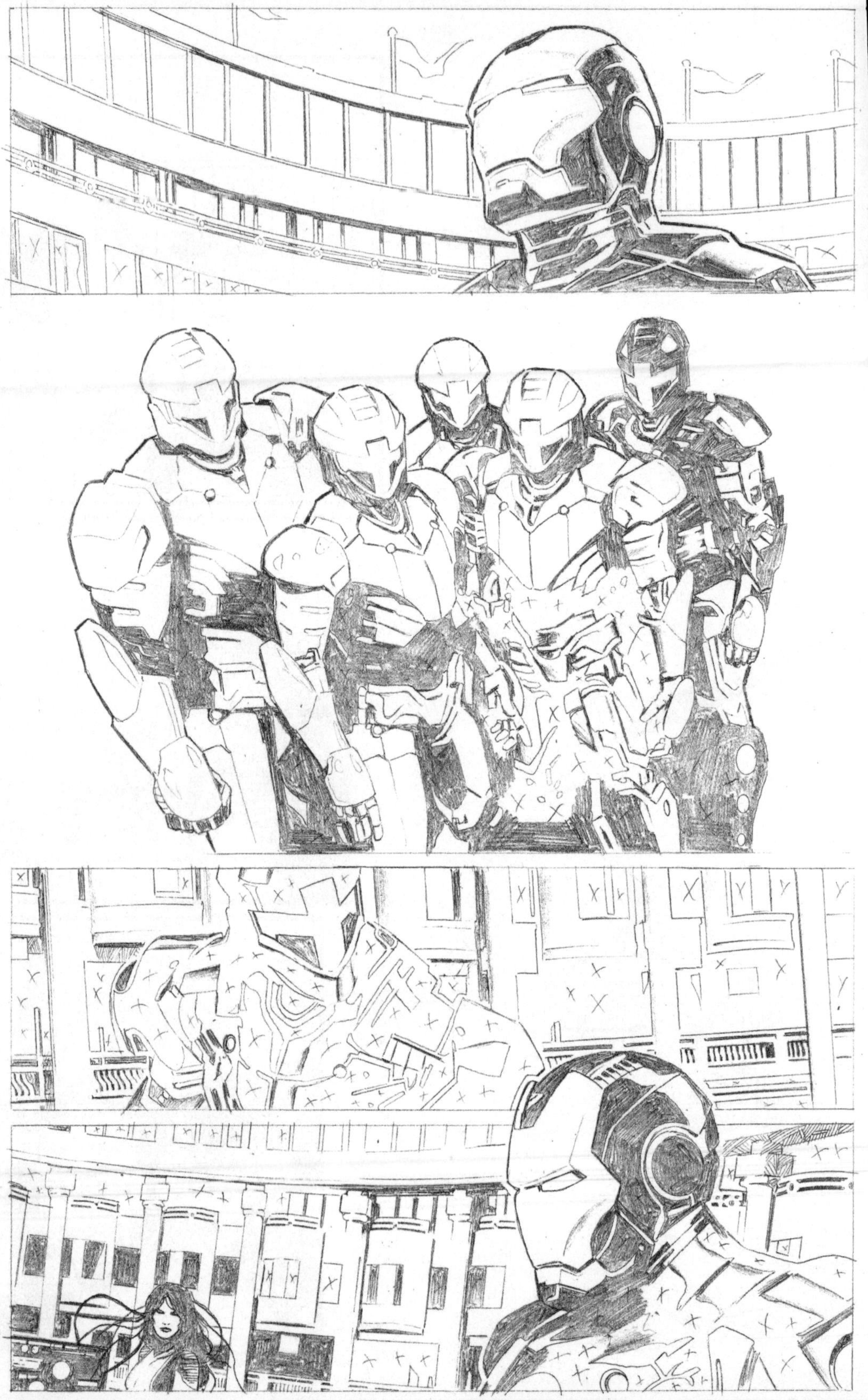

PENCILS BY GREG LAND & INKS BY JAY LEISTEN

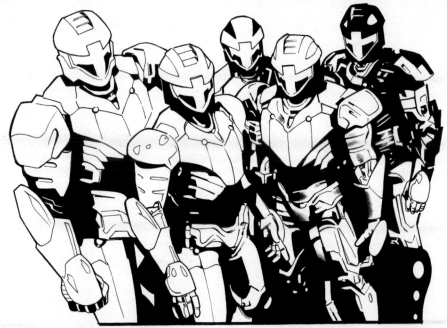

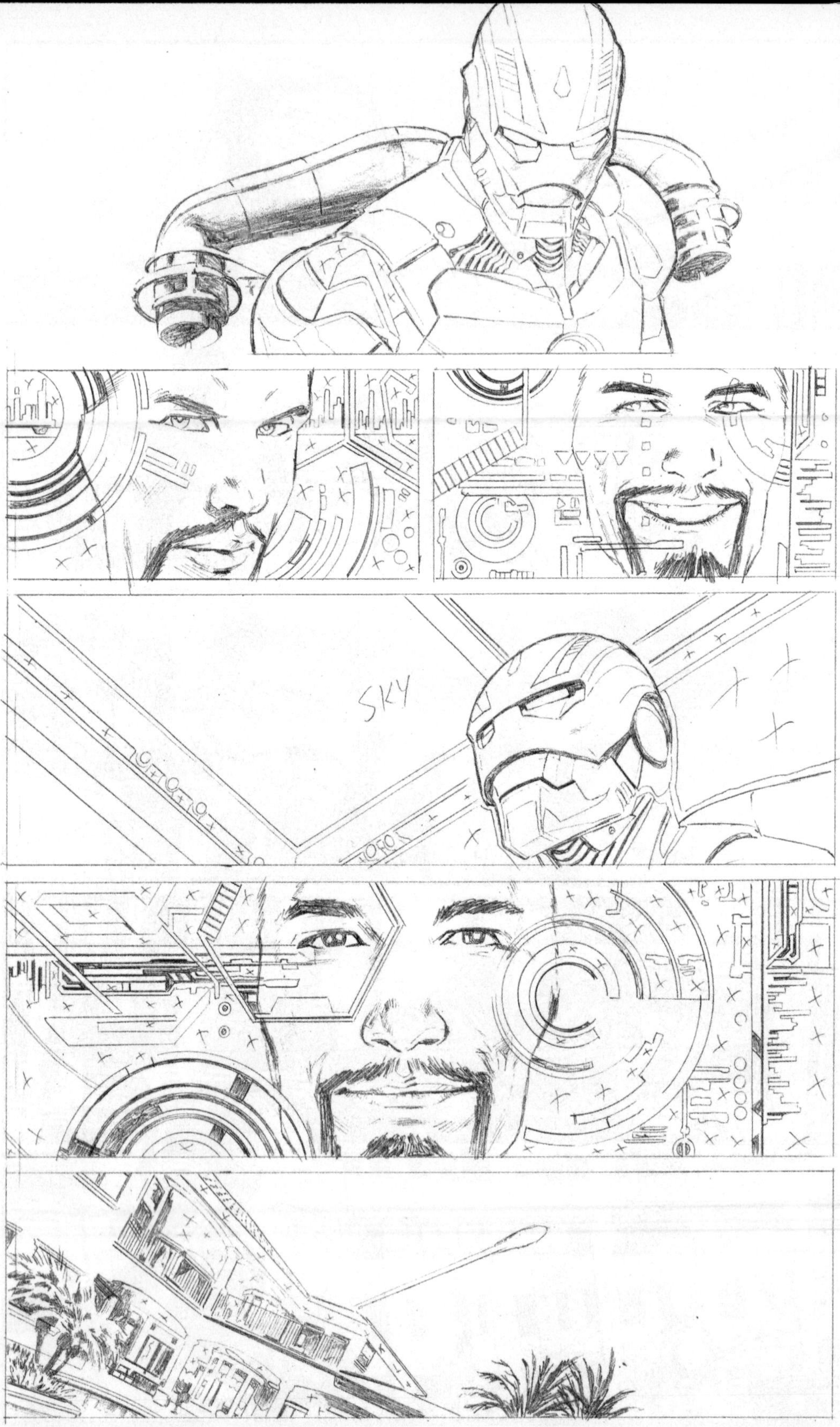
SKY

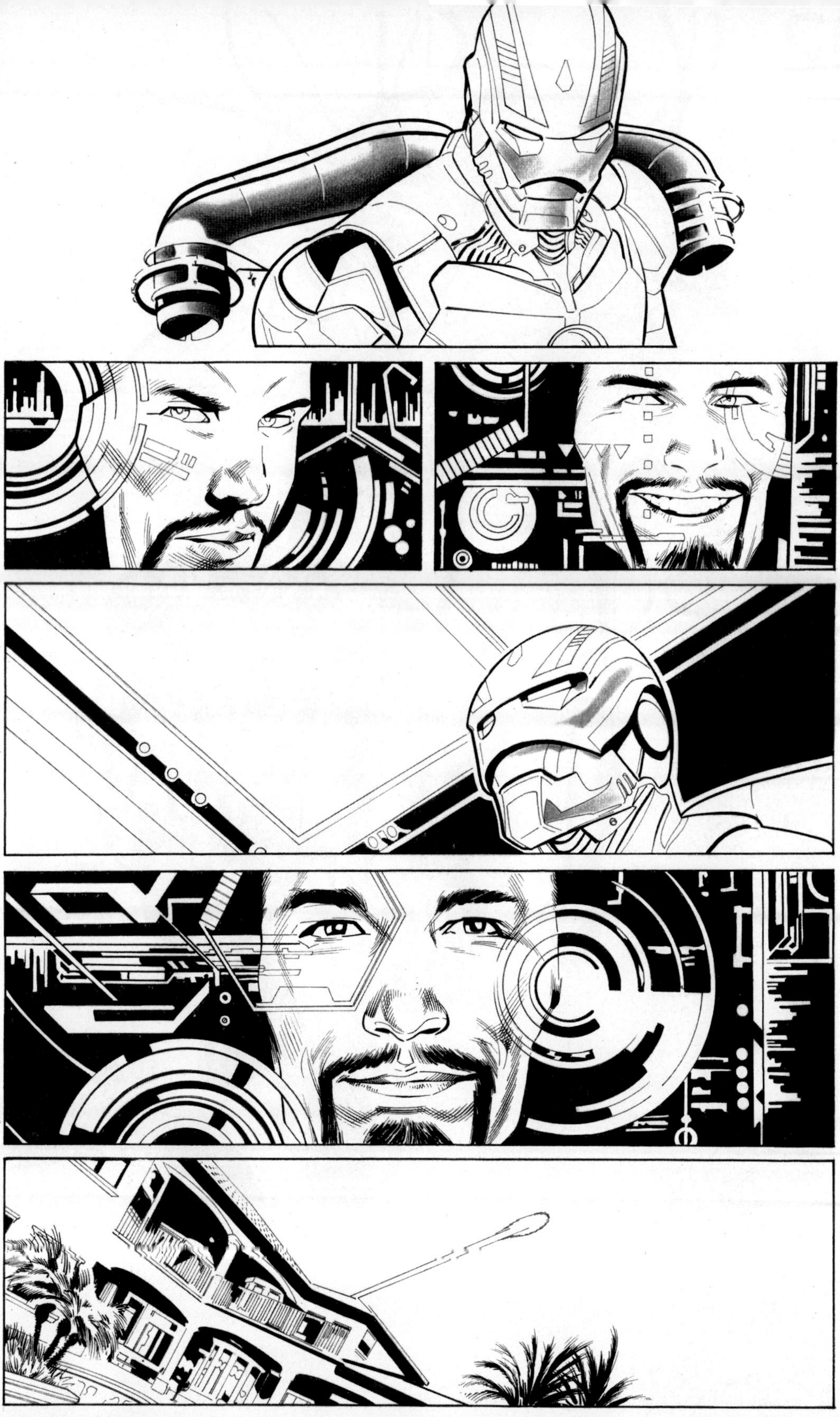

02

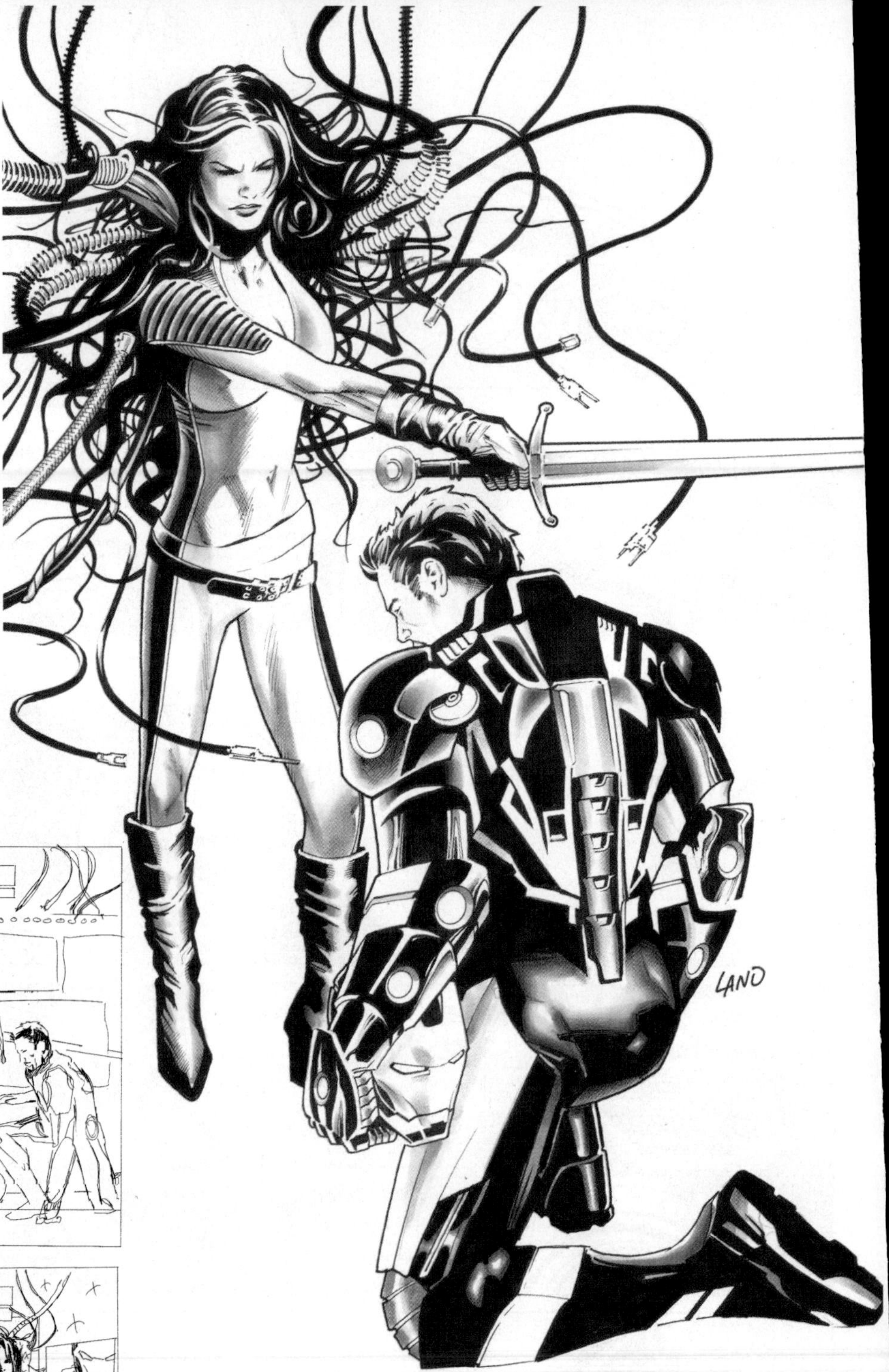
LAND

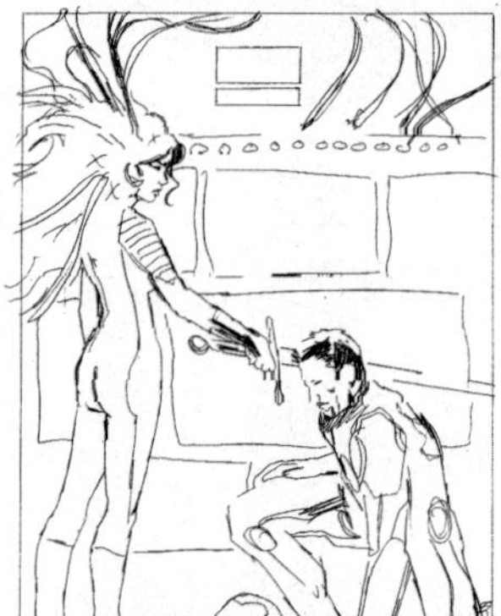

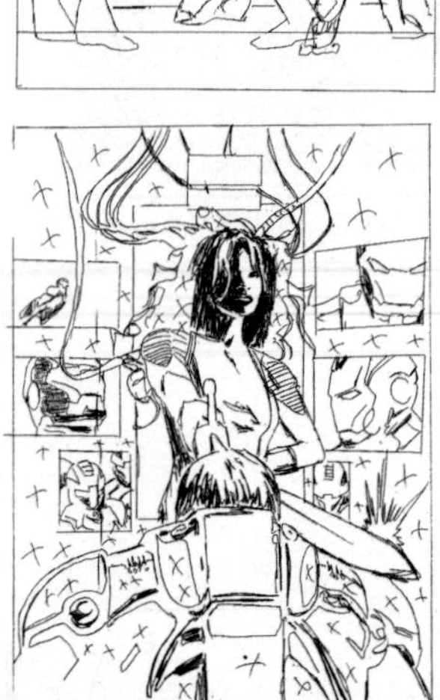

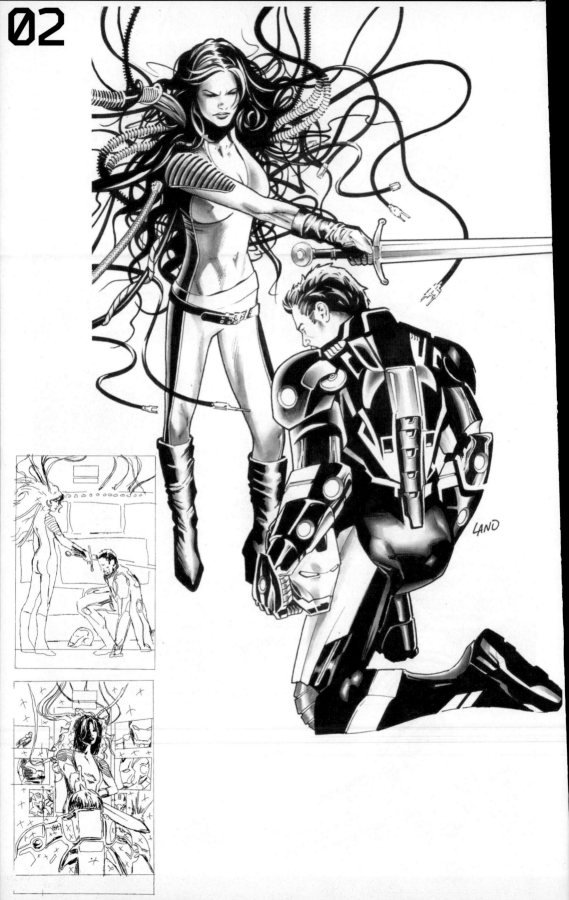

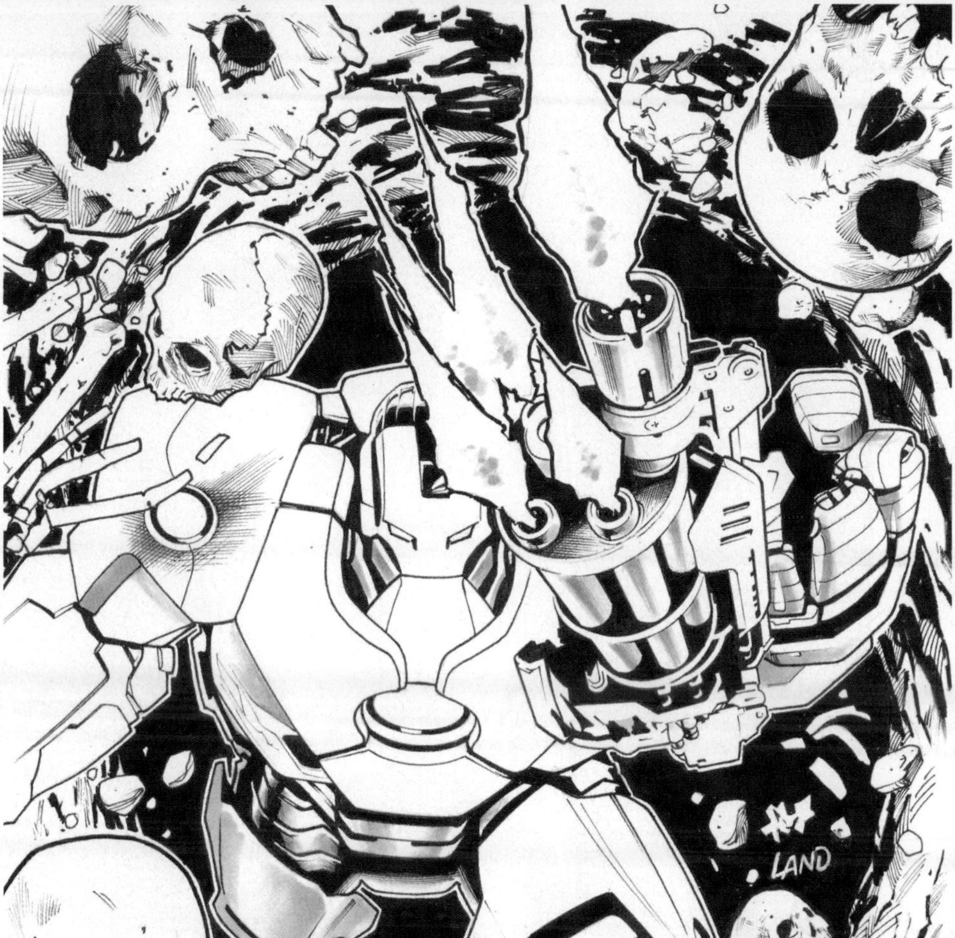
LAND

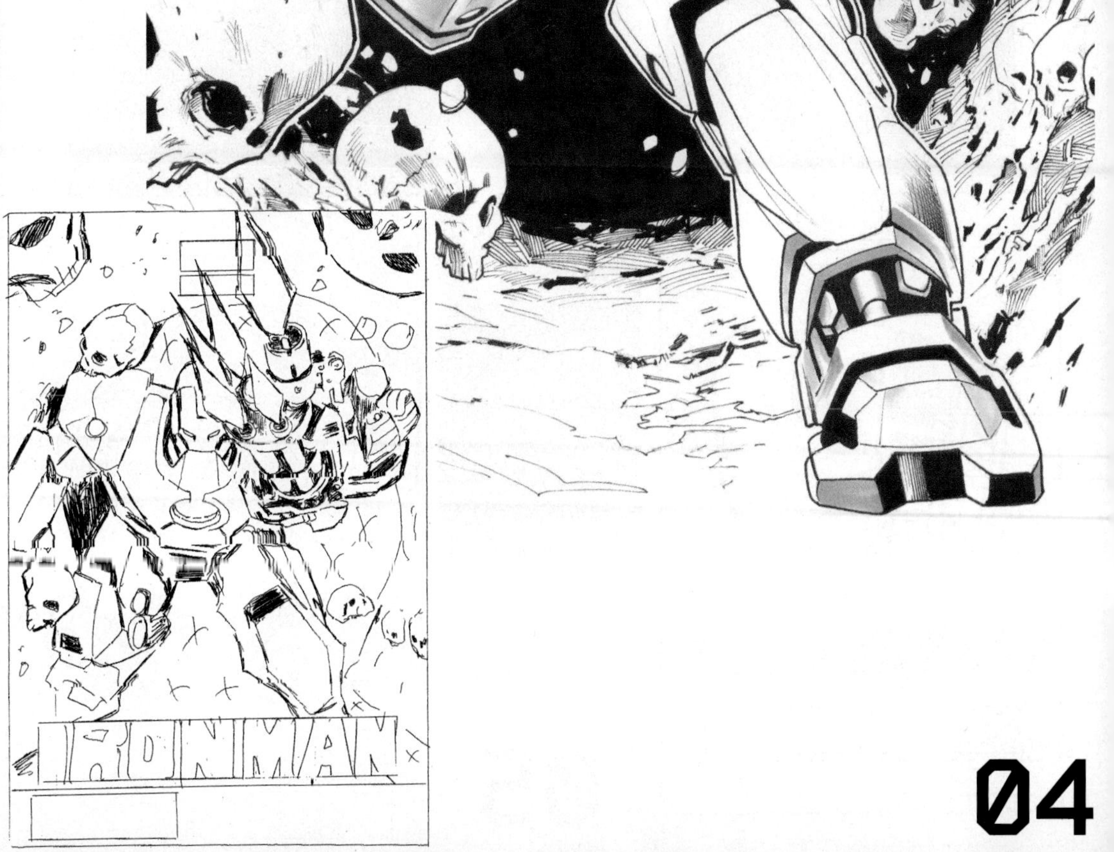
IRONMAN

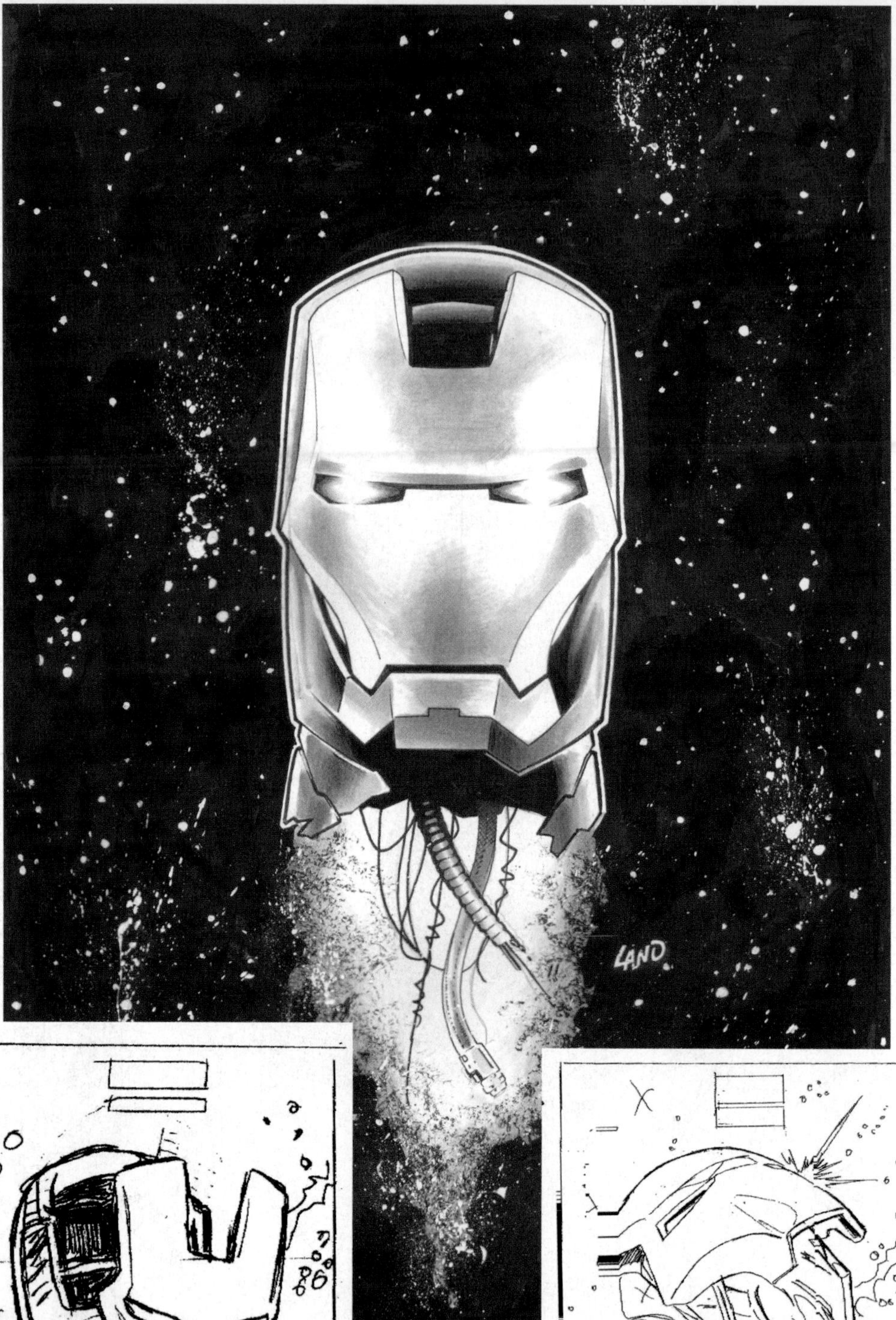
LAND

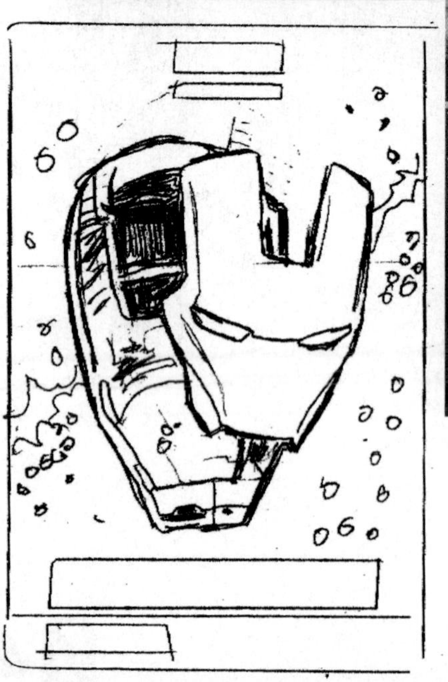

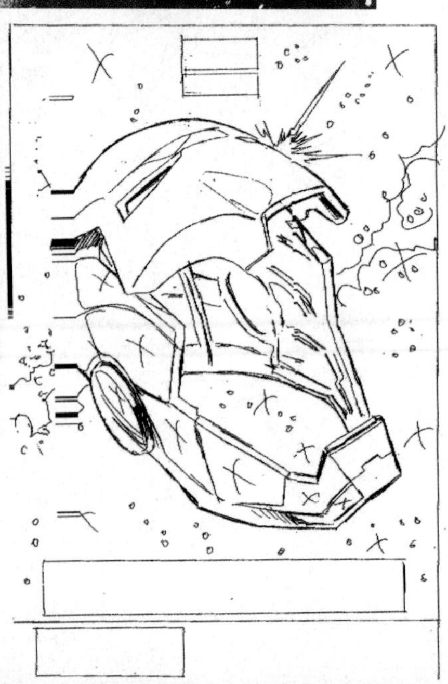

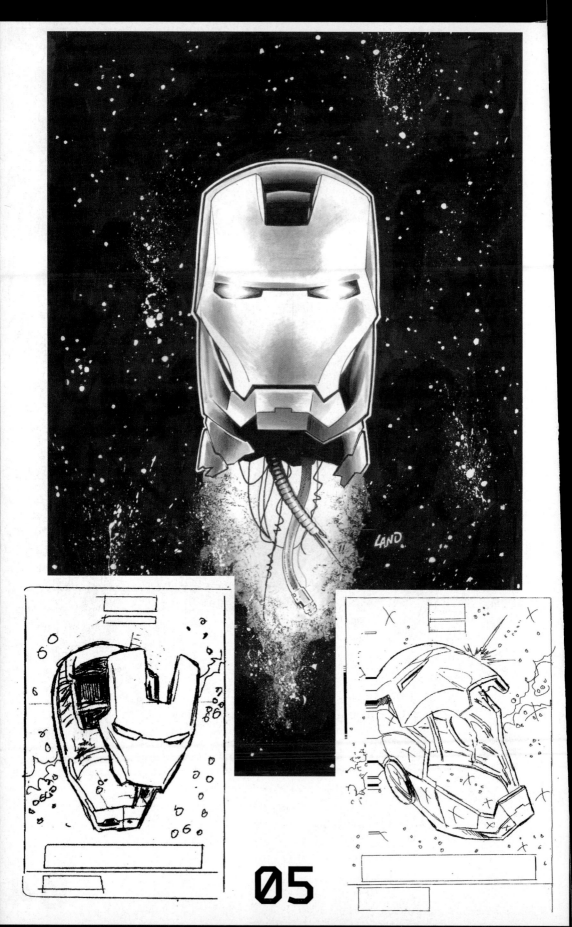

05

TO ACCESS THE FREE *MARVEL AUGMENTED REALITY APP*
THAT ENHANCES AND CHANGES THE WAY YOU EXPERIENCE COMI

1. **Download the app for free via marvel.com/ARapp**
2. **Launch the app on your camera-enabled Apple iOS® or Android™ device***
3. **Hold your mobile device's camera o any cover or panel with the AR gra**
4. **Sit back and see the future of comics in action!**

***Available on most camera-enabled Apple iOS® and Android™ devices. Content subject to change and availability.**

IRON MAN AR INDEX

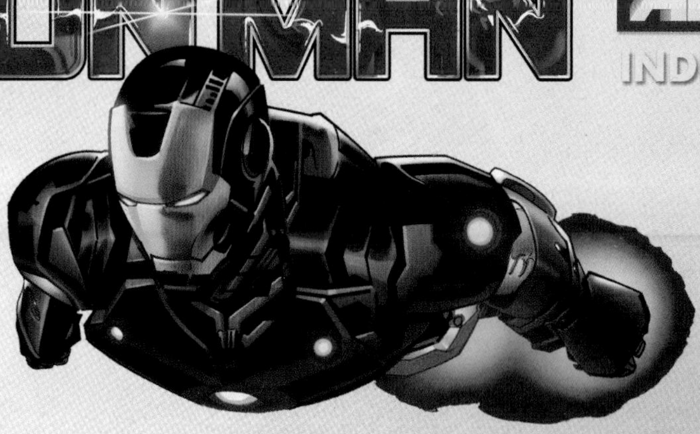